Introducti[illegible] to VM

A Beginner'[illegible]

Trevor Eddolls

NCC Blackwell

MANCHESTER • OXFORD

This book is dedicated to
Jill, Katy and Jennifer,
and my Mum and Dad

British Library Cataloguing in Publication Data

Eddolls, T.
Introduction to VM: a beginner's tuning guide
1. Computer systems. Operating systems.
I. Title
005.43

ISBN 0-85012-780-7

Published for NCC Publications by NCC Blackwell Limited.

Editorial Office: The National Computing Centre Limited, Oxford Road, Manchester M1 7ED, England.

NCC Blackwell Limited, 108 Cowley Road, Oxford OX4 1JF, England.

Typeset in 11pt Times Roman by Laser 27 Limited, Manchester; and printed by Hobbs the Printers of Southampton.

ISBN 0-85012-780-7

Acknowledgements

I would like to thank all the people who have written about VM and its subsystems, in particular those who have contributed to the monthly technical journal *VM Update* published by Xephon*.

I would especially like to thank my family who offered help and support throughout the period when I was writing this book: my wife Jill who supplied cups of tea; my two children, Katy and Jennifer, who offered distractions when I got tired; and my Mum and Dad who regularly phoned up to see how I was getting on.

**Xephon Technology Transfer are based at 27-35 London Road, Newbury, Berkshire RG13 1JL.*

Foreword

With an estimated 23,000 or more VM licences worldwide there are many people who are coming to VM for the first time and need some way of not only understanding what is going on, but also of being able to control what is happening.

At many sites new systems programmers, senior operations staff or more interested application programmers have experienced difficulty in getting detailed and accurate information about VM and its major subsystems. Their only available choices were IBM manuals or senior system programmers.

IBM manuals, although correct in their content, tend to suffer from the same problem as most other manuals in that it is very hard to derive the piece of information required from their texts. There also seems to be a great variety of manuals, any of which might contain the information required. Deciding which one to look in first presents yet another problem.

Senior systems programmers tend to be very busy and, although they are often willing to help, do not have enough time to field all the questions that might be thrown at them and sometimes have a tendency to avoid people who are seeking information altogether.

Another potential solution is to send people on training courses. However, restricted budgets and work rotas might preclude this, or organised courses might not run at the time required.

It is also possible for sites to rent video training courses or PC-based information and question-type courses. While these can offer a great deal of information, the one main problem with using them is that they require special hardware (video machine and TV or dedicated PCs).

This book is intended for people who are relative newcomers to various aspects of VM, who need to know the basics about the system, and who also want to take this information a stage further and make improvements to the way that the system performs. This book explains the basics and contains many suggestions about areas to look at when considering tuning of these particular areas.

Contents

Page

Acknowledgements

Foreword

SECTION I 1

1 Introduction 3

General 3

Hardware Requirements 5
Mainframe 5
Tape Controller 8
Tape Drive 8
DASD Controller 11
DASD 13
Mini-disks 13
Console 16
Terminal Cluster Controller 16
Terminals 17
Printers 17
Communications Controller 17
Other Hardware 19

Software 19

2 Background 23

VM History 23
VM Versions 25
VM/IS 25
VM/SP 27
VM/SP HPO 27
VM/XA SP 27

Future 28

Reasons for Installing VM 30

Workloads 30
VM/IS 31
VM/SP 31
VM/SP HPO 31
VM/XA SP 31

SECTION II 33

3 VM Basics 35

CP-owned DASD Areas 35
PERM 36
TEMP 38
TDSK 40
DRCT 41
DUMP 43
OVRD 43

System Modules 43
DMKRIO 44
DMKSNT 44
DMKSYS 46
HCPSYS 48

Control Blocks 50

Load Map 51

4 Operational Considerations 53

System Start-up 53
AUTOLOG1 54
VMUTIL 55

MAINT 55
PROP 55

Assists 57
VMA 58
ECPS 60
IUCV Assist 60
STBA 61
PMA 61
PMAV 61
SIE Assist 61

Set Commands 62

5 Installation, Maintenance and Problems 69

Installing VM 69
LOADLIST 70
Loading VM 70

Maintenance 71
APAR 71
PUT 72

Modifications 73
Update Files 74
AUX Files 75
CNTRL Files 75
TEXT Files 76
Building Modules Summary 77

Problem Diagnosis 77
Disabled Wait State 77
Enabled Wait State 79
Loops 80
Dumps 80

Debugging Running Systems 81

Disaster Recovery 81
Stand-alone Modules 83

Program Testing 83

SECTION III 85

6 Processing 87

Processor States 87
Supervisor State 87
Problem State 87
TVRATIO 88

Wait States 88
CP Wait States 88
Guest-operating Systems Wait States 89

Active Waits 90

Interrupts 90

SRM 91

Scheduler 91

Q1 93

Q2 94

Q3 94

Timeslice 94

Queuing Sequence 94

Despatcher 95

Deadline Priority 96

Priority Calculation 96

XA Scheduler 97

7 Virtual Storage Overview 99

Virtual Storage 99

Real Storage Layout 103
Nucleus Area 105
Optional guest-operating System 109
Dynamic Paging Area 110
Trace Table 111
Free Storage Area 112

Saved Systems and Segments 115
Saved Systems 116
Discontiguous Saved Segments 116
XA and Saved Segments 116

Maximising DPA Space 118

8 Paging 121

Page Frames 121

Swapping 122

Tables 122
Core Table 123

Maintaining Freelist Pages 123
DMKSEL Routine 124

Hardware Considerations 126
Real Storage 126
DASD Considerations 127

Guest-operating System Paging 129
Non-paging Mode 131
Pseudo Page Fault 131
V=R Guests 131
Shadow Page Tables 131
XA Guests 135

SECTION IV 137

9 CMS 139

CMS Environment 139
Directory 140

CMS Memory Allocation 144

Accessing CMS 147
Terminal Status 148

Files 150

VSAM Files 150
Entry Sequenced Datasets 153

Relative Record Datasets 153
Key Sequenced Datasets 153

Using the Spool 154
Spool 154
Printing 154
Punching 157
Reading 157

CMS Commands 158

CMS Command Usage 163

Maximising CMS Performance 165

10 CMS Facilities 167

Profile EXEC 167

Using XEDIT 167
XEDIT Profile 168
XEDIT Commands 168

REXX 172
Maximising REXX Performance 177

ISPF 177

VM Batch 178

PROFS 181
Maximising PROFS Performance 182

SQL/DS 183
Maximising SQL/DS Performance 185

CICS 186

Shared File System 187
DFSMS/VM 188

SECTION V 191

11 I/O and DASD 193

Disks 193

Mini-disks 194

Recovery Procedure 195
  Temporary Mini-disks 195
  Accessing Mini-disks 198

Files 199

I/O Path 199

Channel 201

I/O Sequence of Events 201
  Queue time 201
  Seeking 202
  Connect time 203
  Protocol 204

Start I/O 204

Path Selection 205

Resource Consumption 207

Maximising I/O Performance 207

12 Communication 211

Software Overview 211
  Terminals 211
  Passthrough 212
  RSCS 213
  VTAM 214
  IUCV 220
  VMCF 221
  NetView 221
  TCP/IP 223
  Communications Controller 224
  LANs 224

Group Control System 225
  GCS Facilities 225
  GCS Components 229
  Problems with GCS 231

Errors 232

Maximising Network Performance 233

Other Terms 233

SECTION VI 239

13 Security 241

Security Requirements 241

Native Security 242
- Access Security 242
- Disk Access Security 243
- Restrictions on Commands Available 244
- Address Space Security 244

Directory 244

Security Problems 245
- User Location 245
- Passwords 245
- Other Problems 246

User Improvements 246

VM Security Products 247
- ALERT/VM 248
- CA-ACF2/VM 248
- CA-TOP SECRET 249
- OMNIGUARD 249
- RACF/VM 250
- VM/SECURE 250

Other Considerations 250

Selecting a Security Package 251

14 Performance Considerations 253

Benchmarks 253

Problems in Benchmarking VM 254

Types of Monitor 256
- On-line Monitors 256
- Historical Monitors 257

CP Monitor 257
INDicate 257
Query 259
Analysing the Monitor Data 261

VM/XA Monitor 263
Data Collection 264
Domains 265
Data Volume 269

Performance Information 270
CPU Usage 271
I/O 272
Network 272
Paging and Swapping 272
Spooling 273
User Information 273
Performance in General 273
Additional Measurements 273

Data Evaluation 274

Appendix 1 — Glossary 277

Appendix 2 — Bibliography 311

Index 313

SECTION 1

Introduction and Background

The first section of this book describes how a VM system appears to its users in terms of the hardware that is required and the software that it involves. It includes a short history of VM and a description of the versions of VM that are currently available. It also looks to the future of VM systems. Lastly the reasons that are usually given for installing VM are discussed along with the workloads that each VM version is best used for.

1 Introduction

GENERAL

IBM currently market for mainframe computers two true operating systems which are called VSE (Virtual Storage Extended) and MVS (Multi Virtual Storage) respectively. The third product for mainframes, which is usually grouped with these two, is VM (Virtual Machine). However, VM is not an operating system in the true sense of the phrase and can perhaps be more correctly described as a 'hypervisor' (superior supervisor software — see p.21).

The VM Control Program (CP) looks after and controls all the real hardware that is installed and allows operating systems to execute as guest systems under its control. One obvious way in which VM differs from an operating system is in the way that it deals with a user's request for a tape drive. An operating system would allocate a tape drive to that user. With VM, a message asking for a tape drive is displayed on the operator console and the operator then keys in a command to allocate a tape drive to a user. When the user has finished with the tape drive the operator keys in a command that deallocates the drive. It is not done automatically.

Although VM controls all the real hardware, guest systems that are running under it have the appearance of controlling their own hardware. This hardware does not really exist, but only appears to exist for these guest systems. Because of this they are referred to as virtual machines. The majority of users of VM will be working with CMS (Conversational Monitor System) and all the hardware that they think exists for them is provided by VM from the existing hardware.

In this way a CMS user will appear to have his own disk drives, tape drives, console and printer. The disk drives are in fact mini-disks, ie parts of real disks. The tape drives do not exist, but real tape drives can be assigned by the operator to occupy the virtual address of the user's tape drives and then they can be used. The console for the CMS user is, in fact, the terminal that he or she is working from. The printer does not exist, but print files can be sent to the real printer if a hard-copy is required (the method for doing this is discussed on p.155). In addition to these devices a CMS user will have a virtual card reader and a virtual card punch. These represent real devices that are almost never found at an installation these days. The virtual card punch can punch holes in virtual cards, and the virtual card reader can read virtual punched cards. Although this may sound strange it is a useful way of storing files and sending files to other CMS users. This set-up is illustrated in Figure 1.1.

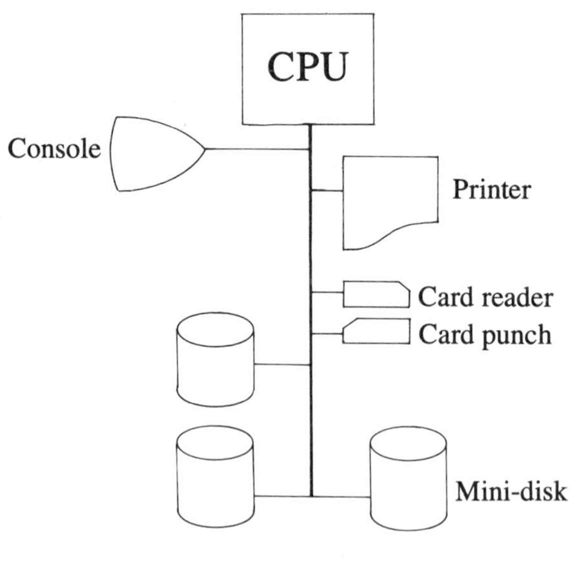

Figure 1.1 CMS Virtual Machine Configuration

Not all virtual machines will have a console (terminal) while running. These virtual machines are said to be running disconnected.

HARDWARE REQUIREMENTS

For VM to be installed the following devices are usually available and connected:

- Mainframe;
- Tape controller;
- Tape drive;
- DASD controller;
- DASD;
- Console;
- Terminal cluster controller;
- Terminals;
- Printer.

More than one of each of these can be installed and there are other devices in addition to the ones listed that could be installed. The basic configuration is illustrated in Figure 1.2.

Mainframe

The mainframe is a large (when compared to a mini or micro processor) processor. It is variously referred to as a CPU (Central Processing Unit), a processor, or a Central Electronic Complex (CEC). Inside the processor is an area that can be used to store the user programs etc that are to be executed. This area is called main storage. It also known as core storage, or real storage. The situation is further complicated on the newer processors (3090E models etc) where main storage can be divided into an area called central storage and an area called expanded storage.

Associated with the area containing the programs is an area that carries out the instructions, ie actually performs the adding up. On older processors this was called the Arithmetic and Logic Unit (ALU). On the modern processors it is referred to as the execution element. On

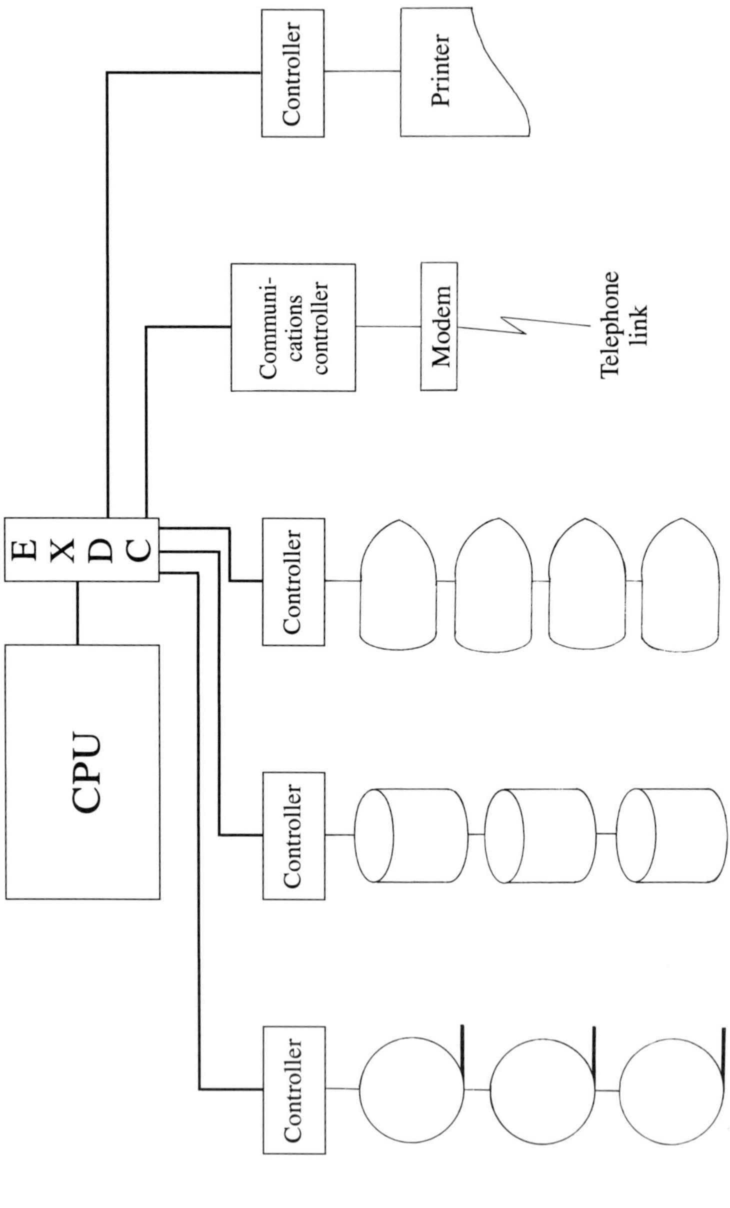

Figure 1.2 Real Machine Configuration

a uniprocessor (eg 3090-300) there is only one execution element, on a dyadic processor (eg 3090-150) there are two execution elements, and on quad processors there are four of them.

The third area within the processor is often referred to by its old name of control register area. This, as its name would suggest, is used to store registers associated with processing programs. On more modern processors it is referred to as an instruction element. These components are illustrated in Figure 1.3.

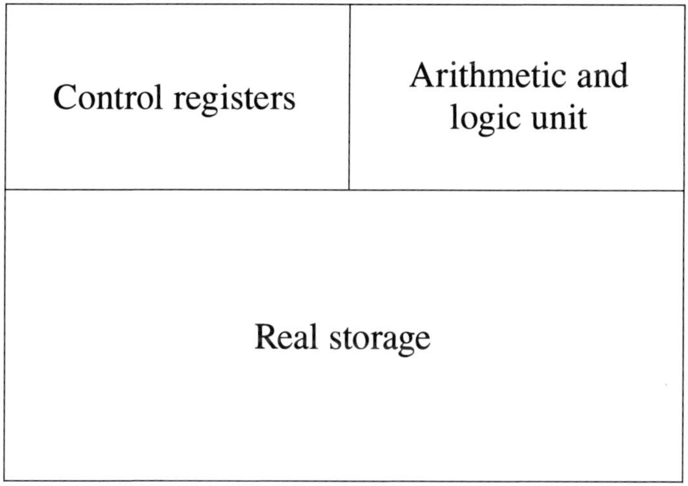

Figure 1.3 Diagram of a CPU Internals

Associated with the processor and controlling the flow of data into and out of it is the EXDC. EXDC stand for EXternal Data Controller. This is divided into a Channel Processing Element (CPE) and two or three Data Server Elements (DSEs) and a number of Interface Adaptor Elements (IAEs). To complicate matters the IAEs are not physically located with the other components of the EXDC. They are located with the processor control unit (3082, 3092). It is to the IAEs that cables connecting control units and other physical devices are attached. They represent the channels, or on XA systems the channel paths that are used for I/O. (Channels are discussed more fully in the chapter on I/O.)

Tape Controller

The function of the tape controller is to separate the data sent from the channel or channel path and direct each packet of information to the appropriate tape drive. Its other function is to interleave the messages coming from the tape drives and send them to the channel. Data travelling between the channel and the control unit, and back again, is multiplexed using time-division multiplexing. This is illustrated in Figure 1.4. In effect, a small packet of data for each tape drive is sent in such a way that the line is fully utilised and every drive gets an equal opportunity to have data sent to it. The communication between the channel and the control unit is full duplex. This is illustrated in Figure 1.5. Messages can be sent from the channel to the control unit and in the reverse direction at the same time.

Tape Drive

Two types of tape drive are currently available. There is the 3420 reel-to-reel type and the 3480 cartridge type. Both can be used to store data which can be taken off-line. This can be a useful way to store infrequently used files so that valuable disk space is not filled up. Although this will make access times for these files slow, it is generally beneficial for other more frequently accessed files stored on the hardware.

Tapes are also used as a medium for storing back-up copies of files. Files are copied to tape at regular intervals and are then stored. If the data in the original disk file becomes corrupted, or the disk itself becomes damaged so that the file is inaccessible, the file can be reloaded (restored) from the back-up tape. Back-up tapes may be stored offsite so that the data can be recovered in the event of the data centre being damaged. They may also be stored at a disaster-recovery site, so that, in the event of a disaster, data at the recovery site will match data that was at the old site, and the recovery site can continue processing users' work.

Tapes are also used as a storage medium for archival data. Data that is no longer current and, therefore, in regular use can be removed from disk and stored on tape. In the event that information about something in the past is required the archive file can be reloaded and read. Otherwise it can be stored in a safe place (tape library or fire safe, etc) and

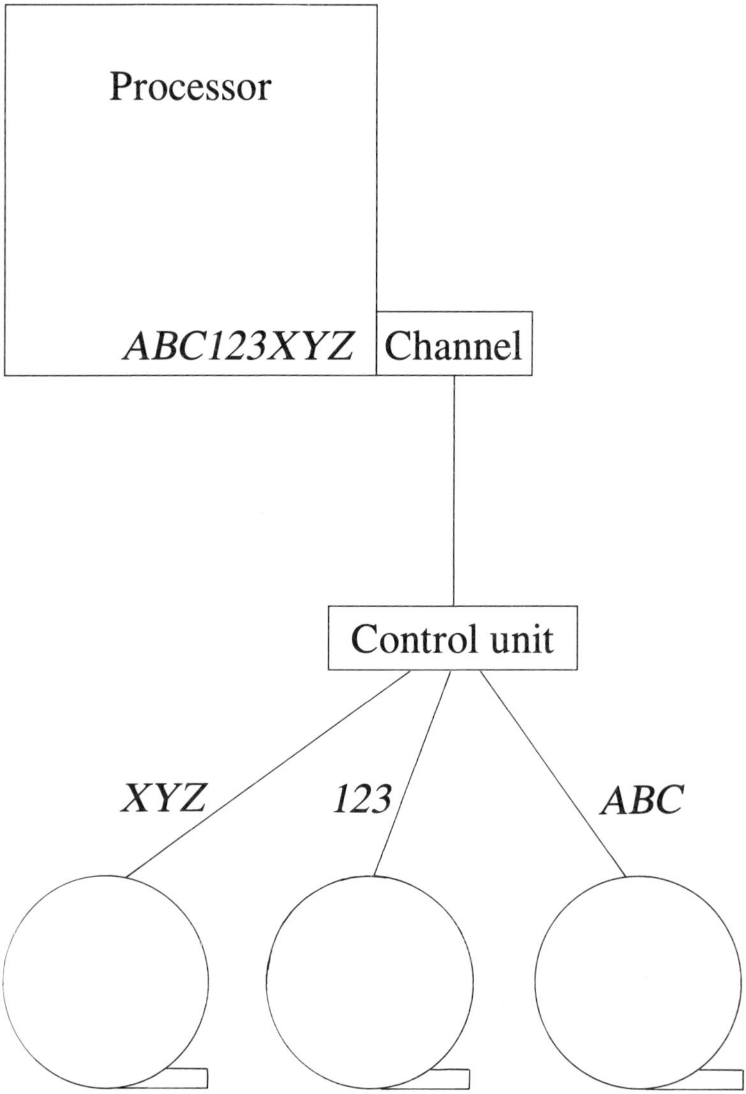

Figure 1.4 Block Multiplexing

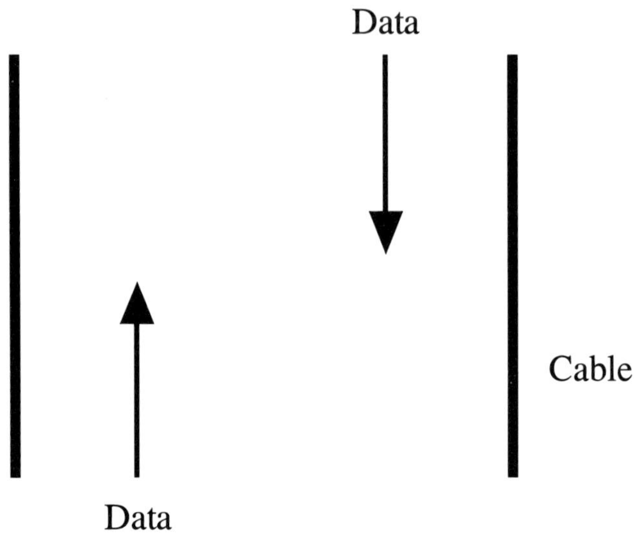

Figure 1.5 Full Duplex Communication

the space on disk originally occupied by the file becomes free for use.

Reel-to-reel tapes typically store data at storage densities of either 1600 bpi (bits per inch) or 6250 bpi. These figures represent how close together the data can be fitted on to the tape. A standard tape is 2400 ft long and stores bytes of data across the tape. There are eight bits to a byte; the extra bit that is stored on a nine-track tape is the first check for data integrity. It is called the parity bit and ensures that all the bits across a tape add up to an odd number (or it could be an even number depending on what is specified as the method for parity-bit checking). This is illustrated in Figure 1.6.

The cartridge tapes are 18-track tapes, which allow two bytes to be written at the same time across the tape. The density of the cartridges is 19,000 bpi. They are often used in preference to reel-to-reel tapes because the drives are smaller and occupy less floor space and the cartridges require less storage space and are easier to load.

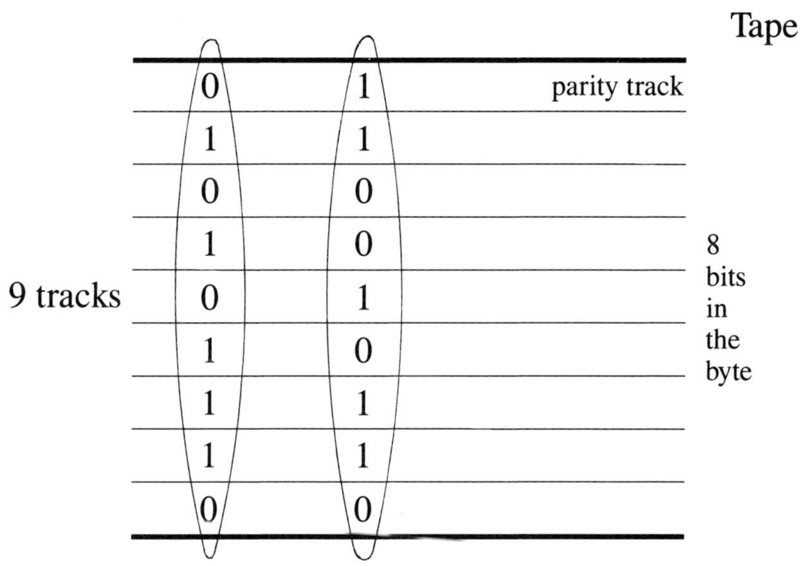

Figure 1.6 Diagram of a Nine-track Tape

DASD Controller

With more modern DASD (eg 3380s) the DASD controller is called a storage director. Its function is similar to the function of the tape controller in so far as it ensures that data from a channel is sent to the right disk and data from the disks is interleaved to be sent to the channel.

The more sophisticated storage directors (eg 3880s) can have cache associated with them. This is illustrated in Figure 1.7. To reduce the time taken to access files on mini-disks it is possible to take a copy from the disk and store it in the cache controller. Any user who needs to access that mini-disk can access the version that is in cache. The cached version is loaded into real storage and can be used. This method of accessing is much faster than having to access the mini-disk on a DASD. Provided that data is only read there is no requirement to write out the data once it has been read. However, if the data is updated, a copy has to be written to cache and a copy has to be written to disk. There is little saving to be achieved by caching mini-disks that are regularly updated. Cache memory sizes currently range from 8MB to

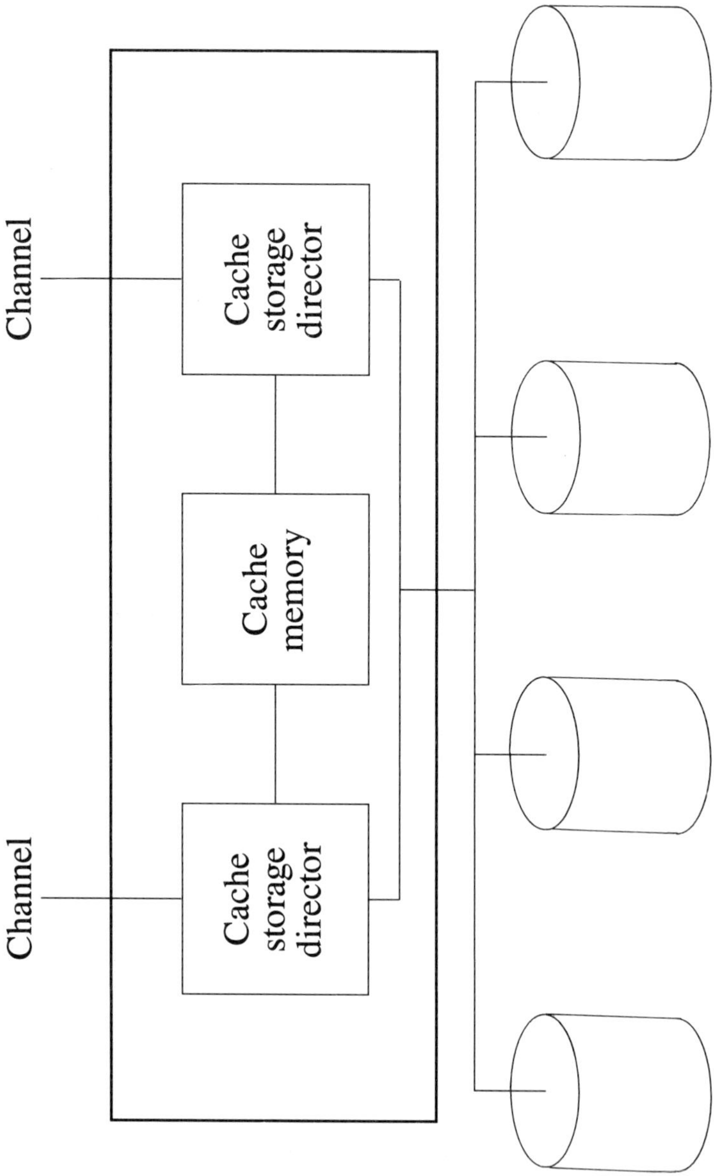

Figure 1.7 Cache DASD Controller

64MB, depending on the control unit model and the vendor.

DASD

Direct Access Storage Devices are typically disk drives, but could be solid-state devices. IBM do not currently make a solid-state storage device, but third party (eg Storagetek) suppliers do. A typical disk device is illustrated in Figure 1.8. The disk spins at 36,000 revolutions per minute and the read/write heads move across the platters, remaining very slightly separate from them. If the heads and platters should collide, this is referred to as an HDA (Head Disk Assembly) crash and results in the data on the disk becoming unusable.

Disks may be divided into tracks and cylinders or into sectors. In the first case they are called CKD (Count Key Data) devices, in the second case they are FBA (Fixed Block Architecture) devices. CKD format is illustrated in Figure 1.9. A track is defined as the area that can be written to or read from by one head without the head moving. A cylinder is defined as the area that can be written to or read from by all the heads without the heads moving. Tracks nearer the spindle occupy less space than those towards the outside of the platter. However, the amount of data that can be written on any track on a platter is always the same. This is because the density of the data is greater nearer the spindle. With CKD disks, there is an optional key area in front of the data, and in front of that is a count area. The count area can be used to ensure that the correct block of data is being accessed. Between the count area, the optional key area and the data area is a gap. If many blocks of data are stored there will be a lot of gaps on the track and so space will be wasted on the disk.

FBA disks are divided into fixed-size sectors. The advantage they have over CKD disks is that the user does not have to be concerned about block sizes because all blocks are 512 bytes long. A 3370 disk can hold 558,000 blocks.

Mini-disks

Mini-disks occupy part of a real disk, although some mini-disks are so large that they occupy a complete disk. Mini-disks are allocated to users, and each user has a directory entry for those mini-disks that

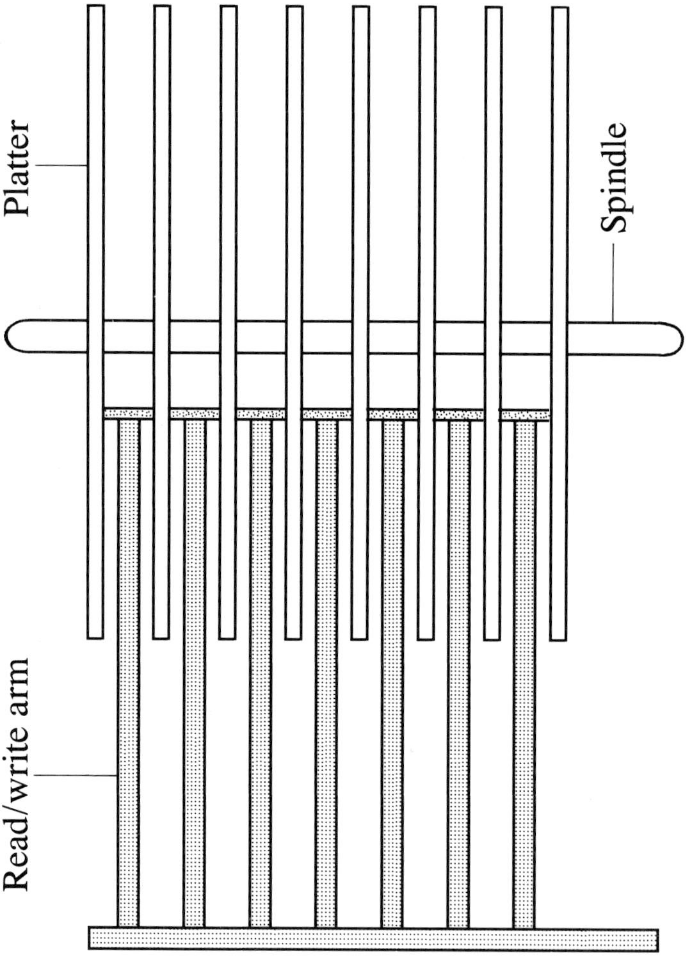

Figure 1.8 Diagram of a DASD

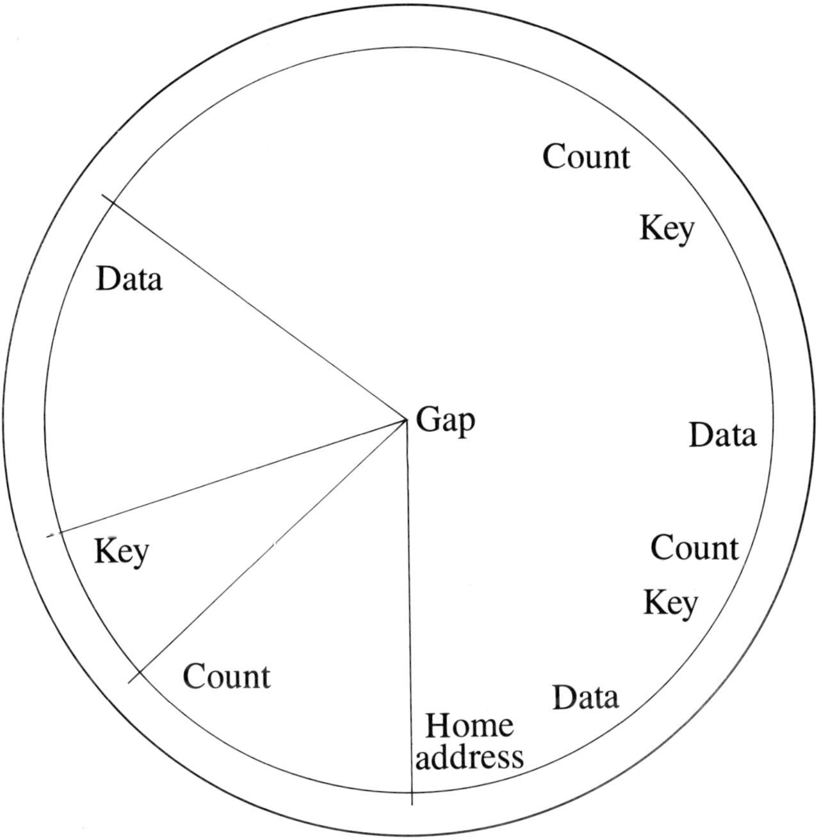

Figure 1.9 Count Key Data Format

are available to them. Most CMS users have a mini-disk at address 191 with a filemode of A, and this usually contains the EXECs and data files for that CMS user. An S disk (the systems disk), a D disk and a Y disk are also allocated.

When a user logs on, control blocks associated with any mini-disks allocated are stored in the Free Storage Area (FSA). When a user accesses a mini-disk, these control blocks are used to translate the virtual address of the mini-disk into a real address so that the request for access can go to the correct real disk. A user can allocate temporary mini-disks at any time. A temporary mini-disk can be used as a temporary file, and space is allocted from TDSK space.

Users often need to access mini-disks belonging to other users in order to use or make a copy of a particular file. This can be done using the LINK and ACCESS commands. They are released after use with the RELEASE and DETACH commands.

Console

The console is in fact a terminal (also known as a VDU — Visual Display Unit — or CRT — Cathode Ray Tube). The system console is attached to the processor itself and displays information about the system. It is this console that displays the System Activity Display (SAD) frames. The system console should not be confused with the operator console.

The operator console displays messages from VM (or other operating system). This is the console that the operator uses to enter various commands, eg:

ATT 481 user-id 280

This allocates a real tape drive at address 481 to a user who has a tape drive at virtual address 280.

Terminal Cluster Controller

In the same way that tape drives have a tape-drive controller between them and the channel, and DASD have a DASD controller between them and a channel, so terminals (CRTs or VDUs) have a terminal cluster controller between them and the channel. It performs a similar job in buffering data input and output to the terminals. It also ensures that data packets are routed to the right terminal and it will multiplex data from the terminals to the channel.

The cluster controller (eg 3274) could be attached to a modem which is linked through the telephone network to another modem and the second modem could be connected through a communications controller (eg 3725) to a channel. If this is the situation the cluster controller and terminals are described as remote. This is illustrated in Figure 1.10. If the cluster controller is directly attached to a channel it is described as being local.

Terminals

The terminal device that the majority of users work from is a screen and keyboard either in full colour or green. The user types commands or programs, etc, in at the keyboard and the screen shows what has been typed. It also shows any response from the system when commands etc are entered. Some users may have local printers so that they can take screen dumps or hard copies of output from the machine.

Printers

Printers may be high-speed impact printers or laser printers. They may be restricted to printing on 11-inch multiline paper, or they may be able to deal with special stationery. They may be attached to a channel, in which case they are called local printers, or they may be located at the end of a communications link, in which case they are considered to be remote printers. Printers are used to produce the output from the spool that has been put there as a result of a piece of work having been completed. Print files that are stored on the spool are not always printed.

Communications Controller

The communications controller acts as a Front End Processor (FEP) in that it controls I/O to and from modems and telephone communication links. It is a necessary piece of equipment if a site requires links to remote devices. An example of a communications controller is a 3725. Much of the work of running a network can be performed by a communication controller and the processor can get on with processing useful work. Software that is found in a communications controller includes NCP (Network Control Program) and EP (Emulation Program).

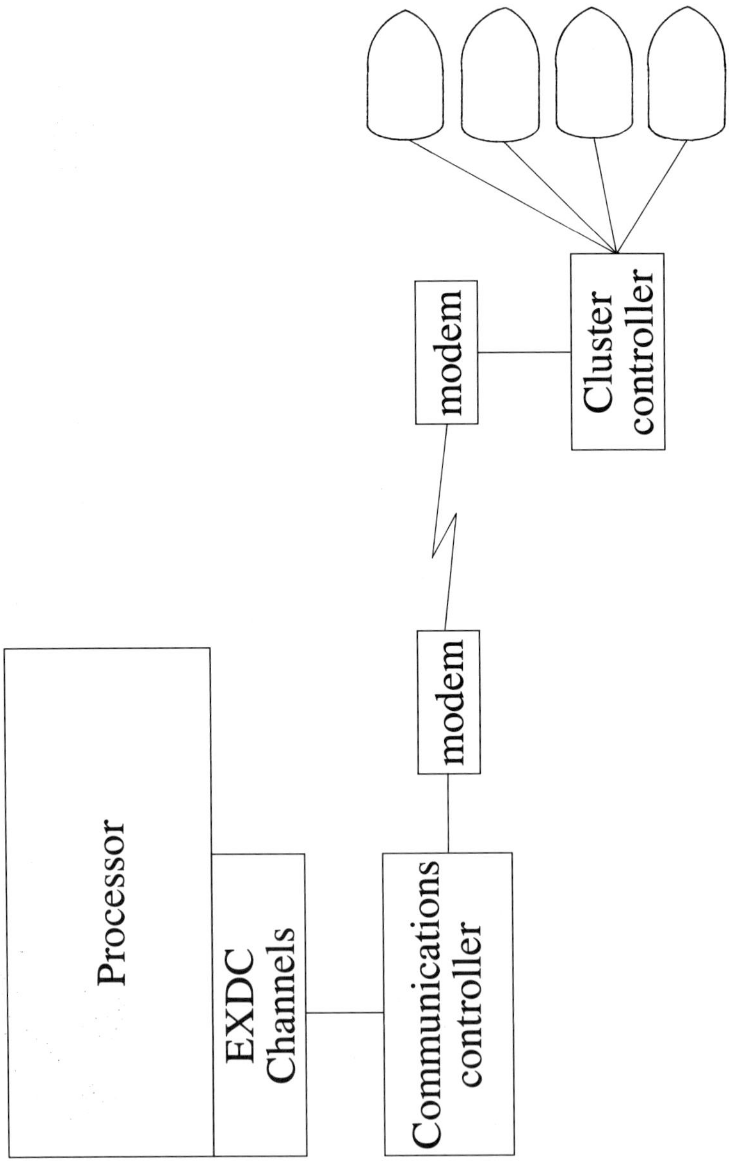

Figure 1.10 Communication Link

Other Hardware

Other hardware components that can be found in a machine room include:

- Solid-state DASD devices — These are not made by IBM, and can be used to speed up data access.
- Power units — These (eg 3089) supply power to all the components of the computer.
- Coolant Distribution Units — These are used at sites with water-cooled processors (eg 3087).

SOFTWARE

The VM control program is required to run a VM system. This contains modules that are stored in the system nucleus. These modules control the real hardware and control the way that systems running under VM are processed. For example, the SRM, which is made up of a scheduler and a despatcher, will control when a virtual machine that wants to be processed will gain control of the CPU and be processed. VM also supplies modules that allow systems running underneath it to communicate.

With VM comes an operating system called CMS. This is what the majority of people who come into contact with VM are using. It offers a range of commands, it has a file-storing capacity, it contains a file editor (XEDIT) and many systems such as SQL/DS and PROFS can run under it. CMS can be used for a whole range of activities and these are discussed in Chapters 9 and 10.

In order to transfer print files to remote sites and to receive reader files a facility called Remote Spooling Communication Subsystem (RSCS) can be used. This is used primarily to communicate with Remote Batch Terminals (RBTs), or Remote Job Entry stations (RJEs).

The fourth component of VM is IPCS which stands for Interactive Problem Control System. This runs under CMS and can be used by system programmers as a way of resolving system problems. With VM/XA this product has been superseded by the Dump Viewing Facility (DVF).

Other software that is associated with VM includes:

- SMART — This is the Real Time Monitor (VM/RTM) that can be used as an on-line monitor to report any exceptional conditions to the operator or systems programmers.
- VMMAP — This is an historical monitor and reporting tool.
- PROFS — The PRofessional OFfice System is the office automation product for VM. It is usually run with PASF (PROFS Application Support Feature), which contains a set of enhancements to PROFS. It runs under CMS.
- SQL/DS — The most frequently installed database product at VM sites is the Structured Query Language/Data System. It is an example of a relational database product. It runs under CMS.
- VTAM — The Virtual Telecommunications Access Method is teleprocessing software that allows SNA (Systems Network Architecture) communication across a network. It runs under GCS.

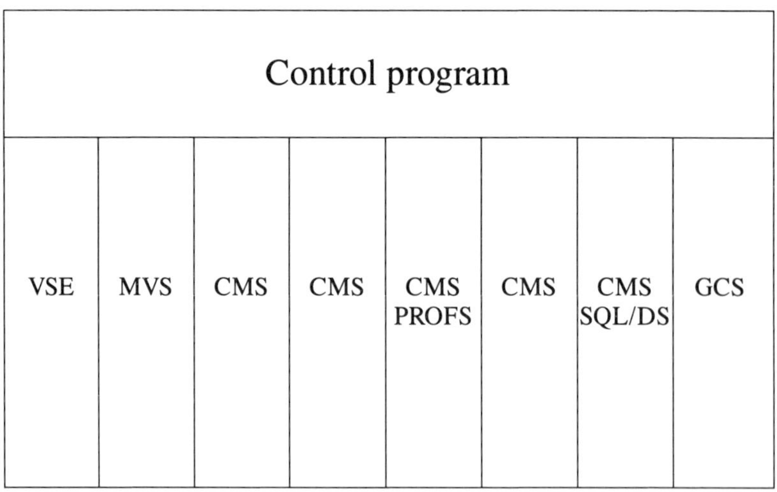

Figure 1.11 Example System Set-up

- GCS — The Group Control System is layer of software that runs under VM. It is under GCS that most of the communications software runs, for example VTAM, RSCS and NetView.
- PVM — The introduction of Passthrough (PVM) allowed terminal users to access easily whichever system they required.

The VM hypervisor allows address spaces, or virtual machines containing other software to be run under it. The instructions in the virtual machines are executed under the control of SRM (Systems Resource Manager — see p.91). In addition to the software mentioned above, it is possible to run other operating systems (eg VSE or MVS) under VM. In addition the IBM version of Unix (AIX/370) will only run under VM. An example of the system set-up is shown in Figure 1.11.

2 Background

The first part of this chapter looks at the history of VM and is followed by a discussion of the various versions of the product that are currently available. A short section suggesting the probable future of VM follows that. The final part of the chapter looks at the reasons that users have given for installing VM, and which version of VM is best for which type of work.

VM HISTORY

Before any attempt is made to modify or tune any operating system it is necessary to understand how the operating system works, ie what the specific task is of each component of that system and how those components interact. Part of this understanding can come from an appreciation of the history of the system and knowing what pressures or constraints it had to contend with in the past.

During the early to mid-1960s a team of scientists at Cambridge in Massachusetts (USA) was working on a system that would allow each user to operate what had all the appearance of being an individual computer system. Although there was only one set of hardware, every user would be able to work as if he or she were the only user on that hardware. In this way, multiple copies of the hardware would appear to exist, ie they would virtually exist as opposed to really existing. The users would work from a terminal, which would be the console for that virtual machine, and control their own disks, tapes and unit record devices. Unit record devices included printers, card readers and card punches. The software was called at that time CP/40.

At the same time, other scientists were working on a user-friendly operating system which they called the Cambridge Monitor System (CMS).

CP/40 was further developed to become CP/67, and this was sold commercially with CMS in the late 1960s to run on IBM 360/67 machines. These machines used the old 360 architecture which IBM marketed by claiming that, just as there were 360 degrees in a circle, so their processors could encompass any workload. However, IBM found 360 architecture somewhat limiting and brought out a new improved architecture called 370 architecture. This architecture is, to a great extent, the basis of all current IBM mainframes. The marketing department could not have 370 degrees in a circle, so they said that, just as 360 architecture was the architecture for the 1960s, so 370 architecture would be the architecture for the 1970s.

To go with 370 architecture, CP/67 was renamed as VM/370 (where VM stands for Virtual Machine). At the same time CMS became the Conversational Monitor System, which was considered to be a way of highlighting its interactive nature rather than its original source (ie Cambridge). Bundled in with VM/370 was a problem control system that ran under CMS; this was called the Interactive Problem Control System (IPCS). There was also a communications package that would allow card decks to be submitted from remote sites, and would allow output to be sent to remote sites; this was called Remote Spooling Communication Subsystem (RSCS).

Although VM was available throughout the 1970s, it was not marketed very actively and many people at IBM, it is suggested, would have preferred it to have been forgotten. However, in the late 1970s VM/SP was released, which contained all the good features of VM/370 release 6 plus all the extra add-ons that people usually required. These add-ons had previously been sold separately as SEPP and BSEPP (System Extension Program Product and Basic System Extension Program Product). The emergence of this new VM coincided with the arrival of the 4300 series of processors and the fortunes of both soared.

There have been a number of releases of VM/SP and a High Performance Option (HPO) is available for users who are running high-performance operating systems under VM. With the introduction of MVS/XA, IBM produced an XA version of VM so that sites could run MVS/XA as a VM guest. More recently IBM have released a fully functional version of VM/XA, which offers all the added facilities available with the extended architecture. IBM have also produced a cut-down version of VM/SP which sold as the version of VM to run on their lacklustre 9370 processors. A summary of VM's history is shown in Figure 2.1.

VM VERSIONS

Currently IBM are marketing four versions of VM which offer different facilities and are aimed at users with varying requirements.

The four versions of VM are:

- VM/IS;
- VM/SP;
- VM/SP HPO;
- VM/XA SP.

VM/IS

VM/IS (Virtual Machine/Integrated System) is clearly aimed at users of smaller processors who need some of the facilities that are available with VM but are not planning to make any alterations to VM itself at the systems programming level. The typical profile for sites with VM/IS would be one where the processor was a 9370 and there were few programmers.

VM/IS is supposed to be easy to install and the process is made even simpler by IBM's SolutionPacs. A user is supposed to identify the facilities that will be required and IBM bundles together suitable software packages with compatible release levels and VM/IS into a SolutionPac. The SolutionPac is supposed to be easy to install and the required system can be up and running within a short period of time and with almost no difficulties experienced. VM/IS is in almost all respects a version of VM/SP and like VM/SP it supports up to 16 megabytes (MB) of real storage (working space inside the processor) and 16 channels (used to communicate between the processor and I/O devices).

Although VM/IS may be very easy to install, any site that wants to tune its VM system is, at some point, going to have to employ a system programmer.

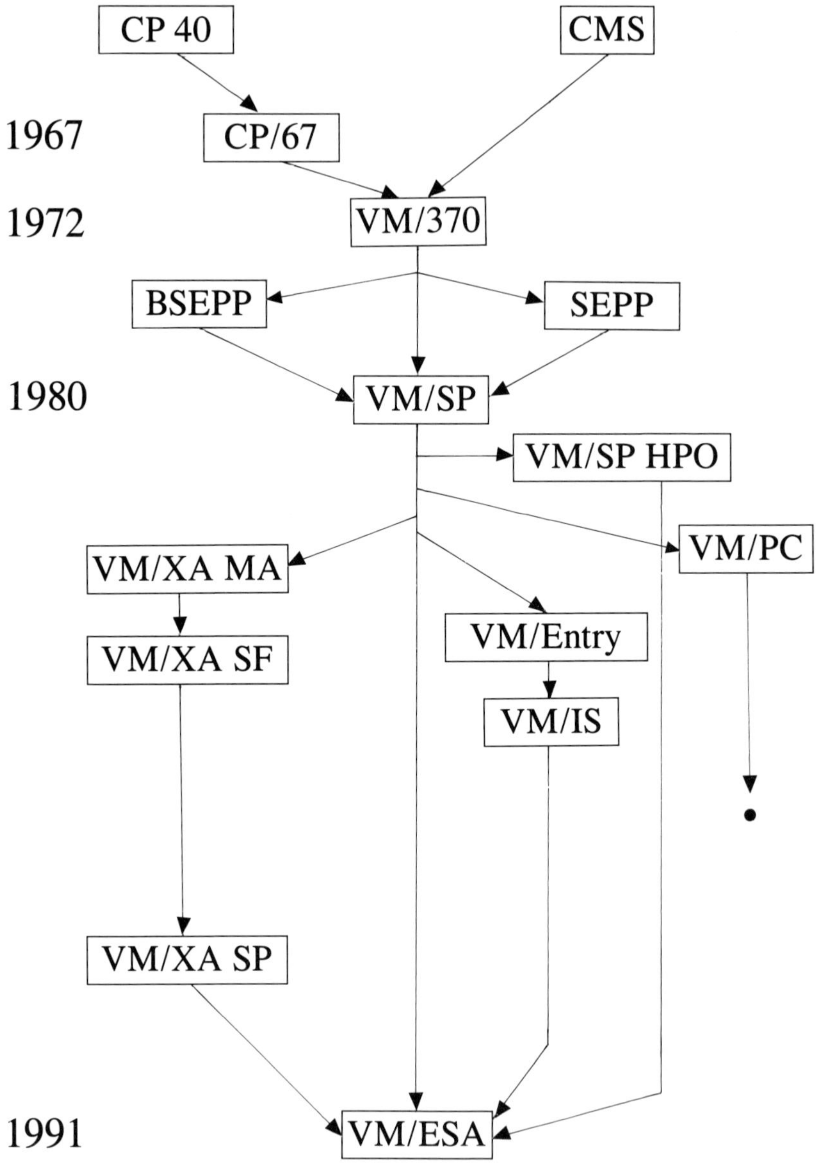

Figure 2.1 History of VM

VM/SP

VM/SP (Virtual Machine/System Product) is the standard VM offering from IBM. It is sometimes referred to as the vanilla version of VM. It contains all the facilities that are associated with VM and some extra ones that are only now becoming available with other VM versions, eg the Shared File System (SFS) and APPC/VM VTAM Support (AVS).

VM/SP is usually installed on medium-sized processors, typically the 4300 series machines. VM/IS, which usually runs on smaller machines, is a version of VM/SP. The majority of sites which run VM/SP also run a VSE-operating system as a guest system under it. VM/SP can support up to 16MB of real storage but cannot make any use of expanded storage where this is available. VM/SP is also restricted to only 16 channels for I/O, and it cannot use cache in DASD controllers (3990s etc).

VM/SP HPO

VM/SP HPO (Virtual Machine/System Product High Performance Option) is a version of VM designed for larger processors operating at sites where processor performance is treated as being of great importance. Although the O on HPO would suggest that this is an option, in fact sites that require high performance have the option to install it or have degraded performance. In other words it is really no option at all.

HPO is usually installed on 3080 and 3090 series processors where a high-performance guest-operating system is running. Typically, the guest-operating system is MVS/SP although it could be a later version of VSE. These systems have multiple address spaces and HPO has facilities to speed up the way that multiple address spaces are handled by VM in real storage. VM/SP HPO will support up to 64MB of real storage and can allocate up to 16MB sections to individual virtual machines. HPO can make use of expanded storage where available. It also increases the number of channels that are available from 16 to 32 and can make use of DASD controllers that have cache.

VM/XA SP

VM/XA SP (Virtual Machine/eXtended Architecture System Product) is a fully functional version of VM and it is able to make use of all the advantages of XA architecture, including 31-bit addressing. As yet, there are not very many sites that have XA SP installed. This is probably due to the fact that version 1 was a controlled release, which means that not very many sites were able to get hold of it. Version 2 was released in December 1988 and the number of sites where it has been installed is growing all the time.

The typical VM/XA SP site would have a large processor (typically a multi-engined processor — eg 3094) and would be running MVS/XA or MVS/ESA as guest systems under VM. Such sites would put a premium on performance and would expect to spend time on tuning and capacity-planning exercises. VM/XA will support up to 2GB of real storage and expanded storage and it will allow each virtual machine to have up to 999MB of virtual storage. It can support up to 3000 CMS users who can be running in either 24- or 31-bit mode. With XA the concept of channels is replaced by a subchannel system and XA SP can support up to 256 subchannels. It can also exploit cache DASD controllers.

FUTURE

Predicting the future is always a hazardous activity and yet it is one that every site has got to engage in if there are plans to install any piece of hardware or software. A site needs to choose hardware that the manufacturer is still developing so that the model installed can be upgraded at a later date if need be, or resold while it still retains some second-hand value rather than being useful only as scrap.

Selecting software has similar pitfalls to selecting hardware. If a version of VM seems to fit exactly the specified requirements at the present, what will be the situation in the future? Will the version be capable of handling increased workloads or running on larger, faster machines? The other problem is whether the version of VM selected is still going to be around in a few years' time.

At the present, it appears that IBM are slowly phasing out the HPO version of VM. The evidence for this comes from the fact that new facilities, eg the Shared File System (SFS) and APPC/VM VTAM Support (AVS), have been made available with SP first, before HPO. In the long term it appears that IBM would prefer users of high-performance systems to run them as guest systems under VM/XA. However, there is not yet enough third-party software available to make the XA alternative as attractive as perhaps it will be in the near future.

The future of a VM system in some form seems assured, in the medium-term future, because IBM have included it in their set of proposals and specifications known as SAA (Systems Application Architecture). Some more cynical pundits have predicted the demise of VM because there is no reason for it to exist any more. The rationale for this argument is that VM was used mainly for three reasons. The reasons given are:

- conversion;
- running multiple VSE systems;
- using CMS.

It is suggested that the conversion from one operating system to another one can be carried out using two logical partitions (LPARs) on a 3090 (or above) processor with PR/SM (Processor Resource/System Manager) installed.

The requirement to run multiple VSE systems became no longer necessary with the introduction of VSE release 3.2, which raised the number of address spaces that could run under VSE from three to nine. This means that programs could run in the address spaces provided under one copy of VSE rather than requiring multiple copies of VSE to present enough address spaces for them all to run.

CMS, although a part of the VM system, could be made a part of the MVS system or VSE system and this would remove the third major reason sites give for installing VM. It would mean that VM could be axed completely. However, this last proposal is not one that IBM appear to be working on and it is unlikely that IBM would axe the VM system when it is generating so much revenue for them.

Some six years after the introduction of MVS/XA came the introduction of VM/XA. With the introduction, in 1988, of MVS/ESA many pundits now predict the arrival of a VM/ESA product. This would certainly seem to be in line with IBM thinking, but the delay before a working version of VM/ESA is available may be considerable. The future of VM/IS seems assured so long as there is a VM/SP version and small machines to run it on.

The other suggested future for VM is one in which the functions of the control program are written as microcode and stored in the hardware. The evidence for this is in the use of PR/SM (Processor Resource/System Manager) on the 3090s. PR/SM can be used to partition a multiprocessor into up to seven logical partitions on which different operating systems can run. This feature is almost exactly the same as the Multiple High Performance Guest (MHPG) feature of VM/XA. MHPG allows up to six guest systems to run with near-native performance under VM. Both systems make use of the SIE (Start Interpretive Execution) microcode in the hardware. Also many of the VM instructions are carried out faster by including them in the microcode. This is the basis for assists such as PMA. If this trend were to be continued then all of the code could be microcoded and the need for VM as a hypervisor would be removed.

The true future of VM is probably being worked out by the Advanced Systems Development group at Kingston, in New York state. The group was originally called the Advanced VM Development group, but changed its name shortly after being set up.

REASONS FOR INSTALLING VM

The reasons given for installing VM at sites are many and various, and this is a reflection of the uses that can be made of VM. The most frequently given reasons are to enable multiple guest-operating systems to run on one set of hardware, and to take advantage of the personal computing facilities that are available, in particular with CMS, but also with APL (A Programming Language). A slightly less frequently given reason for installing VM is for the development and testing of software. The other reasons that sites have for installing VM include:

- using it for conversion (eg VSE to MVS);
- storage relief;
- a need to run VSE on hardware installed;
- upgrading guest-operating system.

WORKLOADS

It is necessary to select a version of a VM system that best suits the type of work that is to be run under that system. When the system is installed it is best to try to restrict the type of work that is to be run to the types that the system does best. Some guidelines are given below.

VM/IS

VM/IS is designed to run on small processors, eg 9370s or 4341s, and at sites that do not have a full-time systems programmer. It will not support a guest-operating system. It is considered to be a fairly cheap (in comparison with others) solution to the problem of needing to supply processing capability possibly across a wide geographical area.

VM/SP

VM/SP is considered to be suitable for small to medium mainframes that require support for a VSE guest-operating system. It is preferred to IS if there are to be more than 128 CMS users, a 3800 laser printer subsystem is installed and program development is being carried out.

VM/SP HPO

VM/SP HPO is suited to larger processors (3080s or 3090s) or 4381s with more than 16MB of memory. The guest system that benefits most from HPO is MVS/SP, but VSE systems using VAE can also benefit. HPO also suits sites that are running a demanding Information Centre and a CMS-intensive environment.

VM/XA SP

VM/XA SP is suited to the largest processors (3090-600s) and offers a system that makes best use of expanded storage. It supports up to six preferred guest systems, which could all be MVS/XA or MVS/ESA. The bimodal CMS makes best use of the extra addressable storage space, and the system is suited to highly intensive and demanding workloads.

SECTION II

VM Basics; Operational Considerations; and Installation, Maintenance and Problems

The second section of the book covers those areas that make up the technical background knowledge of systems programmers at any VM site. The first chapter in the section looks at the CP-owned DASD areas, describing the function of the areas and how they are set up. It then examines the various system modules that define the VM environment at a site. Finally, it describes some of the control blocks that are commonly referred to. The second chapter looks at the operational aspects of VM, describing the different start types, the use of AUTOLOG1, VMUTIL, MAINT and PROP. It also looks at the use of assists and the various commands that are available to modify system performance. The third chapter concentrates on how VM systems are initially installed and how they are maintained. The final section of that chapter looks at various problem situations, how to identify what is happening and how to resolve the problems encountered.

3 VM Basics

This chapter describes the 'nuts and bolts' of a VM system, concentrating on those basic components that VM systems programmers need to understand for their systems to function well, and before any tuning activities can take place.

CP-OWNED DASD AREAS

When the processor is powered off, the system programs, saved systems and other control blocks or pointers that need to be available when the VM system is next IPLed (including the directory) are stored on a non-volatile medium which is typically a disk. In addition, when the system is running it needs somewhere to store pages that are on auxiliary storage, and spool files etc. These are all stored on special areas of disks. The disks are called CP-owned DASD.

CP-owned DASD contain four main areas. These are:

- PERM;
- TEMP;
- TDSK;
- DRCT.

There may also be two additional areas, DUMP and OVRD (on later releases of VM).

The areas are allocated using the CP FORMAT/ALLOCATE program DMKFMT. An example of this is given in Figure 3.1 and an example of the resulting system set-up is shown in Figure 3.2.

```
FORMAT,481,3380,VMDSK1,000,403
ALLOCATE,481,3380,VMDSK1
DRCT,001,002
PERM,003,095
TDSK,096,403
END
```

Figure 3.1 Example of FORMAT and ALLOCATE Commands

The location of areas such as nucleus, checkpoint, warm start, saved system, paging, spooling, TDSK, DRCT are specified in the allocation map in cylinder 0 of each DASD formatted using DMKFMT, and in the SYSRES and SYSPAG macros in DMKSYS. (DMKSYS is described on detail on pp. 46-8.) They must be on CP-owned DASD which are specified to CP by the SYSOWN macro.

PERM

The PERM area is subdivided into a number of areas including CP nucleus, warm start, saved systems areas and error recording. The areas are allocated using the SYSRES macro.

CP Nucleus

The CP nucleus part of the PERM area (SYSNUC) contains the systems programs that are loaded at IPL time into the nucleus area of real storage and into the pageable nucleus.

Warm Start

The warm start area (SYSWRM) is used to allow a warm start of VM (as opposed to a cold start). The area contains all the information about the state of the system when it was shut down. This information includes pointers to spool files, etc. When VM is re-IPLed it will load this information and continue processing as if it had never stopped.

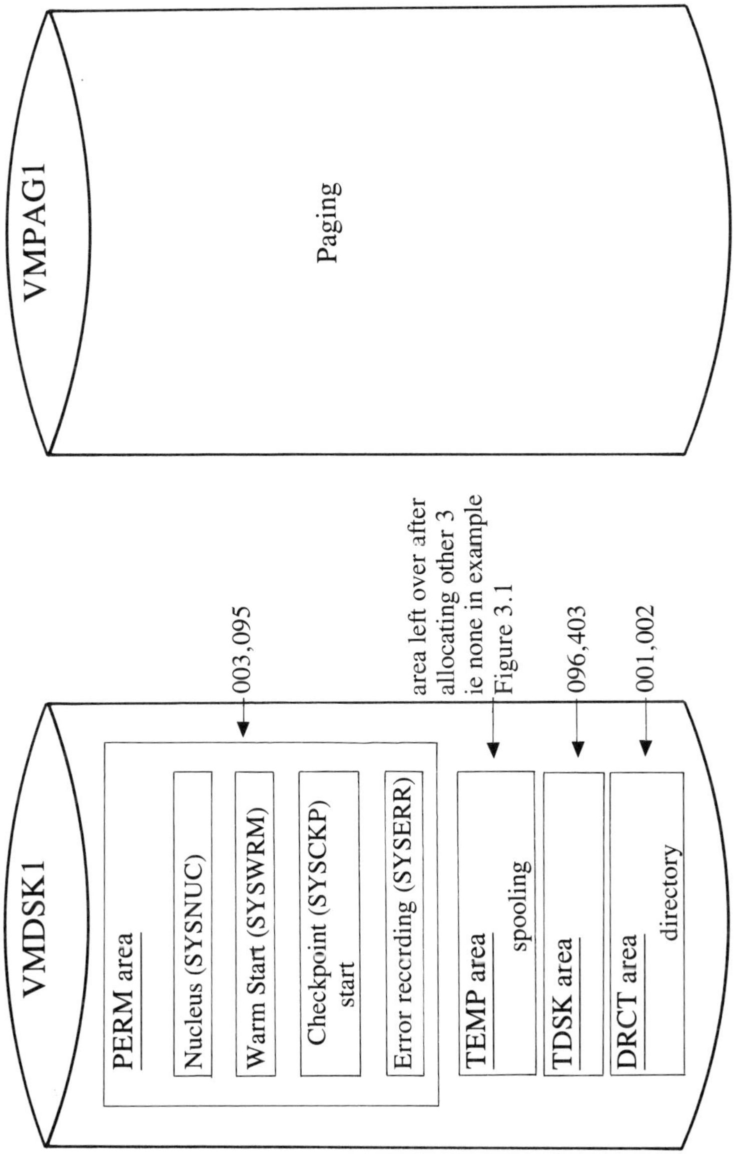

Figure 3.2 System Areas on Disk

Saved System Areas

Saved system areas (SYSCKP) contain code that can be used by a number of users. It is loaded into storage once, so that users do not have to load from disk every time they want to use it. CMS is an example of a saved system. With XA saved systems are stored in the spool area.

Error Recording

The error recording area (SYSERR) has information about hardware errors and some software errors that occur on devices written into it. The majority of errors recorded are I/O errors and machine check errors. The stored data can be processed using the CPEREP command. This will produce various reports and may be optionally used to initialise the area. The CPEREP program is run at most sites on a regular basis.

TEMP

TEMP space is used for spooling and paging space. Any space on CP-owned DASD not allocated is assumed to be TEMP. CP is informed about the space allocated using the SYSOWN macro (illustrated later).

Both spooling and paging transfer data in units of 4K and the spooling subsystem uses the paging subsystem to perform all its I/O. The spooling manager uses the same CCPD designation as paging when writing out a spool page. With SP and HPO there are no separate counters and it is impossible to separate I/O for paging and I/O for spooling. The IND PAG command always includes spool paging in its output. High values may not therefore mean high amounts of paging, but may indicate high amounts of spooling. With XA there are four counters that can be used to separate spooling activities from paging activities. These are PLSPIOPR, PLSPIOPW, PLSPIOSR, PLSPIOSW. PAGE and spool areas can be kept separate using CP FORMAT/ALLOCATE PAGE. Using this type of set-up separate information about spooling and paging can be obtained.

Paging and spooling I/O always takes precedence over other I/O. If S and Y disks are placed on the same packs as either paging or spooling areas the response to CMS users may deteriorate enormously. Paging will spill into spool (TEMP) space if there is not enough PAGE space. This will prevent the system from crashing, although performance will deteriorate. Spool files will not overflow into paging areas.

Paging is described fully in Chapter 8

Spooling

The spool area on disk is formatted into 4K pages and is used to store print files, reader files and punch files created by every virtual machine on the system. Several problems may be encountered with the spool. Some of these are given below:

- Messages (DMK401I and DMK400I) are only sent to the operator when the spool is 90 per cent full and 100 per cent full (usually too late).
- If the spool area fills up, users will receive 'intervention required' messages on virtual unit record output devices. More importantly, accounting and monitoring data may be lost.
- Some users treat the spool as a mini-disk overflow area, and store data as spool files. It is not easy to find out who is doing this or to charge them for doing it.
- A full spool degrades overall system performance because of the resulting large numbers of spool file control blocks (SFBLOKs) in the Control Program's work areas. Another problem that can occur is when a checkpoint (CKPT) or force start is required. Verifying spool chains can make the IPL process take a long time. A checkpoint start of VM may take up to 15 minutes while spool file chains are validated.
- There is no user facility for backing up and restoring spool files. If a user inadvertently deletes a spool file the operator must use the SPTAPE command to restore the file from a back-up (assum ing SPTAPE back-ups of spool files exist).
- The SPTAPE command must be used regularly to dump spool files to tape.
- There is no audit trail of what happens to spool files (eg who deleted them etc).
- Spool space availability and spooling activity are generally difficult to investigate.

With HPO release 5 and above, the system can support up to 9900 spool files per user. In practice this number may be reduced. The total number of spool files supported is specified with the DMKSYS SYSSPL option on the SYSRES macro. There is a restriction on the number of spool files supported which is enforced by the size of the checkpoint area. Also with HPO release 5, reader SFBLOKs (spool-file control blocks) are stored in new SYSSPOOL address space, and the performance of both checkpoint and force starts is improved with the use of overlapping I/O.

Although it is often considered to be a good idea to clear down unwanted spool files on a regular basis, some users can experience problems with this arrangement, particularly after long illness or holidays. The best performance can be achieved if enough spool space is made available and spread across as many DASD as possible. However, this is not possible at many sites.

With XA, spooling is used for the following:

- CP monitoring data;
- virtual machine spooling;
- DCSSs (DisContiguous Saved Segments) and NSSs (Named Saved Systems);
- DUMPs;
- printer FCBs (Forms Control Blocks) and UCSs (Universal Character Sets);
- user class override file.

XA can support up to 9999 files per user, although the total number of spool files for an individual user can be limited by the SPOOLFILE MAXSPOOL directory entry. As with HPO the total number of spool files supported may be restricted by the size of the checkpoint start area. It is worth remembering that one 3380 cylinder can support almost 154,000 spool files.

If user mini-disks are not placed on disks with spool files, the spool disks will not need to be backed up with the nightly back-ups. This can save time. However, if things are arranged in this way it is a good idea, at least occasionally, to perform SPTAPE back-ups of the spool files.

TDSK

The TDSK area contains temporary mini-disks. These act as scratchpad areas and can be allocated by any CMS user. They are de-allocated when a user logs off, or uses the CMS command to de-allocate them.

Many sites have more than one TDSK extent on several CP-owned volumes. In this case, when VM is IPLed the SYSOWN macro of DMKSYS is read from left to right and ALOCBLOKs (control blocks containing information about areas allocated on disk) are created for TEMP, PAGE and TDSK extents allocated by DMKFMT in cylinder 0 of each pack. For the TDSK extents, each new ALOCBLOK created is chained on the top of the TDSK ALOCBLOKs chain, and is pointed to by DMKPGTxx (where xx = 7A for 3375 devices, 8A for 3380, etc). The first (from left to right) TDSK extent found on the SYSOWN list becomes the last on the chain (ie a LIFO chain).

When a temporary mini-disk is created, the first ALOCBLOK in the chain is searched and if enough space is found, the temporary mini-disk will be created in that area. If there is not enough space on it, the second block will be searched, and so on. Temporary mini-disks are created using the DMKDEF module.

If DASD volumes are coded on the SYSOWN macro in ascending order of the size of TDSK extents they own, then after an IPL they are scanned in the opposite order. Therefore, the largest extent is used first, typically by small temporary mini-disks. Should a user require a large temporary mini-disk, the largest extents will have become fragmented by several small mini-disks.

Performance improvements can be gained by specifying DASD volumes in the SYSOWN macro in descending order of TDSK extent size. This forces CP to allocate the small temporary mini-disks on the first and smaller extents, leaving the larger ones free for large temporary mini-disks that may be needed later.

DRCT

The DRCT area contains the system directory. The system directory contains an entry for every virtual machine that can log on to VM. There are, in fact, two versions, one that is compiled and in use and as such unavailable for modification — called the object directory — and one that is in a text format and can be updated by systems programmers.

An example of an individual user's entry is given in Chapter 9.

Directory Maintenance

The source directory is a CMS file with a filetype of DIRECT. It is usually kept on one of MAINT's disks. The source directory can be read and modified. The DIRECT command can be used to create the object directory. When the DIRECT command is used it will optionally read a file called RPWLIST DATA which contains 'illegal' passwords. If a password is found in the file the directory is updated to prevent the user from being able to log on. This feature was made available by IBM as a way of forcing sites to change the default passwords shipped with the system.

The first control statement that is not a comment in the directory must be the DIRECT statement. This specifies the location of the object directory and is usually a virtual address. If the real address of the directory disk volume is coded this allows the source directory to be used with the stand-alone directory utility. Because the source directory file is so large at most sites it is cumbersome to maintain and most sites use a package to help. The package most frequently used is DIRMAINT from IBM. The directory maintenance package requires two virtual machines. One is called DIRMAINT and is the directory manager. The other is called DATAMOVE and it performs copying and formatting tasks.

Before a new entry can be made it is important to run DISKMAP. DISKMAP is a REXX EXEC that produces a CMS output file listing all disk allocations in the directory (REXX EXECs are described in more detail in Chapter 10). The DISKMAP output will show where there is space on a disk for the new mini-disks to be defined. It will also show areas of overlap of mini-disks. Apart from MAINT and the machine for DDR back-up there should not be any overlap. Overlaps between users' mini-disks can lead to security and data integrity problems.

Because special DASD areas are allocated using DMKFMT rather than MDISK statements in the directory it is possible to 'forget' which areas have already been allocated. MDISK statements are used in the directory to allocate mini-disks to virtual machines (users). To overcome the problem dummy user-ids are set up with mini-disks that overlay the system areas. The naming convention is to prefix and suffix the name of the area with a dollar sign ($), eg $PAGE$ for the PAGE area etc.

When a new directory (containing all user-ids) is compiled CP is told to use it by the DIAGnose X'3C' command. Some items in the object directory can be updated by a privileged user, using the DIAGnose X'84' command. (DIAGnose instructions are described in the Glossary.)

XA provides the facility to use several directories: a primary for the production system, and one or more alternatives for test or emergency use. The search for a directory starts at the system resident volume and continues through the list of all volumes defined as CP-owned until a valid directory is found and brought on-line. If no valid directory is found an OPERATOR user-id is created which may be used to bring a directory on-line.

DUMP

The DUMP area is used to store system dumps when they occur. If a separate DUMP area is not defined, dumps are written to the TEMP area.

OVRD

The OVRD area is the user class override area. It is used to store tables if the CP command privilege classes are customised at a site.

SYSTEM MODULES

System modules are used to define the environment within which CP will run. CP modules are prefixed DMK, or HCP with XA. CMS modules are prefixed DMS. SP and HPO have three important system modules within the CP nucleus; XA has one. The SP and HPO modules are:

- DMKRIO;
- DMKSNT;
- DMKSYS.

The important XA module is HCPSYS, which is similar in function to DMKSYS. There is an HCPRIO module, but it contains much less than DMKRIO.

DMKRIO

The DMKRIO module identifies all the real I/O device that CP can use, and their location in relation to each other. The DMKRIO module is made up of a number of macros. These include:

- RDEVICE macros which refer to real devices;
- RCTLUNIT macros which refer to real control units;
- RCHANNEL macros which refer to real channels.

The macros are used to build control blocks which are stored in main storage and used by CP when it needs to identify a real address etc. Whenever new devices are installed they have to be defined in DMKRIO before they can be used by CP.

DMKRIO also contains the RIOGEN macro, which lists the operator consoles. If the first one in the list is unavailable at IPL time it will try the next in the list. If none are available CP loads a disabled wait code of 5 into the PSW and stops. All consoles listed should be in the machine room, and should be on as many control units as possible. Note that the VM system operator is the first user-id to log on with privilege class of A.

With VM/XA, DMKRIO has been replaced by HCPRIO. This no longer contains information about control units or channels, just I/O devices. Another change with VM/XA is thc use of four-digit addressing and the use of subchannels instead of physical channels. Because of this the way it deals with real devices and addresses is different. With XA, all devices are specified in the Input Output Configuration DataSet (IOCDS) which is resident on the processor controller unit (3082 or 3092). New devices must also be specified on the IOCDS before CP can use them.

DMKSNT

The DMKSNT module contains a number of resource definitions. These include space allocation for saved software, a specification of how much of the software is shared amongst users, network control programs, 3800 printer data arrays and national language repositories. The names of the macros associated with these functions are NAMESYS, NAMENCP, NAME3800 and NAMELANG. If changes are made to DMKSNT it usually requires a SYSGEN and IPL to implement them. The

NAMENCP macro loads the appropriate Network Control Program into the Communications controller (eg 3745). The NAME3800 macro is used to define 3800 laser printers, and is only required if a 3800 printer is installed. The NAMELANG macro is used to define additional languages at sites where languages other than English are used.

An example of the NAMESYS macro is shown in Figure 3.3.

```
NAMESYS  SYSNAME = CMS
         SYSVOL = VMSRES,
         SYSTART = (006,1),
         SYSPGNM = (0-8,14-34,3824-4095),
         SYSPGCT = 302,
         SYSHRSG = (239-255),
         SYSSIZE = 256K,
         VSYSADR = 190,
         SYSCYL = 502,
         PARMRGS = (0,15),
         VSYSRES = VMSRES
```

Figure 3.3 Example NAMESYS Macro

SYSNAME is the name of the shared program (eg DCSS). SYSVOL gives the volume serial number of the pack containing the program. SYSSTART specifies the location of the shared program on the disk, ie page 1 of cylinder 6. SYSPGCT specifies the size of the program in pages.

With VM/XA, DMKSNT has been removed. Named Saved Systems and DisContiguous Saved Segments are kept in the spool area. They are defined and generated on-line without a SYSGEN having to be done, and may be manipulated by ordinary spool commands (ie QUERY, PURGE, SPTAPE). They are not erased during a cold start.

Forms Control Blocks or Buffers (FCBs) and Universal Character Set Buffers (UCBs) are buffers associated with line printers except 3800s. With XA the modules DMKFCB, -UCB, -UCC and -USS are replaced. This means that FCBs (Forms Control Blocks) can be added without a SYSGEN being done. The modules may exceed 4K in size because they are no longer part of the CP nucleus.

DMKSYS

The DMKSYS module most directly affects the performance of VM. If inappropriate values for system definitions are specified (and these may be different at different sites) the overall performance will be poor. Some of the macros within DMKSYS are:

- SYSCOR;
- SYSFCN;
- SYSJRL;
- SYSMON;
- SYSOPR;
- SYSOWN;
- SYSPAG;
- SYSPCLAS;
- SYSRES.

SYSCOR

The SYSCOR macro specifies the maximum size for main storage. An example of how it is done for an SP system is given in Figure 3.4.

```
SYSCOR RMSIZE=16M
```

Figure 3.4 Specifying Main Storage Size

SYSFCN

The SYSFCN macro is used only if the command class structure is extensively modified. The basic command class structure is described in Chapter 9.

SYSJRL

The SYSJRL macro is used to specify journalling options. The choice of options determines which accounting records are kept about resource usage. An example is the JOURNAL = YES option. This causes accounting records to be produced for unsuccessful access attempts.

SYSMON

The SYSMON macro identifies those parameters that are to be used in the collection of performance monitoring data. After collection the data is sent to a virtual reader.

SYSOPR

The SYSOPR macro specifies the user-id of the system operator and the user-id that is to receive the system dump after a system restart has occurred.

SYSOWN

The SYSOWN macro tells CP which of the CP-owned DASD have been formatted using DMKFMT. These DASD contain the DRCT, PERM, TDSK and TEMP areas. Examples of the macro are given in Figure 3.5.

```
SYSOWN (VMDSK1,TEMP),(VMPAG1,PAGE)
```

Figure 3.5 Example SYSOWN Macro

SYSPAG

The SYSPAG macro is used with HPO only to specify the SWAP and PAGE areas on disk etc. The space on the disks must first be formatted using DMKFMT. If extra disks are to contain PAGE or SWAP areas performance will degrade if the SYSPAG macro is duplicated to add these extra devices. This is because the additional devices specified will only be used when all devices listed in the first macro are full. Therefore, any extra packs should be added to the first macro. Performance will also be improved if, when there are four or more packs to be specified, they are specified on different channels. This will help to balance the system.

SYSPCLAS

The SYSPCLAS macro allows a site to specify that one or more printer output classes are to have a description printed at the top and bottom of every page. For example class S output may cause the words TOP SECRET to be written at the top of every page.

SYSRES

The SYSRES macro is used to specify to CP the DASD that are to be used for the major system areas and where on the DASD they are to be located. This is illustrated in Figure 3.6. An example of the way that they are defined is given in Figure 3.7.

SYSVOL specifies the VOLSER of the pack to be used. SYSRES gives the real address of the disk. SYSTYPE specifies the device type. SYSCLR=YES means that temporary disks should be reformatted with 0s before being allocated to another user. SYSNUC is the CP nucleus area, the start cylinder and the number of cylinders used are specified in the macro. SYSWRM is used for warm starts. During a normal shutdown various pointers to spool, network information and accounting information are stored in this area. SYSERR is the area used for recording hardware errors and is used by EREP. SYSCKP is the checkpoint area. It contains similar information to the warm start area, but it is written to while the system is running and used when the system is restarted after an abend. Performance improvements may be obtained by placing the SYSWRM (warm start), SYSCKP (checkpoint start) and SYSERR (error recording) files on the spool pack.

HCPSYS

With VM/XA to be ATTACHed to the system at IPL all the disk volumes

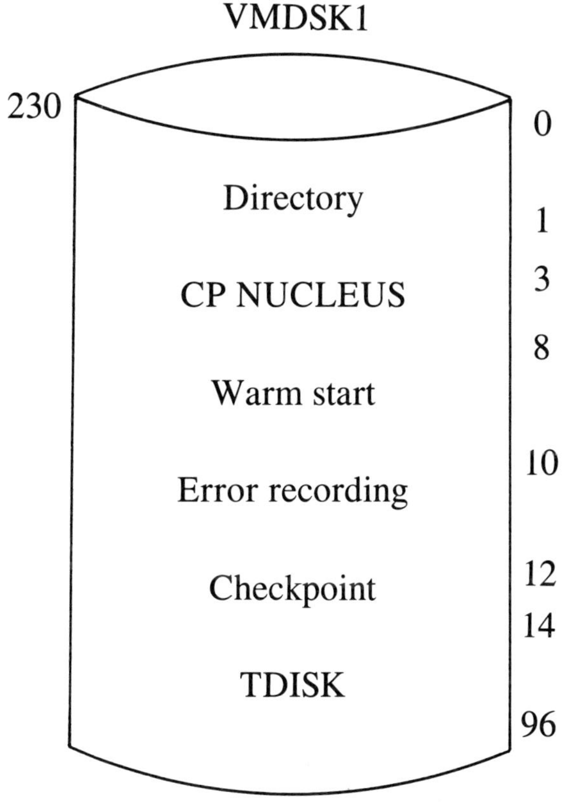

Figure 3.6 Formatted System Disk

```
SYSRES   SYSVOL = VMDSK1,
         SYSRES = 230,
         SYSTYPE = 3380,
         SYSCLR = YES,
         SYSNUC = (3,4),
         SYSWRM = (8,2,VMSRES),
         SYSERR = (10,2,VMSRES),
         SYSCKP = (12,2, VMSRES)
```

Figure 3.7 Example SYSRES Macro

(not just CP-owned volumes) have to be specified in HCPSYS. Alternatively AUTOLOG1 can be used to attach the disks to the system at IPL. The advantage of this second method is that disk volume labels can be added or changed without requiring a SYSGEN every time.

CONTROL BLOCKS

In order to keep track of what is happening in an active VM system, CP maintains control blocks. Control blocks are special areas of storage used to store information. A summary of some of these control blocks and their function is given below.

With SP and HPO, a control block called the VMBLOK is used to describe the attributes of a given virtual machine, including its running status. This control block is built in real storage when a user logs on and is removed when the user logs off. With XA the equivalent control block is VMDBK.

The Prefix Storage Area (PSA) is a CP control block that maps page zero of memory and contains pointers and flags used by CP.

When DMKRIO is assembled it generates a series of control blocks called RCHBLOKs, RCTBLOKs and RDEVBLOKs. RCHBLOKs contain information about the status of every real channel; RCTBLOKs contain information about the status of every real control unit; RDEVBLOKs contain information about the status of every real device.

The Virtual ConTroL unit BLOcK (VCTLBLOK) is a control block that contains the status of each of the control units in a particular virtual machine. The Virtual CHannel control BLOcK (VCHBLOK) contains the status of each of the channels in a particular virtual machine. The Virtual DEVice BLOcK (VDEVBLOCK) contains the status of each of the I/O devices in a particular virtual machine. With XA the hardware control block that contains much of this information is the HCPDEV control block.

When a mini-disk is accessed a control block is built called the ADT (Active Disk Table). The ADT contains details such as block sizes on the disk, number of files, etc. The control block is removed when the mini-disk is released.

When a file on disk is opened a control block called the AFT (Active File Table) is built. It is removed when the file is closed.

When a file on disk is accessed the FST (File Status Table) is read from the disk into virtual storage with the file. The FST is a control block that describes a CMS disk file.

SFBLOKs (Spool File control BLOcKs) are used to store information about spool files. The more spool files that exist, the greater the number of SFBLOKs that are stored.

ALOCBLOKs are created by the DMKFMT program for PAGE, TDSK and TEMP areas of CP-owned DASD and are stored in cylinder 0. ALOCBLOKs are grouped together in chains so that CP ‘knows’ where the different areas are located.

LOAD MAP

CPNUC MAP is the default name for the load map on disk. It contains ALOCBLOK anchors and other pointers to CP modules and shared segments in storage.

4 Operational Considerations

This chapter covers more of the basic information concerning the way that VM is set up and features those areas that operations staff are likely to come directly into contact with. It covers starting the system, the use of MAINT and PROP, assists, and commands that can be used on virtual machines to improve system performance.

SYSTEM START-UP

Very occasionally the processor will have to be powered on. This invokes the Initial Microcode Load (IML) sequence, which will load in microcode either from diskette or from its location on the processor controller. This will enable the system console to be used in order to start the IPL (Initial Program Load) procedure.

IPLs occur much more frequently than IMLs, and may be required for any number of reasons. The operator will select an address on the disk (or tape) that contains the bootstrap program. The microcode in the system will cause the first program on the selected disk to be loaded into storage. This contains the address of the nucleus programs and an instruction to load them in. Once these programs are starting to be loaded the operator will see information messages appearing on the console, and will be prompted for responses to other messages. The first message checks the system date and time. If necessary the TOD (Time Of Day) clock can be reset. The software will check to ensure that all CP-owned DASD are available. If not, a message will be sent to the operator (this rarely occurs with fixed disks). The Control Program will initialise all its storage tables (eg core table). Next CP requests the operator to enter the start type required. The choices available are:

- COLD;
- WARM;
- CKPT;
- FORCE.

The other choices are to press the enter key, which defaults a warm start, or the operator can choose from the menu DRAIN or SHUTDOWN.

A COLD start is used after a FORCE start or after new software has been installed. It initialises pointers to the spool area, which means that no spool files will be available from the previous VM session.

A WARM start allows the system to continue in the same state it was in when it was shut down. All spool files and accounting records are saved.

A CKPT (checkpoint) start is performed if a WARM start fails for any reason. A checkpoint start usually gets the system running, but accounting data and possibly some spool files will be lost.

A FORCE start is used in emergencies when WARM and CKPT have failed. There is typically some kind of serious problem and the procedure after IPL is to copy spool files to tape, shut down and re-IPL using the COLD start option.

The DRAIN option is used in combination with one of the previous four, and will DRAIN all unit record devices (usually there are only printers). The effect of this is to stop the printers from doing any printing until directly commanded to do so by the operator. It is used if a particular file must be printed first and it is suspected that a large file is top of the print queue.

The SHUTDOWN option is used to shut down the system straight away. It will write warm start records so that the next warm start should be easily performed.

The next stage is for CP to log the operator on to the console and start AUTOLOG1.

AUTOLOG1

AUTOLOG1 is a shared virtual machine that is known to CP and automatically logged on when CP is IPLed. It typically contains the start-up commands for a number of systems that are to run under VM. Because the commands are invoked automatically, the operator does not need to remember to key them in in the correct sequence and this removes a potential source of error. It also reduces flexibility about what is to be started and when. AUTOLOG1 can also contain various SET commands to define the VM environment for that session and may contain WAKEUP commands which will perform predetermined activities at predetermined times. A PROFILE EXEC on AUTOLOG1's A disk can act as a system-wide profile. When the profile has been executed and started other system resources, AUTOLOG1 can be logged off.

VMUTIL

VMUTIL is part of IPF (the Interactive Productivity Facility) and runs as a service machine. It acts as a general time-of-day event processor. It is controlled by the WAKEUP module with a parameter file giving the actions to be performed.

MAINT

MAINT is a CMS user-id that is used by all systems programmers for system maintenance. The MAINT user-id is set up at most sites so that it can issue all the CP and CMS commands. All CMS users have a link to the S and Y disks that belong to MAINT. These disks usually contain important software that other users need to have read-access to. At most sites there are more disks assigned for MAINT. The recommended set-up for MAINT is shown in Figure 4.1.

With HPO, disks 196, 296 and 396 are installed to contain HPO versions of files stored on 194, 294 and 394 disks respectively. The disks should be accessed in the order HPO, CP, CMS.

PROP

The PRogrammable OPerator (PROP) was introduced with VM/SP release 2. It provides a convenient way of combining consoles from many systems. It directs console output from selected virtual machines or VM systems through the Programmable Operator (PROP). PROP logs all messages and, using a table, forwards selected messages to a

Address	Use
190	CMS S disk — contains CMS commands, EXECs and library files
193	Base version of CMS object code and macro libraries
194	Base version of object code and macro libraries
293	CMS source updates and current PUT tape's version of object code and macro library files
294	CP source updates and current PUT tape's version object code and macro library files
295	Local customisation files (may be done on 191)
393	Base version of CMS source code
394	Base version of source code

Figure 4.1 Recommended MAINT Set-up

logical operator (LOPER). LOPER sees filtered messages from all PROP-controlled machines. With PROP running on the system-operator virtual machine, messages can be routed to any workstation, eg those responsible for printers, tapes and the network. PROP ensures that they can be sent only information that is relevant to their respective functions. Routine information can be filtered out and recorded in the PROP log file, for later analysis if required.

If a site needs to route a particular message to multiple users it can be done because PROP supports the usage of the CMS TELL command and therefore will allow a nickname to be defined for a list of users through the CMS NAMES command.

It is also possible to define the PROP virtual machine as a secondary user for disconnected service machines, eg RSCS, Passthrough and VCNA. This means that all of their activities are recorded in the PROP log which, therefore, provides a single reference point for all VM system activities.

PROP does not currently have a time-driven event scheduling facility. To overcome this omission it is necessary to run a separate disconnected service machine to trigger events by time-of-day or day-of-week, using the IPF WAKEUP module.

Other problems with PROP include:

- Each message sent from PROP to LOPER causes a beep and constrains a system and user-id. This both wastes space on the display and makes it impossible to use a beep to attract the operator's attention.
- When sending commands to machines controlled by LOPER the operator must prefix each command with unwieldy extensions. For example, to send a simple QUERY NAMES command 'MESSAGE OPERATOR CMD SEND user-id QUERY NAMES' must be sent.
- The console log, as stored by PROP, has all users interwoven in a file too wide to display easily on a 3278.

ASSISTS

Assists are microcode and they are incorporated in the hardware of CPU models. Different processor models have different assists and assist levels installed. Before the purchase of a processor it is important to check that the required assists are available. (This is quite important when selecting non-IBM processors.)

Assists are used to perform certain instructions that would otherwise be performed by CP. This, therefore, saves CP from performing them and results in their being performed more quickly, thereby improving overall system performance. The more frequently used instructions are the ones usually microcoded into assists. A copy of the instructions is retained by CP in case it is run on a machine that does not have the assist installed. If this is the case, then at IPL time CP will overwrite the E6 instructions with No-op instructions, and control passes to the old Assembler code.

In addition to ensuring that a particular assist is installed it is also useful to check that the assist has been activated. If it has not, it may be the cause of a performance problem.

Assists that are available include:

- VMA;
- ECPS;
- CPA;
- EVMA;
- VITA;
- IUCV;
- STBA;
- PMA;
- PMAV;
- SIE assist.

VMA

Virtual Machine Assist (VMA) was the first assist available and was introduced to make the then new 370 operating systems (DOS and VS/1) run faster when executing under VM. Using VMA has reduced the time taken to execute certain privileged operations (privops) considerably. Examples of time saving are shown in Figure 4.2. Later implementations of VMA contain enhancements and additional instructions. Because

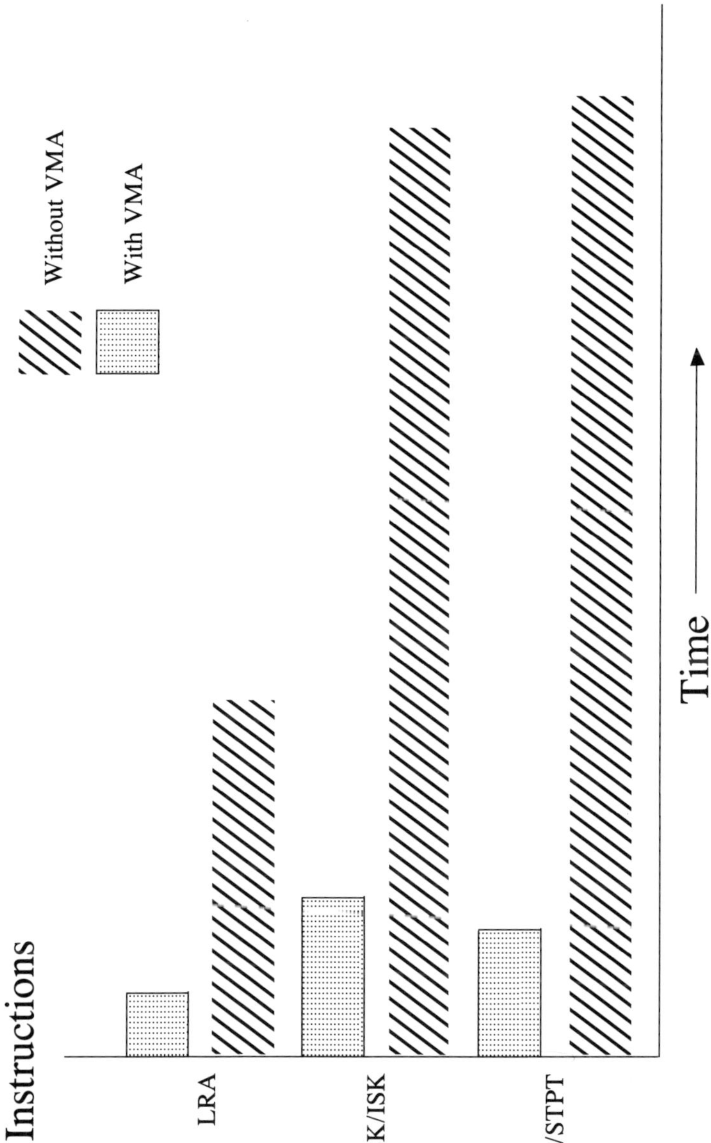

Figure 4.2 Performance Improvements Using VMA

CMS is an operating system it too can benefit from the use of VMA. To find out which instructions are assisted by VMA it is usual to look at privop counts in VMMAP or SMART. Most of the time, any privops with zero counts are handled by VMA or are not used by the guest system.

ECPS

The Extended Control Program Support was introduced after VMA. It is not available on 3080 and 3090 processors. It has three components, which are

- CPA;
- EVMA;
- VITA.

CPA

The Control Program Assist contains single instructions that are invoked by op-codes in the form of X‘E6nn’.

EVMA

The Extended Virtual Machine Assist assists more privileged operations than VMA. In addition, it allows partial assists for those instructions that the assist cannot completely handle.

VITA

The Virtual Interval Timer Assist was used to ensure that a virtual machine’s interval timer was maintained with an accuracy similar to that of the real system’s interval timer. Because current operating systems use the more accurate System/370 CPU timer for accounting purposes it is now rather unimportant.

IUCV Assist

The IUCV (Inter-User Communication Vehicle) assist is available on 4381 and 9370 processors. It improves the performance of software that uses IUCV, including VTAM and SFS (Shared File System).

STBA

The Shadow Table Bypass Assist is available on some CPUs, for example the 4381. Performance improvements are brought about by the way that it facilitates those instructions (eg LCTL) necessary to handle guests with multiple address spaces, eg MVS. The STBA is invoked using the SET STBYPASS VR command.

PMA

The Preferred Machine Assist allows MVS/SP and, more recently, VSE users to attain near-native performance when running under VM/SP HPO. When PMA is active, control passes to CP in one of only three conditions. These are:

- at the end of a time slice;
- when an interrupt is received from a device on a VM channel;
- when the guest system goes into a wait state.

PMA extends V=R support allowing a guest to attain performance figures around 95 per cent of what could be achieved if the system were to be run native (ie without VM). Channels can be allocated to the guest system by omitting them from the VM SYSGEN. The preferred guest treats the channels as if they were directly attached to it. The benefit of this is that there is no VM overhead.

PMAV

The PMAV is an improved PMA. In addition to the usual PMA facilities it allows the guest to issue VM commands using the DIAGNOSE instruction. To indicate to the guest system that it is a PMAV guest, after the guest issues a Store CPU-id instruction, CP returns a response starting X'FF'.

SIE Assist

The Start Interpretive Execution assist was introduced with VM/XA. The SIE assist automatically handles three-level address translation, which means that guest-virtual to guest-real address translations can be handled using the guest system's page tables. Guest system real to XA real address translation is handled by XA's page tables.

Performance improvements are achieved by removing the need to build and maintain shadow page tables for guests who have multiple address spaces. This is illustrated in Figure 4.3.

The SIE assist also reduces the overhead of I/O instructions issued by the preferred guest to dedicated devices. This is because dedication is at the device level, not at the channel level as in HPO PMA. This also makes XA easier to configure than HPO with a PMA guest. The SIE assist is also used to allow LPARs (logical partitions) to be created on machines with the PR/SM (Processor Resource/System Manager) facility, eg 3090E.

SET COMMANDS

The performance of virtual machines that are executing under VM can be altered by the operator or other authorised user issuing a SET command. The use of SET commands can directly affect the response times for a virtual machine and many other performance-related factors. It should be remembered that if one machine has a positive improvement in performance this may be to the detriment of all the other users of the system. It is usually thought best to monitor the system after any changes have been made, to ensure that only the expected change has taken place. It is also better to make only one change at a time otherwise it is impossible to know which change brought about the increase/decrease in performance. SET commands are described in detail in various IBM publications, but a summary of some commands that can be used are given below.

Some of the modern processors (3080s and 4300s) have hardware features that can improve performance. These can be started by the command:

SET 370E on

To ensure that in a multiprocessor environment the service virtual machine is despatched on the processor with the FEP (Front End Processor) and terminals attached to it, the following command is used:

SET AFFINITY user-id nn

In BTAM (Basic Telecommunications Access Method) environments performance improvements can be achieved by reducing the overhead involved in testing whether BTAM CCWs (Channel Command Words)

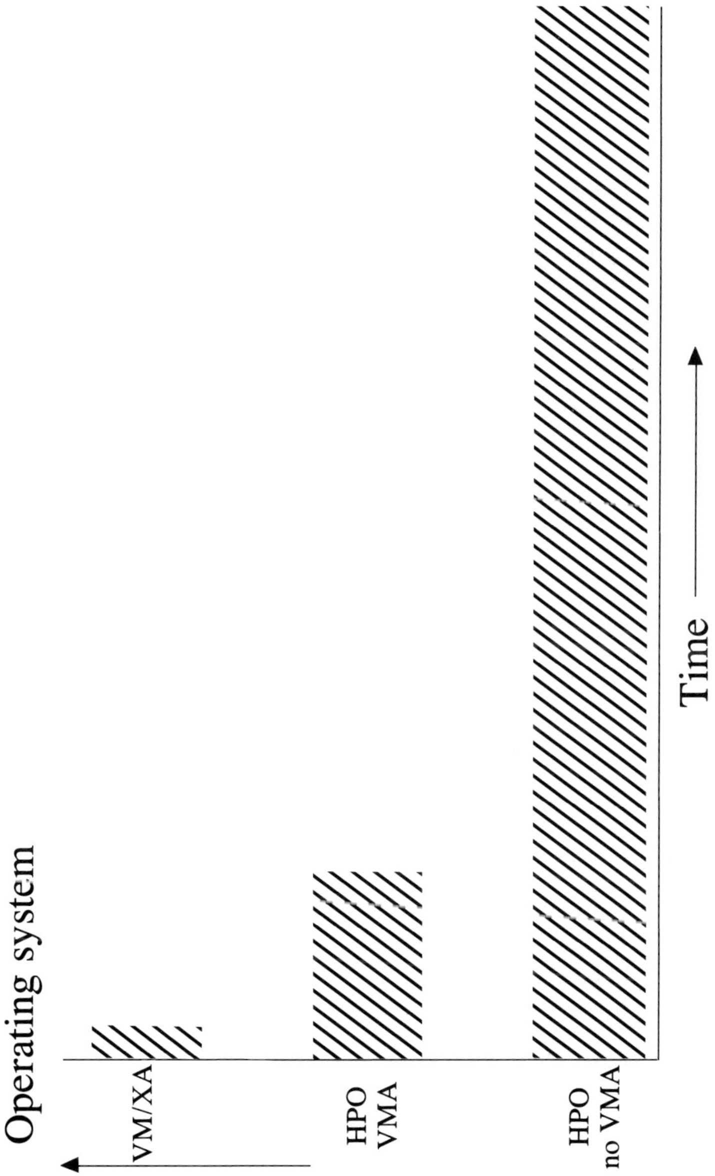

Figure 4.3 Performance Improvements Using VM/XA

have been dynamically modified. This is done by:

SET AUTOPOLL on

Performance improvements in I/O can be achieved by specifying channels as block multiplexor channels rather than as selector channels. This can be done using the command:

SET BMX on

The performance of a given virtual machine can be improved by using the FAVOR command. By specifying a percentage value CP will try to give the specified virtual machine that percentage of the system CPU resource. The command format is:

SET FAVOR user-id nn

With VM/XA, a guest-operating system can make use of SIE assists by using the following command:

SET IOASSIST guest-id

With XA, the load on the system can be controlled by specifying the maximum number of virtual machines that can be active. The command format is:

SET MAXUSER nn

HPO users can specify the minimum size for the working set that the scheduler will use for the whole system or for a specific user-id. The command can be used to reduce the number of page faults for a specified user-id and so improve the performance of that virtual machine. The command format is:

SET MINWS user-id nn

With VSE guest systems performance improvements can be achieved by activating handshaking facilities. This improves the way that pseudo page faults are dealt with. The command format is:

SET PAGEX on

With SP the paging rate can be controlled and, indirectly, the multi-programming level. If excessive paging rates are observed the following command can be used to reduce them and improve the performance of the active virtual machines. The command format is:

SET PAGING nn

Another way of improving the performance of a user is to increase the priority of that user. The default value is 64 and values nearer 1 improve performance, while values nearer 99 decrease performance. The value does not directly affect the deadline priority, which is calculated using a complex formula described in Chapter 6. The command format is:

SET PRIORITY user-id nn

The amount of paging that takes place for a particular user-id can be reduced by stopping the usual queue-drop procedure occurring for that user. The command format is:

SET QDROP user-id off

With XA, there is no FAVOR command and the equivalent to the FAVOR command without the percentage value is the SET QUICKDSP command. This means that user stays in queue 0. The command format is:

SET QUICKDSP user-id

The response times for remote terminals can be improved by specifying the REMOTE on option. This optimises data streams for remote transmissions. The command is placed in an XEDIT profile and its format is:

SET REMOTE on

The pages in real storage belonging to a particular user-id can be retained as a method of improving the performance for that user. With SP only one user can have pages retained; with HPO more than one user can have pages retained. The command format is:

SET RESERVE user-id nn

XA does not have the SET FAVOR nor the SET PRIORITY command. The equivalent to the SET FAVOR with the percentage option is SET SHARE ABS. The equivalent to SET PRIORITY is SET SHARE REL. The ABS percentage values cannot add up to more than 99 per cent. If they do, they are proportionately decreased. The command format is:

SET SHARE user-id REL/ABS nn

With SP systems the scheduler can be given a value for the number of page frames to use in the calculation for available page frames. Low values reduce paging and multiprogramming levels. The command format is:

SET SRM APAGES nn

With XA it is possible to limit the number of users of each type that are allowed onto a queue at any one time. By limiting the number of heavy concurrent users, performance for others can be improved. The command format is:

SET SRM DSPBUF nn mm pp

With XA the performance of interactive users can be increased at the expense of other users. The command format is:

SET SRM IABIAS nn% mm

The time that a user spends in the interactive buffer and the size of the buffer required can be controlled. If the size of the buffer is increased it improves the performance of interactive work at the expense of other work. The command format is:

SET SRM IBUF bufftime tt maxsize nn

With XA, if a large number of paging actuators are in use it is possible to control the number of heavy paging users on the system. The command format is:

SET SRM LDUBUF nn% mm% pp%

With HPO it is possible to specify the percentage of the preferred paging area that may become full before page migration takes place. The command format is:

SET SRM MAXPP nn

With SP it is possible to specify the maximum number of pages in a user's working set that will be considered by the scheduler in its calculations. The command format is:

SET SRM MAXWSS nn

With HPO it is possible to specify the minimum number of swap sets that are to be used. It can be used to ensure that enough page frames are available for page-in and swap-in operations and so improve performance. The command format is:

SET SRM MINNUMSS nn

With HPO it is possible to specify how full a paging device is to become before page migration automatically takes place. The command format is:

SET SRM PGULL nn

With HPO it is possible to specify the number of swap sets that are to be swapped in when a user is added to the swap queue. Different values can be specified for queue 1 and queue 2 users. The value for queue 2 is usually set to 1. The command format is:

SET SRM PREPAGE Q1 xx Q2 yy

With XA it is possible to specify what percentage of storage is to be available to users in the three queues. It is possible to overcommit storage in order to improve performance if paging rates are low and there are many users in the eligible queue. The command format is:

SET SRM STORBUF nn% mm% pp%

With HPO the length of time that interactive and non-interactive users can keep a page frame in real storage before it becomes a candidate for swapping out can be controlled. For interactive users a value around 20 is used; for non-interactive users a value nearer 5 is preferred. The command format is:

SET SRM SWPQTIME intuser-id time nonintuser-id time

Performance of guest-operating systems can be improved by using the SET STBYPASS command. If the guest system is to run in real storage the command format is:

SET STBYPASS VR

This will prevent VM building shadow page tables to despatch the guest system and will also start STBA if it is available on the hardware. If MVS/SP is despatched in virtual storage rather than in real storage, further performance improvements can be achieved by using the command:

SET STBYPASS nnK

This specifies that VM need not build shadow page tables for nn K amount of storage. This can be a saving because of the way that MVS address spaces are arranged. Parts of each address space are common. Therefore there is no need to recreate a new shadow page table for those parts of the address space that are the same.

It is possible to specify the number of shadow page tables that VM will maintain. There is a trade-off between the amount of storage space that is used up by each shadow page table and the time saved by not having to build a shadow page when a new MVS address space is despatched. The command format is:

SET STMULTI nn USEG mm CSEG pp

5 Installation, Maintenance and Problems

This chapter provides an overview of what is required in order to install a VM system, maintain and modify it, and also gives some suggestions about dealing with system problems.

INSTALLING VM

Typically, a site where VM is being installed for the first time will have the hardware installed and connected, but will be unable to use the boxes supplied until some kind of operating system is loaded in. The site will receive a 'starter' tape from IBM. Using this the system programmers must format and define DASD to the system. Programmers will also have to specify which options are to be used with the modules DMKRIO, DMKSNT and DMKSYS (see Chapter 3). These modules are central to the way that the VM Control Program (CP) will perform. Once the various options are stored in the modules (in fact they are object code not source code) the basis of the system is ready. Modules prefixed DMK are CP modules. CMS modules are prefixed DMS.

The next stage is the generation of the CP nucleus by means of the VMFLOAD program. VMFLOAD uses two input parameters: the first is a LOADLIST and the second a control file name. The LOADLIST contains a list of the modules that are to make up the VM nucleus programs. Any modules on the tape that would not be used at a site can be excluded at this point. Frequently used modules are placed in the nucleus area of real storage. Less frequently used modules are placed in the pageable nucleus, which occupies DPA (Dynamic Paging Area) space. In the LOADLIST, resident nucleus modules are placed before the DMKCPE statement; others are after it but before DMKCKP. DMKCPE is the name for the nucleus resident control program module and is made up of the other specified modules. The control file allows a hierarchy of filetypes to be specified for the modules in the LOADLIST. This means that a selection order can be specified at a site for modules where more than one version exists. In effect, a recently modified version of a module will be selected in preference to an older version with a similar name. VMFLOAD locates the modules specified and removes any comments from them (they are at this stage in text format). It then treats them as one large program rather than a number of separate modules. This process creates what is called a load deck. A loader is attached by VMFLOAD to the load deck and this results in the creation of the VM nucleus. The use of SolutionPac/VM on 9370 machines is designed to make all this activity transparent to the users.

LOADLIST

The LOADLIST is used by the VMFLOAD command and lists the modules to use when building the VM and CMS nuclei. For CMS the LOADLIST EXEC is CMSLOAD EXEC. For CP there are LOADLIST versions for each type of VM that can be created (SP/HPO, uni-processor/multiprocessor, etc).

Within the LOADLIST filenames are specified in the order they are to appear in the IPL deck to be created by VMFLOAD. The first file listed is the LOADER. These modules will form the nucleus. If no filetype is specified, VMFLOAD searches the CNTRL file for the specified filename with a filetype of TXTLCL. If none is found it tries the same filename with the filetype of TXTTMP. If it is still unsuccessful it tries a filetype of TEXT.

Loading VM

The stand-alone module CPFMT must be IPLed in order that disks can be formatted and labelled. The Initial Program Load (IPL) procedure for the system can then be set in motion. This will load the nucleus into real storage. It can then be written out to the system residence (SYSRES) disk pack. The next time that VM is IPLed it will be loaded from the SYSRES pack.

Once the system is up and running the system programmer will have to define all the other user-ids and virtual machine definitions in the directory, allocate mini-disks to users, and load in software packages (eg a security package).

MAINTENANCE

Maintenance of the VM system is usually performed by systems programmers using the MAINT user-id. MAINT's mini-disks may contain:

- CP source code;
- CP source updates;
- CP object modules;
- CMS source;
- CMS source updates;
- site-dependent programs.

Maintenance involves installing modifications sent out by IBM. These may be APARs (Authorised Program Analysis Reports) or more usually PTFs (Program Temporary Fixes) and SLUs (Service Level Updates) on PUTs (Program Update Tapes). With XA, maintenance is performed using Serviceability Enhancement Support stage II (SES-II).

APAR

If the systems programmers experience a problem with VM they contact IBM and report the problem with an APAR (Authorised Program Analysis Report). The fix for this problem sent out by IBM is also often referred to as an APAR. These APARs are provided as ZAPs by IBM until a replacement text file is made available as part of a PTF. The system programmer creates a new TEXT file by adding an AUX file entry for it and issuing the VMFASM command (see p.74).

The naming convention for APARs is as in the following example. File DMKDMP A12345DK, for example, would be a fix for a DMK module (indicated by the DK suffix) on an HPO system (indicated by the prefix A). The APAR number is 12345 and the module being updated is DMKDMP.

Associated with APARs are SPEs (Small Programming Enhancements). These are not fixes to problems, but are enhancements to the system itself that are considered by IBM to be so important that they cannot wait until the next release.

PUT

Program Update Tapes (PUTs) contain fixes for problems reported at sites running VM. A fix is referred to as a Program Temporary Fix (PTF). The PUT tape may also contain fixes to earlier PTFs. These are called PEs (PTFs in Error). Thirdly, the tape contains AUX files, which direct the application of the fixes. The tape also contains information about problems that a site may encounter. The tapes have a four-digit number. The first two digits indicate the year that the PUT was released, and the second two digits are a sequence number.

PUT tapes are cumulative and contain SLUs (Service Level Updates). The SLU indicates which version of VM the PUT is for by a three-digit number. The first digit gives the VM version; the other two are sequence numbers. All the fixes on a PUT tape are meant to be applied at once, but many sites ignore the fixes if they have not experienced the problem because all the enhancements are incorporated in the next release of the software anyway.

The PUT enhancements are applied by logging on to MAINT and attaching a tape drive at virtual address 181 and loading thc PUT tape. VMSERV is used to copy the PUT files, including AUX files, to one of MAINT's mini-disks. Using the CMS update process the fixes are applied to the CMS and CP source files. The source file is then reassembled to include the changes and a new, improved version of the object code is available. To avoid potential system problems and having to remove all CMS users when updating CMS files, a duplicated CMS S disk is usually used.

Instead of using VMSERV some sites use VMFPLC2 LOAD to take files from tape to the service disks. The first time VMSERV is run it 'maps' the tape, noting which products it contains. This 'map' is written into a file. It also loads the documentation files for each product. VMSERV also ACCESSes the 194 disk as the A disk and updates SERVICE DISKMAP and VMPUT SERVICE on the 191 disk. VMSERV next issues prompts to select the products to update and for the minidisk addresses to load the new service to. After this the PUT tape can be unloaded.

Next reachahead fixes applied from previous PUT tapes must be removed. Temporary copies of the APARs are erased along with associated TEXT (TXTTMP) files and AUX-file entries. Local fixes need to be reassembled, and modules DMKRIO, DMKSNT, DMKSYS and DMKBOX should be reassembled in case any macros they refer to have been changed. Fixes must be moved to live disks so that they can be used.

Several CP nucleus areas can be allocated on disk (VM release 5 and above). These can be used for testing system changes. Usually multiple CMS nuclei are kept for live and test versions as well.

Buckets

A bucket is supplied on tape by IBM and contains the latest information about a product. The contents of the bucket should be read before a new product is installed. Similarly with PUTs, the bucket's contents should be read before the contents of the PUT are installed. The first file on the bucket tape is called VSPxnnnn BUCKET, where x is the release of VM and nnnn is the PUT number. It contains recent changes to service instructions and recent fixes.

MODIFICATIONS

In addition to changes sent out by IBM, it is possible for the system programmers at a site to make changes to the source code sent by IBM, and most sites make use of this facility. A CMS EXEC called VMFASM is used. This consists of two programs, an update program and an Assembler program. The update program takes the source code and updates it with the required changes. The new code is Assembled. This produces a text deck which is used by VMFLOAD to create a new CP nucleus.

When VM souce code is modified the following steps are taken:

- A control file listing locally created AUX files is created.
- An AUX file pointing to the fix is created.
- XEDIT's CNTRL option is used to create the fix.
- The module is Assembled. At this stage it is important to ensure that the fix is included correctly.

- The fix is tested to ensure that the problem requiring it does not recur (or at least it should be tested at this stage).
- The fix is then ready for use on the production system.

The VMFASM command creates an object module by reassembling a temporary copy of the source module constructed by applying updates to the module's base version. The temporary source file is erased. The update history of the module is placed in the object code TEXT file.

When a COPY or MACRO file is changed a new MACLIB is created by applying updates to those base versions of files using the VMFMAC command. Affected modules are reassembled to pick up the changed definitions.

If a module is not distributed with source code a ZAP must be used in order to modify it. This involves entering hexadecimal values without any method of error checking. If source code is available updates are applied using the UPDATE command. In this case validity checks are applied to its sequence numbers, and by the Assembler.

The VMFASM command used for MODULEs is

VMFASM module cntrl

where module is the name of the source module being Assembled and cntrl specifies the name of the CNTRL file which determines the updates that are to be applied to the module, and the filetype to assign to the resulting TEXT file.

The VMFMAC command used for MACRO and COPY files is

VMFMAC maclib cntrl

where maclib is the name of the MACLIB to be produced and cntrl names an EXEC file containing the names of files to be added to it. When a MACRO or COPY file has been changed the Assembler modules that use it must be reassembled using VMFASM.

Update Files

Update files contain changes that are to be made to VM source code. These are prefixed by update commands, which all begin './' The commands are given in Figure 5.1.

Sequence numbers in columns 73-80 are used by UPDATE commands to indicate where changes are to be made.

./ *	Comment
./ D	Delete a line
./ I	Insert a line
./ R	Replace a line by new code

Figure 5.1 Update Commands

AUX Files

The updates that are to be applied by VMFASM are listed in an AUX file. The first word in each line that is not a comment (starting *) is the filetype of the update to be applied. There are three types of AUX files. AUXSP are IBM standard. AUXTMP contain temporary changes. AUXLCL contain local changes (ie made on-site). New fixes are put at the top of the AUX file. VMFASM puts the contents of the AUX file in the TEXT file so that the history of the module is available.

CNTRL Files

CNTRL files are used to specify

- which AUX files are to be used to update a module;
- which MACLIBs to use during Assembly;
- the filetype to use for the resulting TEXT file of object code.

For CMS two control files are used. These are DMSSP for ASSEMBLE files and DMSMSP for MACRO or COPY files. DMSMSP CNTRL has an entry for an AUX filetype of AUXMSP instead of AUXSP. Control files come in different formats for HPO and non-HPO systems, for different CPUs, and for the optional inclusion of the CP FRETRAP.

For VM/SP the standard CNTRL file DMKSP CNTRL consists of the lines shown in Figure 5.2.

TEXT MACS lists the MACLIBS needed for Assembly, TEXT

```
TEXT MACS DMKSP DMSSP CMSLIB OSMACRO
TEXT AUXSP
```

Figure 5.2 Basic DMKSP CNTRL File

AUXSP tells VMFASM to apply updates contained in an AUXSP file with the same name as the module being assembled, and to name the resulting object code file with a filetype TEXT.

The file DMKSP CNTRL can be made more flexible and can be put on the A disk. The contents can be changed to those shown in Figure 5.3. This can be used to install temporary files, or make on-site modifications. When multiple AUX files are present they are processed from the bottom up, ie first AUXSP, then AUXTMP then AUXLCL. DMKLCL MACLIB is used as a location for MACRO and COPY files updated by local changes.

```
TEXT MACS DMKLCL DMKSP DMSSP CMSLIB OSMACRO
LCL AUXLCL
TMP AUXTMP
TEXT AUXSP
```

Figure 5.3 Modified DMKSP CNTRL File

TEXT Files

If the TEXT file produced from updating a module is not called TEXT it is renamed TXTxxx, where xxx is taken from the name of the AUX file, eg if a temporary file is listed in DMKHVC AUXTMP the resulting file would be named DMKHVC TXTTMP. If a local modification were applied in an AUXLCL file, the file would be called DMKHVC TXTLCL.

When building a nucleus VMFLOAD searches for object-code files using the filetypes in the order TXTLCL, TXTTMP and TEXT.

A TXTLIB is a library of 'text decks', ie compiled programs. A

MACLIB is a library of source code files.

Building Modules Summary

Programmers compile or assemble programs producing TEXT programs. All other programs necessary for execution are LOADed. The module is then BUILT. To include OS macros the MACLIB is used by pointing to it with a FILEDEF command and issuing a GLOBAL command.

PROBLEM DIAGNOSIS

In the event of a system crash,

- the operator's console displays an abend code (xxxnnnn). This can be looked up in the appropriate message and codes manual;
- an auto-dump of the system occurs;
- the system restarts.

If the system is unable to auto-dump, a stand-alone dump should be taken. In the event of a system abend some of the typical abend codes that could be displayed are shown in Figure 5.4. In the event of an application program abending the following steps can be taken:

- The message from CMS describing the problem can be read.
- The DEBUG command can be used immediately to examine failing registers and storage.
- CP VMDUMP can be used to produce a dump of the virtual machine. This could be analysed later.

Some of the system problems that may occur include

- Disabled wait states;
- Enabled wait states;
- Loops.

Disabled Wait State

Disabled waits occur most often during IPL. All work stops and the PSW has bit 14 set on, and no interruptions enabled. An example is shown in Figure 5.5.

FRE/FRT	Free storage management involved
LOK	A fault with multiprocessor interaction
PAG/PGT/PGU	Paging involved
PRG	A program check occurred
PSA002	Processor manually restarted from the system console
SVC003	Usually DASD problem has prevented a pageable module being loaded

Figure 5.4 Typical Abend Codes

000A0000 xxxxxyyy

Figure 5.5 Example PSW

PSWs are displayed on the system console. The part shown in the example as yyy contains the wait state code and this can be looked up in the manual. Examples of wait state codes are given in Figure 5.6.

001/00A/00B	Unrecoverable hardware error
002	Unrecoverable channel error
003	Fatal error when restarting system
005	No operator console
00C	No VM nucleus on IPL pack

Figure 5.6 Example Wait State Codes

Enabled Wait State

In an enabled wait, bits 6 and 7 are set on. Bit 6 on allows I/O interrupts; bit 7 on allows external interrupts. Enabled waits may occur because of frequently occurring timer interrupts. An example of the PSW is given in Figure 5.7.

070Ennnn xxxxxxxx

Figure 5.7 Example PSW

Enabled waits may also occur because there is no suitable work to be performed.

Loops

If the system loops, an attempt should be made to identify the cause. This can be achieved by:

- examining R12 to see if it points to DMKIOS or DMKIOT (these are both modules associated with I/O activity);
- examining the trace table to see whether it is full of I/O entries for a single device.

In the event that either or both the above circumstances are true the problem is usually with a device or control unit. The processor should be stopped, the device or control unit should be reset and the processor should be restarted.

In most other cases the procedure to adopt is to stop the system and then restart it. This will produce a dump which can later be examined.

If an application program is looping a monitor program can be used to identify the user responsible for it. Steps can then be taken to remove the looping program.

Dumps

CP dumps are usually produced by CP after it crashes. VM dumps are produced by the VMDUMP command or DIAGnose X'94'. VM dumps contain data from virtual machines. Stand-alone dumps can be run from tape or disk and are used when VM cannot take a dump of itself (CP dump). The CPDUMP command can be used to produce a dump in readable printed format of virtual machine registers, PSW and storage.

When a dump is taken it is written to the DUMP area of CP-owned

DASD. If no DUMP area has been defined it is written to the TEMP area.

The following steps are usually taken to deal with CP dumps:

- The abend code is looked up in the manual.
- If a program check occurs the instruction and its operands are examined. R12 shows which module contains the code. R11 has the pointer to the VMBLOK (VMDBK with XA) which contains the user-id for whom services were being carried out. In any other circumstance the trace table is examined. This indicates what happened up to the time that the problem occurred.
- All control blocks associated with the operation are examined and corrupted fields, missing or incorrect values or flag settings, etc can be identified.
- If the problem has occurred previously, previous dumps should be compared with the present one.

The following steps are taken to deal with VM dumps:

- The failing components being dumped are identified.
- PSW contents, register contents, control area and data area contents, and the application's trace table are examined.
- The console log is checked for additional information.

DEBUGGING RUNNING SYSTEMS

A running system can be debugged by using the DCP or DISPLAY H (XA) command which displays real processor storage. The CP and CMS debugging commands are shown in Figure 5.8.

CPTRAP can be used to add entries to the trace table. The CMS command TRAPRED can be used to display data from CPTRAP files. XA allows tracing in a similar manner to HPO's PER or ADSTOP using TRSAVE and TRSOURCE. These commands create a list of rules specifying events to trace and actions to take when trace events occur. IO trace (like CCWTRACE), GT trace (for guest systems), and DATA trace (similar to PER) can be performed.

DISASTER RECOVERY

In order that the systems programmers can recover the system in the

CP commands

ADSTOP	stops the machine at a specified address
BEGIN	starts the machine at a specified address
DUMP	dumps virtual storage etc
PER	performs an activity depending on one or more program event-recording events
STORE	modifies virtual storage, registers, etc. STORE STATUS saves the machine's status into low storage
SYSTEM	can be used for restart, clear or reset
TRACE	performs an activity depending on one or more software detectablc events
VMDUMP	dumps virtual storage etc into a file

CMS commands

DEBUG	is unavailable with release 5.5 and above
EXEC tracing	allows EXECs to be debugged by displaying each line as it runs
SVCTRACE	provides a list of SVC calls

Figure 5.8 CP Debugging Commands

event of a disaster occurring (flood, explosion, etc) the following items need to be kept on-site and at the off-site back-up site (where it exists):

- stand-alone version of CP FORMAT/ALLOCATE;
- stand-alone version of DDR;
- stand-alone directory utility and directory source code (stand-alone modules are described more fully below);
- a DDR back-up of the SYSRES pack;
- back-up of all files on the system;
- the IOCP source code if the processor requires it;
- PUT tapes, error bucket and all authorised modifications.

Stand-alone Modules

There are a number of modules that can be used stand-alone to perform various useful functions. These include:

• DDR MODULE	IPL DDR can be used to back-up and recover files to tape.
• CPFMT MODULE	IPL FMT can be used to format DASD.
• DSF MODULE	IPL DSF can be used for DASD analysis.
• DIRECT MODULE	IPL DIR can be used to create a new directory.

PROGRAM TESTING

Non-CMS programs that are to run in a guest-operating system can be tested under VM. Programs that are Assembled or compiled under CMS produce a TEXT file. Any other programs that are to be used must be LOADed in order that a MODULE can be BUILT. MODULES run faster than TEXT files. The MODULE is created using the following command:

GENMOD txtlib

If the programs use OS macros the disk containing the MACLIB must be accessed, the MACLIB can be indicated by using the FILEDEF command, and the use of the GLOBAL command makes the macros available.

If VSAM files are to be used a VM VSAM catalog must be placed on any mini-disk, even a TDSK. It cannot share the mini-disk with CMS files because it must have CP formatting, not CMS. To use files in the catalog the command SET DOS ON must be used and DLBLs must be coded.

SECTION III

Processing, Virtual Storage Overview and Paging

The third section looks at how VM processes work. The first chapter in this section looks at processing in some detail. It looks at supervisor state and problem program state and uses a comparison of the two as a measure of the VM overhead. It looks at the various wait states for both the VM machine and any guest machines running under VM. Finally it describes how VM selects virtual machines for execution, describing in detail the scheduler and despatcher. The second chapter gives an overview of virtual storage. It describes the contents of real storage and explains their function and how overall system performance can be maximised by controlling the size of these components. The last part of the chapter looks at saved systems and shared segments. The third chapter in the section describes the paging mechanism that is used with the different VM systems. It describes paging, swapping, the different tables that are maintained to control paging, and how page frames are made available for use. It also describes the DASD requirements for paging. The chapter ends with a description of guest-system paging.

6 Processing

Processing is the name given to the execution of instructions. This is performed within a hardware complex often referred to as a processor. This chapter summarises the stages that CP goes through in order to process an instruction from a virtual machine. It examines the scheduler and despatcher elements of the Systems Resource Manager (SRM) and describes the way that deadline priorities are calculated. The chapter first describes the processor states and the different types of wait state that are experienced by VM and a guest-operating system.

PROCESSOR STATES

When the processor is carrying out instructions it is described as being in one of two states, which are:

- Supervisor state;
- Problem state.

Supervisor State

A processor is described as being in supervisor state when CP is using it to perform activities such as paging or managing I/O. While CP is active, the virtual machines that it supports cannot be active. This is considered to be an overhead for the systems running under CP. An example of an activity carried out in supervisor state is paging.

Problem State

A processor is described as being in problem state when virtual machines running under CP are using it to execute instructions, rather than the control program using it to carry out its instructions. While in this state the processor is effectively carrying out work. An example would be a short EXEC being processed for a CMS user.

TVRATIO

The TVRATIO is used as a rough-and-ready measurement of the VM overhead. It is the ratio of TTIME against TTIME. VTIME is the total length of time taken for an application to process, ie time spent in problem state and supervisor state. VTIME is the time that the application code itself was processing, ie the time spent in problem state. The difference between TTIME and VTIME is the length of time spent in supervisor state. The TVRATIO cannot be less than one, but the closer the value is to one the lower the VM overhead. The figure produced is useful as a guide to the VM overhead. However, it should be realised that some of the work carried out by CP would have to be carried out by a guest-operating system if CP was not running (eg paging). Also, changes to the microcode may reduce TTIME and VTIME. This would, in fact, increase the TVRATIO value and make the system appear to be less efficient.

WAIT STATES

When guest-operating systems are being run under VM, there are two sets of wait states. CP itself can go into a wait state, and so can each of the guest-operating systems.

CP Wait States

If CP is unable to continue processing for any reason other than serious hardware malfunction or power failure, it is put into what is called a wait state. There are three wait states it could go into. These are:

- Idle;
- I/O;
- Page.

Idle

This indicates that there is no work for CP to perform, and therefore no work is being processed.

I/O

This indicates that the system is waiting. However, it is not in an idle wait or page wait.

Page

A page wait indicates that half or more than half of the virtual machines are themselves in a page-wait state. This makes identification of paging problems much harder, and they can be identified most easily by looking at page rates and queues on the paging volumes.

Guest-operating Systems Wait States

If a guest-operating system is unable to process, it may be in one of four wait states. These are:

- EX;
- I/O;
- Page;
- PSW.

EX

An execution wait (EX) is also known as a console-function wait. It occurs whenever VM simulates an instruction for a guest-operating system, or whenever VM executes a CP command for it.

I/O

An I/O wait occurs when the guest system is suspended while VM starts an I/O for it. Typically these days, most guest systems use SIOF (Start I/O Fast) and an I/O wait is therefore rarely seen.

Page

A page wait occurs when the guest system is suspended while the control program performs a page-in operation for it. With handshaking (see Chapter 8), page waits are rarely seen, so that, unfortunately, a guest system that is doing a lot of paging cannot be identified from page waits.

PSW

A PSW wait is also known as a voluntary wait. It occurs when a guest system has no work to do. The guest system will load a wait PSW. The situation occurs when the guest system is waiting for an I/O operation to complete. If handshaking is used the guest system may be waiting for a page. If many PSW waits occur, they may be caused by the guest-operating system having no work to do or by an I/O problem or a paging problem. It is not possible to differentiate between these.

ACTIVE WAITS

Since release 3.4 of VM/SP HPO, active waits have been available with multiprocessor configurations. Without the use of active wait an inactive processor will load a wait state and spend a lot of time checking with the other processor to see whether there is any work it could do. When active wait is in use the inactive processor will attempt to take work from the queue of the other processor. One positive benefit of this is that the second (working) processor will not be continually interrupted by the first. If the first processor finds no work it will keep on checking.

With XA SP release 1 active wait is required for 3080s, 3090s and 4381s. This results in the System Activity Display (SAD) frame showing 100 per cent busy, which may confuse inexperienced operations and systems people. A simple method to make the display more meaningful is to set it up in such a way that work that is not supervisor and associated with storage key 3 is separated from the rest.

INTERRUPTS

An executing task will continue to execute until an interrupt occurs. With 370 architecture there are six types of interrupt. These are:

- external — interrupt 'button' pressed;
- I/O — I/O transfer completed;
- machine check — hardware malfunction;
- program — 'problem' program has attempted something illegal, or an address not in real storage is being located;

- restart — restart 'button' pressed;
- SVC — 'problem' program has requested supervisor services.

When an interrupt occurs the instruction that is being executed is allowed to finish, but instead of the next instruction being processed, control is given to another task. Associated with the current instruction is the current PSW. This contains the address of the next instruction to be processed (as well as other information).

In addition to the current PSW there are six old and six new PSWs that are stored and these correspond to the six types of interrupt. This is illustrated in Figure 6.1. When a task is interrupted the current PSW is loaded into the old PSW box associated with that type of interrupt. The PSW from the appropriate new box contains the address of the appropriate interrupt handling routine. When the task is restarted the PSW is loaded from the old PSW box and this contains the address of the next instruction. The structure of a PSW is shown in Figure 6.2. In Figure 6.2, D shows whether DAT (Dynamic Address Translation) is turned on or off; I/O shows whether I/O interrupts are enabled or disabled; E shows whether external interrupts are enabled or disabled; P specifies the access-control key for storage access; EC indicates extended control mode; M shows whether machine-check interrupts are enabled or disabled; W indicates whether the machine is in a wait state; P refers to problem program execution; C is a two-bit condition code; PM shows whether program check interrupts are enabled or disabled; IA is the address of the next instruction to be processed.

SRM

All virtual machines that are logged on to the system fall under the control of the Systems Resource Manager (SRM). The SRM has two main components which are the scheduler and the despatcher.

SCHEDULER

The scheduler (module DMKSCH) looks after idle users (dormant) and eligible users. An idle user is one who has no work to process. An eligible user is one who has some work to process and wants to be despatched but has not yet been selected. The scheduler's job is to organise the

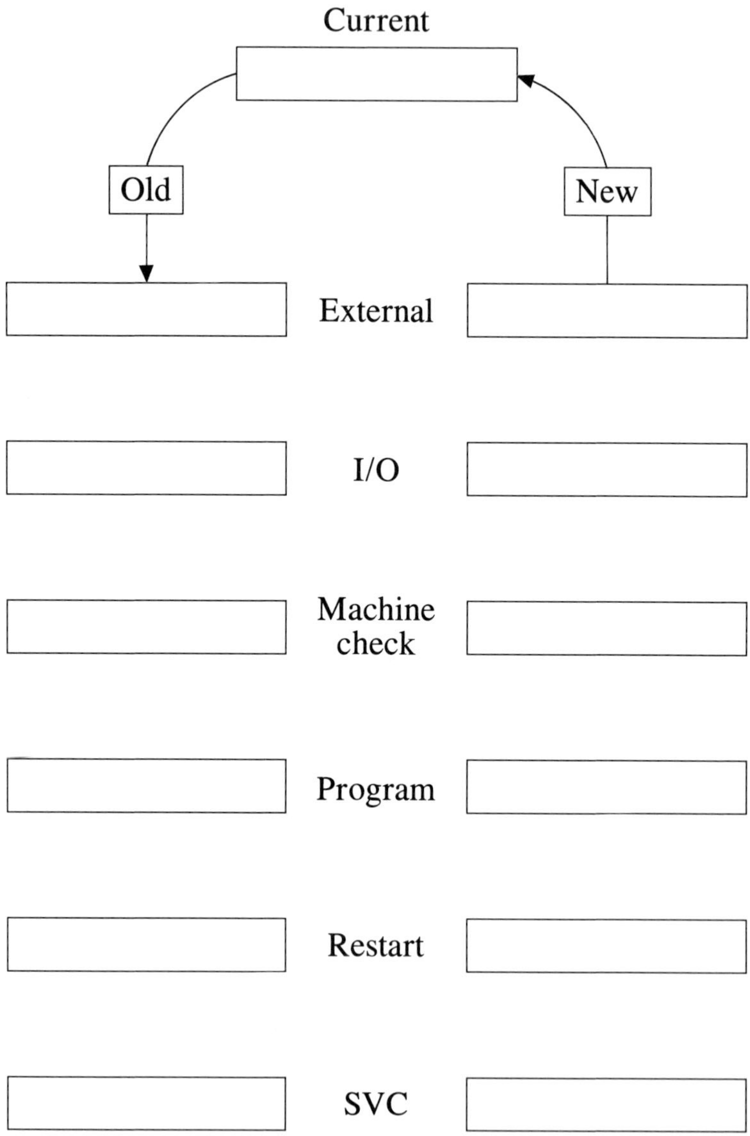

Figure 6.1 Program Status Words

competing virtual machines to make the despatcher's job as straightforward as possible. To do this the scheduler maintains two lists and three queues. The function of the scheduler is to maximise system throughput and to maintain user-response times by the discretionary allocation of CPU resources. The first of the two lists contains those virtual machines that are eligible for despatching but cannot start because their working-set requirements (ie the number of real storage page frames that they require) are greater than the number of page frames currently available. This list is called the eligible list. The second list contains those virtual machines whose working sets are in real storage and could be selected for processing by the despatcher. It is called the despatchable list.

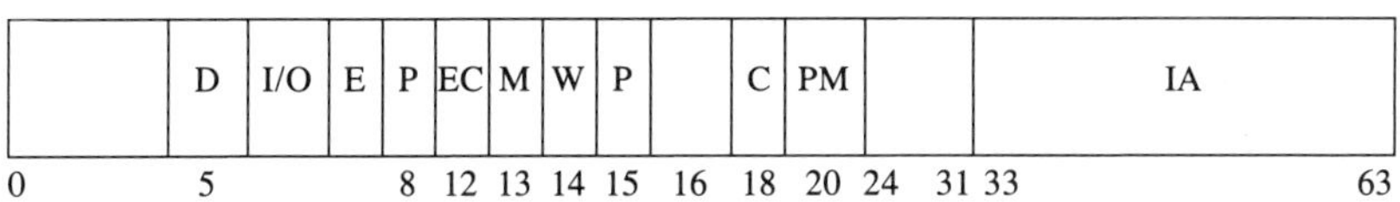

Figure 6.2 Program Status Word Structure

A virtual machine that is waiting to execute will be placed in one of three queues which are known as Q1, Q2 and Q3. All new users are put on Q1. The user is called an in-queue user. Any movement between queues is controlled by the scheduler. There are separate lists for each of the three queues. When a user changes from one queue to another he is placed on the eligible list for that queue rather than the despatchable queue. Queue drop is the name given to what happens at the end of each virtual machine's timeslice. A user is dropped from the run list and put on the eligible list. At qdrop a virtual machine is placed on Q1 if it has returned from a long wait, otherwise Q2 or Q3. The scheduler will calculate the working-set requirements for the next timeslice, and the deadline priority for all in-queue users. The method for calculating the deadline priority is described later.

A virtual machine will move to the run list when it is the top priority on the eligible list and there is enough room for its working set in real storage. Movement between queues is described later.

Q1

A virtual machine in queue 1 is allocated the shortest time interval or timeslice. For example, a virtual machine executing in Q1 might be allocated 5 milliseconds to complete all instructions before being interrupted. Queue 1 will typically contain interactive users who do not utilise the processor for long periods of time, eg CMS users. The size of queue 1 is dependent on the multiprogramming level.

Q2

A queue 2 virtual machine is given the second shortest time interval. For example, a virtual machine executing in Q2 might be allocated 40 milliseconds (ie eight times longer than the Q1 value). Q2 will typically contain non-interactive users who use considerable amounts of processor time, but are rarely interrupted for slow speed I/O operatons.

Q3

A queue 3 virtual machine is given the longest time interval. For example, a virtual machine executing in Q3 might be allocated 320 milliseconds (ie 64 times the Q1 value). Q3 will contain virtual machines that require very large amounts of processor time. Q3 will almost certainly contain guest-operating systems such as VSE or MVS.

TIMESLICE

The timeslice (sometimes known as quanta) that is used by each processor may be different, and is certainly different for different processor models. During the IPL, CP executes around 6000 machine instructions and the total time taken is divided by the number of instructions processed to find the average instruction execution time. This is compared to the average time taken on an S/370 145 processor. If the time taken is less (ie the new processor is faster) the default value for the timeslice of 50ms is reduced accordingly.

QUEUING SEQUENCE

All virtual machines start in eligible Q1. They are scheduled for despatching, and put in despatchable Q1. The fair share despatcher selects a virtual machine for processing when it is the highest-priority virtual machine in the queue. If, at the end of the timeslice (DSPSPLICE) allocated to the virtual machine, it has not completed all its instructions, it is moved to eligible Q2; otherwise it stays in Q1.

The scheduler moves the virtual machine from eligible Q2 to despatchable Q2 when there are enough page frames available for the virtual machine's working-set requirements to be met. Again, when a job has the highest priority in the queue it is despatched. A virtual machine in Q2 that executes for between five and eight consecutive timeslices without becoming idle before the end of the allotted timeslice is moved to eligible Q3. Otherwise it stays in queue 2.

A virtual machine in eligible Q3 passes to the despatchable Q3 only when all the usual requirements can be met. It then waits in despatchable Q3 until it is selected for processing. With XA, the total length of time spent in a queue is varied to ensure that 85 per cent of transactions complete while the user is in Q1.

DESPATCHER

The despatcher (module DMKDSP) is known as the fair-share despatcher, and looks after those virtual machines that are active. The currently active virtual machine is called the runuser. When it despatches virtual machines it takes no account of any internal activity that might take place, for example within a guest-operating system. The order in which virtual machines are despatched depends on their despatching priority. The despatcher selects a Q2 user eight times less often that a Q1 user. It will select a Q3 user 64 times less often than a Q1 user. However, these users are allocated longer timeslices in which to process.

The despatcher selects the the first runnable user and then:

- retrieves the user's virtual PSW from an internal control block in memory;
- a special PSW is built to protect CP;
- the user's virtual PSW is modified to put it in problem state with all interrupts enabled, and the appropriate storage key is set;
- internal timers are set to go off a short while later;
- CP's registers are saved and the user's registers are loaded;
- the special PSW is loaded to the real hardware PSW.

A virtual machine that is despatched will continue processing instructions until one of the following events occurs:

- it reaches the end of its timeslice;
- a privileged operation requires CP simulation;
- a real machine interrupt occurs (eg an I/O interrupt).

If the interrupt is an SVC interrupt then:

- control is passed to CP's interrupt handler;
- the virtual PSW is stored in the user's 'SVC old PSW' area;
- the user's 'SVC new PSW' is retrieved and modified;
- registers etc are restored and the modified PSW is loaded.

DEADLINE PRIORITY

At the end of each user's timeslice the priority for its next despatch (ie its deadline priority) is calculated by the scheduler based on the user's activity in relation to other active users on the system. It is placed in the queue in the position that is appropriate to its deadline priority value.

PRIORITY CALCULATION

The priority value assigned to a user within a queue is called the deadline priority and it is recalculated at each queue drop. Deadline priority is based on a number of parameters. A simplified way to calculate deadline priority is to use the formula

$$DP = ToD + (t*u)$$

where DP = Deadline Priority
ToD = Time of Day
t = timeslice
u = number of users.

The calculation is further complicated by the additional items:

$$DP = ToD + (t*u)*au/fs*p$$

where DP = Deadline Priority
ToD = Time of Day
t = timeslice
u = number of users
au = amount already used
fs = fair share
p = user priority.

If 10 active users are on the system, the CPU is 100 per cent busy and a timeslice is 0.1 seconds, a user can expect to take 1 second to get his 0.1 second timeslice. The deadline time for that user would be calculated as time of day plus 1 second. This value would be modified by usage history. Therefore, if the user has been getting less than his fair share, his deadline value will be reduced. If he has been getting more than his fair share, his deadline value will be increased. A reduction in deadline priority will result in improved response time. The usage variables are typically smoothed exponentially over an eight-minute period. The effect of this is that a user who becomes active after a period of inactivity will get better than average service for the first few minutes. Eventually the scheduler will restore the service level for that user to normal. In fact, a user who starts a highly compute-bound job after being idle on a system with very few users on it will get far more than his fair share for several minutes. This will consequently degrade the performance of existing users.

In theory, the fair-share calculations are based on the weighted average of a virtual machine's usage of CPU cycles and storage. The initial setting is to weight the CPU at 100 per cent and storage at 0 per cent. If paging is very light this value might never change. The weight used in calculations is typically varied by the feedback module according to the current system performance.

XA SCHEDULER

XA maintains three lists of logged on users like SP and HPO. Those in the dormant list have no work to perform, ie the users are 'thinking'. Those in the eligible list would like to be selected for despatching, but are waiting for resources. Those in the despatchable list are waiting to become active.

With XA there are three queues, Q1, Q2 and Q3. There is also a Q0 which is a special class of Q1 user. Q0 users are not held on the eligible queue, they are passed to the despatchable queue. The QUICKDSP command puts a user in Q0.

A virtual machine will continue processing until it is interrupted. An interrupt occurs when

- Its timeslice ends — When the virtual machine is next despatched it will continue from where it left off.

- The user becomes idle — This usually occurs because the current transaction comes to an end.
- User has been swapped — This happens when an interactive user requires access to the despatch list and storage is constrained. Non-interactive work is swapped to support more interactive users.
- Growth in working storage size — This occurs when storage space is constrained, and a user acquires more pages than the system expected.

7 Virtual Storage Overview

This chapter provides a simplified account of storage in a VM system. It starts by describing the way that virtual storage is arranged, defining terms such as real storage and auxiliary storage and explaining what a page frame and page slot are. The second part examines in some detail the way that real storage is organised, describing its component parts including the Dynamic Paging Area (DPA). The third part looks at the way Names Saved Systems (NSSs) and Discontiguous Saved Segments (DCSSs) can be used in virtual storage.

VIRTUAL STORAGE

The early series 360 processors produced by IBM had a small amount of core storage. Comparatively speaking they were equivalent to many domestic computers, and could store far less than many of today's PCs. This limitation in space available for programs to execute led to the development of virtual storage. Virtual storage is storage space that appears to be available within the processor, but in reality exists on DASD. A direct consequence of this is that a processor with only 256K of internal storage could process a program that was 1MB in size.

Virtual storage is made up of two components, real storage and auxiliary storage. Real storage occupies space within the processor itself. Auxiliary storage typically exists on disks but may exist on special paging devices or within expanded storage. With more recent processors (3090 Es, etc) the space within the processor is divided into two components called central storage and expanded storage (XSTOR). The area called central storage contains real storage. The area called expanded storage can be used for paging and other functions by some versions of VM.

With some of the older processors, the storage space inside the processor is referred to as main storage.

The real storage space is logically divided up by VM into a number of areas including the Dynamic Paging Area (DPA). The DPA can contain pages from active virtual machines. The pages contain instructions which the processor will perform. All the pages from a virtual machine that are in real storage are referred to as its working set. The maximum size of real storage that can be supported by VM/SP is 16MB, with HPO it is 64MB, and with XA it is 2GB.

When a user logs on to a virtual machine, it is allocated virtual storage space. The amount depends on the value specified in the directory for that virtual machine. This space is formatted into 4K blocks called pages. The pages contain the instructions, data and programs used by that user. All the pages are placed on auxiliary storage. Some are then copied into real storage. It is only the instructions within pages in real storage that can be processed. Real storage is formatted into 4K units called page frames. Auxiliary storage is formatted into 4K units called page slots. This is illustrated in Figure 7.1. The copying of the contents of a page from auxiliary storage into real storage is called a page-in. The copying of the contents of a page from real storage to auxiliary storage is called a page-out. A page-out operation only has to occur if the contents of the page have been changed while in real storage.

VM allows multiprogramming. Multiprogramming is the ability of the processor apparently to process two or more instructions at a time. In fact, it processes instructions from one virtual machine and then processes instructions from another virtual machine, and does it in nanoseconds (10 to the power of minus 9). This means that in one second it will have done work from more than one virtual machine. (In fact it will have processed them one after the other). If a lot of users are logged on, those who have instructions that the processor could carry out are kept in despatch queues and dealt with as quickly as possible.

Some processor complexes (eg 3090-600E) have more than one processor and, therefore, can carry out two (or more depending on configuration) instructions at the same time. This process is called multiprocessing, and requires two or more ALUs.

Demand paging takes place when the next instruction to be processed by an active virtual machine exists in a page that is not in real storage

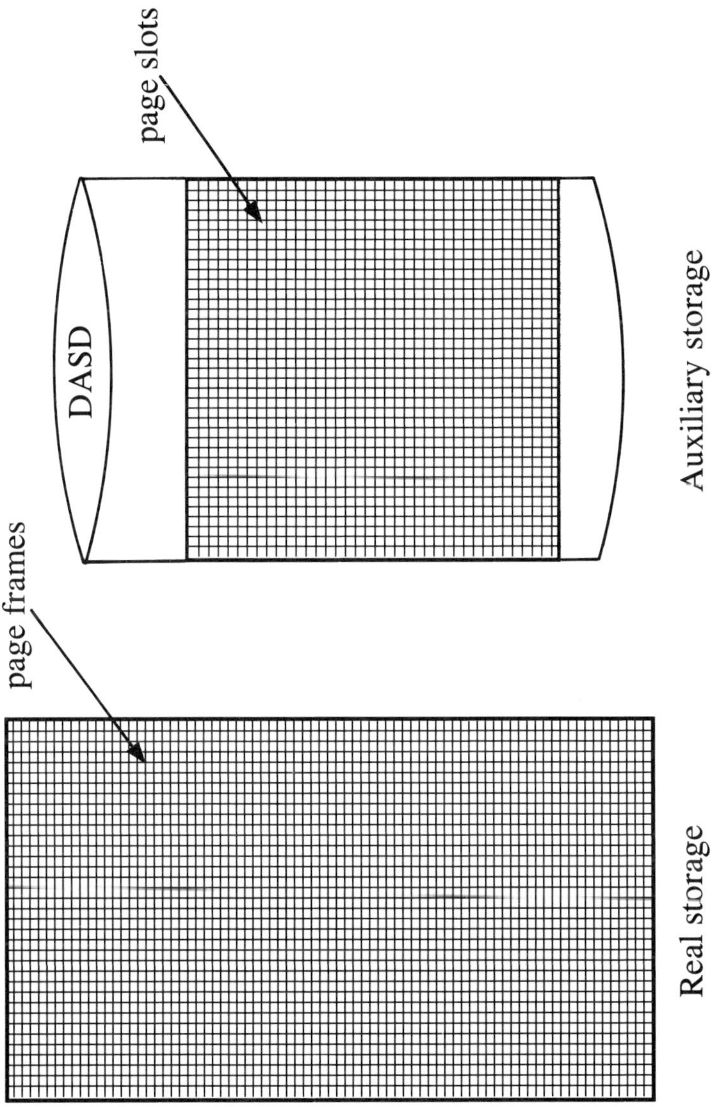

Figure 7.1 Virtual Storage Layout

at that time. The instructions cannot be executed until they are located in real storage and so the active virtual machine is interrupted and another virtual machine becomes active. A copy of the required page containing the next instructions is copied from auxiliary storage into a page frame in real storage and the virtual machine can then be restarted.

When the processor is very busy a situation may occur in which there are no free page frames in real storage available for a page-in activity. To allow work to continue, CP will take an unreferenced page from another user by a process called page stealing. If the situation occurs where CP steals pages from one user to satisfy the working set requirements of a second user, and then almost immediately has to page-in the contents of these de-allocated pages to satisfy the working set requirements of the first user, this is known as thrashing. A situation in which page-ins and page steals become excessive results in the processor spending a lot of time in supervisor state handling paging rather than being in problem state and processing the instructions within the pages. One obvious indication of this situation is that response times for virtual machines deteriorate.

An enhancement to paging was introduced with HPO and called swapping. Swapping improves overall performance in three ways:

- by freeing page frames to allow other users to page-in;
- by reducing I/O for page-in/page-out operations;
- by speeding up the bulk transfer of pages.

The virtual storage for virtual machines is formatted into segments and pages. With SP and HPO a segment is 64K in size. For XA a segment is 1024K. Pages are always 4K in size. In order to keep track of each logged-on virtual machine CP uses segment and page tables. The segment table contains pointers to page tables. The page tables are used to translate virtual addresses into real addresses. Following a page fault the appropriate entries within the page table are updated to reflect the new location of the page.

Every page is given an address so that CP can identify it and also to prevent pages being accidentally overwritten. CP maintains a number of tables to keep a record of pages and their location. With VM/SP, page addresses are 24 bits in size, with HPO they are 26 bits, and with XA they are 31 bits long. The first part of the address points to the segment table, the second part is a page number and the third part gives the displacement from the start of the page of the instruction (ie whereabouts in the page it is). This is illustrated in Figure 7.2. The start location for the segment tables is indicated by a pointer in control register 1. In order that the real location of a page can be located, its address must be translated. If, for example, an address of 42612B is the address of the next instruction to be processed and it falls beyond the range of real storage addresses, CP will look up segment 42 in the segment table. This will give the address of the appropriate page table. It will look up page 6, which might give a virtual address of 81000. Therefore the address of the next instruction is 8112B. This is illustrated in Figure 7.3. The address of the next instruction to be processed is also contained in the second part of the program status word (PSW).

Segment table	Page number	Displacement within the page
0 7	8 11	12 23
0 11	12 19	20 31

Figure 7.2 Address Structure for 24- and 31-Bit Addresses

To keep track of page frames within real storage CP maintains a page frame table which is called the core table. CP uses swap tables to identify the location on disk of the swap set (groups of pages for a user) for each virtual machine, if that virtual machine has been swapped out.

REAL STORAGE LAYOUT

Real storage is used to contain the VM systems programs and the control blocks that it needs to use while the system is up and running, and most importantly it contains pages from logged-on virtual machines so that work can be processed. The more space in real storage that can be allocated for pages from virtual machines, the better the performance will be for those users. If the processor contains space allocated for expanded storage then real storage occupies the area called central storage.

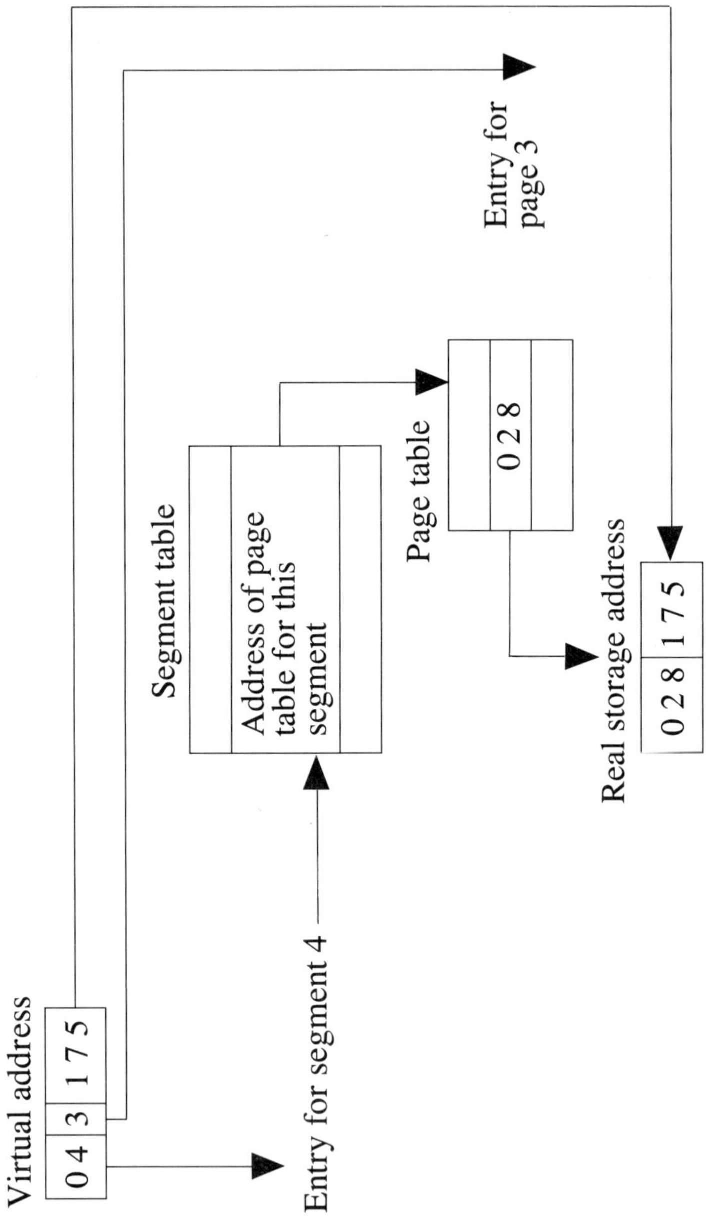

Figure 7.3 Address Translation

With SP the maximum size for real storage is 16MB as this is the maximum size that can be addressed with 24-bit addressing. With HPO the maximum size for real storage is 64MB. This is possible because real storage management uses 26-bit addressing. With XA the maximum size is 2GB, which is the maximum size possible using 31-bit addressing.

The various components of real storage are kept in separate areas. These areas are given below:

- nucleus;
- optional guest-operating system;
- Dynamic Paging Area (DPA);
- trace tables;
- Free Storage Area (FSA).

The actual arrangement of these five components is different for SP, HPO and XA. They are illustrated in Figures 7.4, 7.5 and 7.6.

Nucleus Area

The nucleus area contains some of the system programs that are loaded in when VM is IPLed. The system programs in the nucleus area make up what is known as the resident nucleus (DMKCPE). It contains those programs that must remain in real storage at all times and some others. The other system programs are in what is called the pageable nucleus, and they are loaded into DPA space. The resident nucleus will typically occupy about 100 pages and may be reduced by removing unwanted devices from the DMKRIO module, and removing (ie deleting from the CP LOADLIST) those modules that are not required in the environment where the CP is running. Any savings in space will usually be small and will not significantly increase the size of the DPA. Also, if any attempt is made to use a function that was removed, CP will abend.

With VM/SP release 5 the total saving that can be achieved by removing functions is 66K. The following functions can be removed:

- multiple address space guest;
- SNA(CCS);
- TTY terminals;

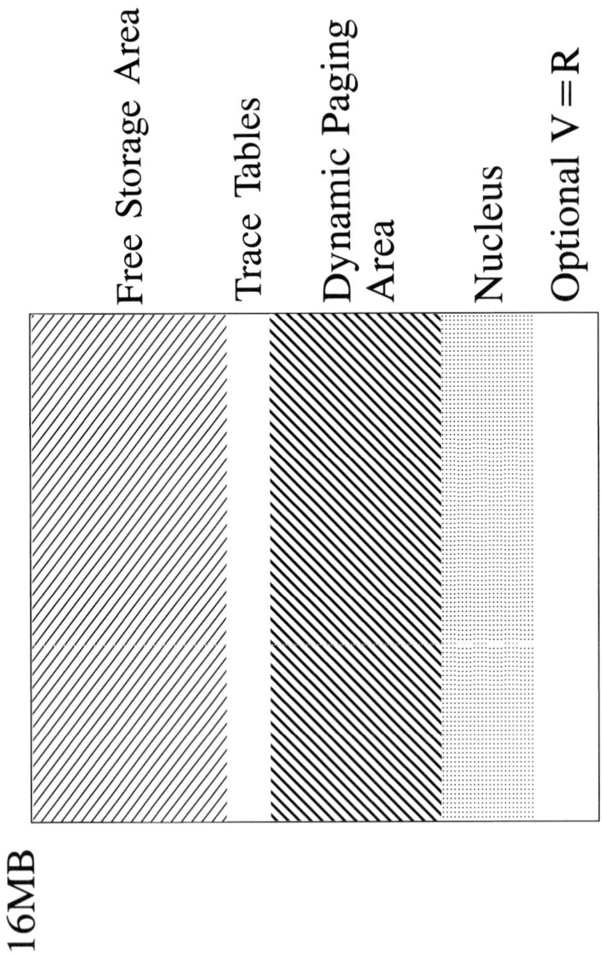

Figure 7.4 SP Real Storage Layout

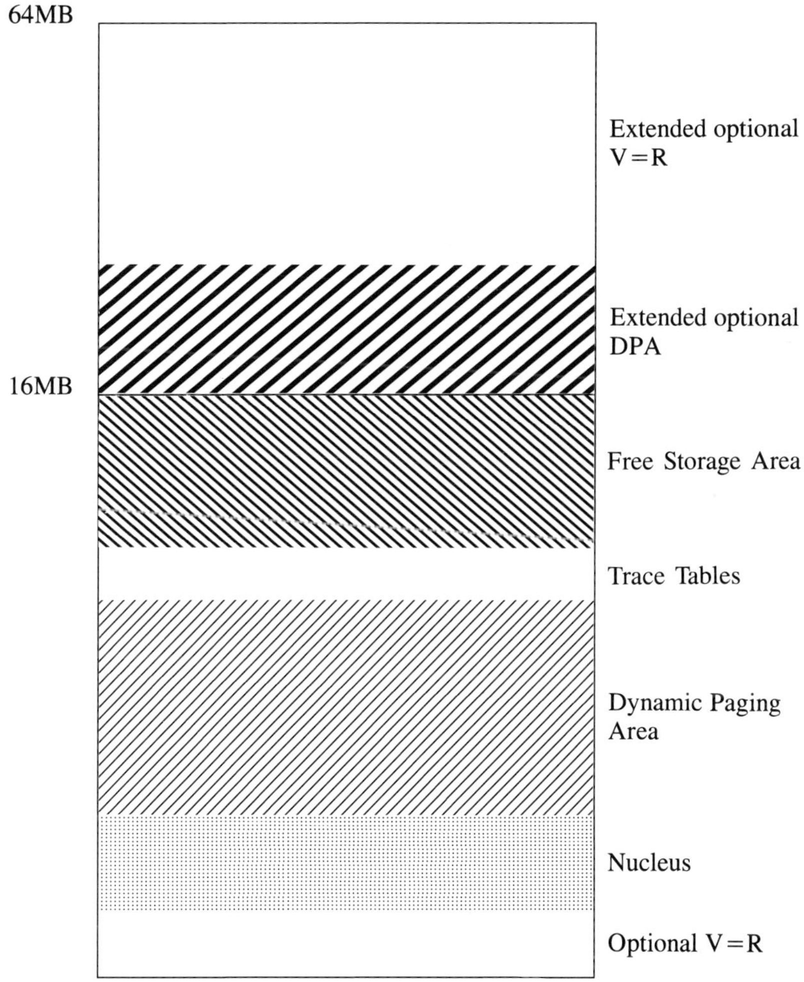

Figure 7.5 HPO Real Storage Layout

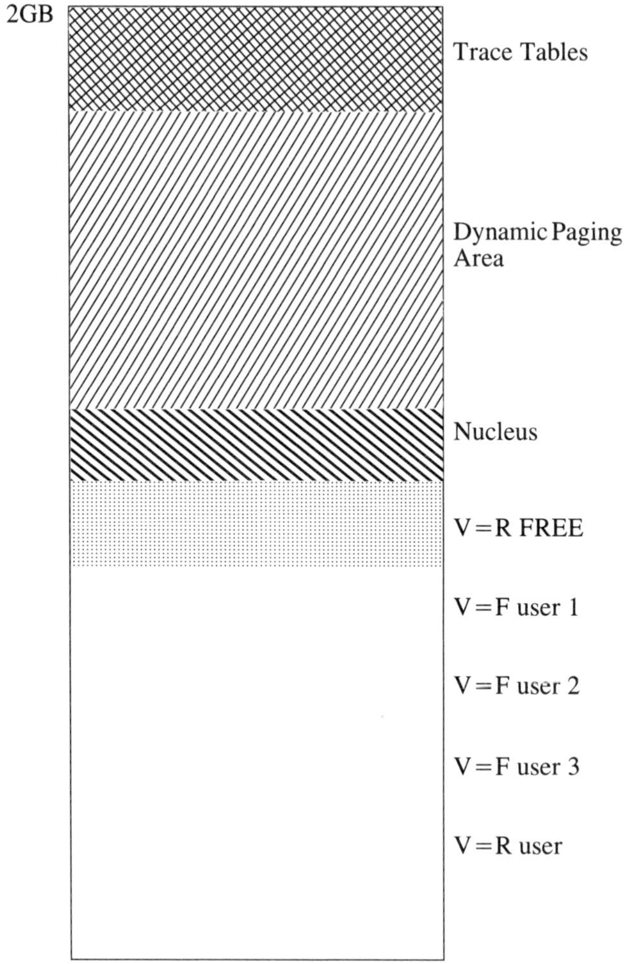

Figure 7.6 XA SP Real Storage Layout

- 3066 device support;
- remote 3270;
- 3375 and 3380 device support;
- 3704, 3705, 3720 and 3725 controller support;
- 3850 support;
- 3800 support.

With HPO release 5 the total saving that can be achieved by removing functions is about 80K. The list is similar to the SP list with the addition of:

- local 3270;
- PMA;
- V=R;
- V=R recovery;
- quiesce command;
- missing interrupt handler.

Not available for removal from the HPO list is 3800 support.

Performance improvements can be achieved by adopting the opposite procedure and moving some nucleus entries from the pageable to the resident nucleus. An example is the IUCV modules. Although this increases the size of the nucleus area and, as a consequence, decreases the space in real storage available to the DPA, it may give positive benefits in performance.

VM/XA maintains its own 2GB address space (called SYSTEM), in which it keeps routines and data. If these routines are not in use they can be stored in expanded storage or on DASD and, therefore, make more real storage space available.

Optional Guest-operating System

Many VM sites will run with a guest-operating system occupying part of real storage. The guest is said to be running V=R (ie Virtual=Real). This is done because it is a way of improving the performance of the guest system. The guest system run in this way will typically be MVS.

The larger the area that it occupies, the less space can be allocated to the DPA. The amount of space allocated is usually decided upon in response to the requirements of the guest system and its users. With VM/SP all the space allocated to this guest will come from the bottom of real storage, ie page 1 upwards. With HPO, space can also be allocated at the top end of real storage. It is always good policy to attempt to balance areas above and below the 16MB line. The space above the line is specified by the RSSIZE parameter of the SYSCOR macro of DMKSYS. With XA one V=R guest can be run and up to 5 V=F guests (ie Virtual=Fixed). However, with XA there is no problem with limitations on the amount of real storage that can be addressed.

V=R FREE area

The V=R FREE area only exists with XA and is used as a guest-operating system-recovery area. The size of this area depends on its usage, but is usually set at between 60 and 80 pages of each V=R and V=F user. The default selected by IBM is 1MB, but this is usually considered to be too large. The size of this area is specified in the HCPSYS SYSSTORE macro VRFREE, and must be big enough to recover V=R and V=F areas automatically in the event of an abend. A usual starting value for its size is around 300K per guest system in real storage. If the space is too small a message is sent to the VM operator console and appropriate action can be taken. The amount of space to be used can be found by entering LOCATE HCPRSMVE. This will give a real address. The command D H*address* is entered and shows the number, in hex, of double words currently in use.

Dynamic Paging Area

The Dynamic Paging Area (DPA) is made up of 4K page frames and is used to contain the working sets of active virtual machines. A virtual machine must have a page in the DPA before the instructions in that page can be processed. The more DPA space that is available the less paging (and swapping with HPO) will be required, and the better the performance that the users will experience. In addition to page frames containing pages from virtual machines, the DPA may contain the pageable nucleus and DisContiguous Saved Segments (DCSSs). With HPO VMBLOKs are also allocated in the DPA. HPO has an advantage over SP in that the DPA area can be split above and below the

16 MB line. One drawback is that if a required page resides above the line it must first be migrated to below the line before it can be used. The size of the extended DPA is specified by the RMSIZE parameter of the SYSCOR macro in the DMKSYS system module. A map of the contents of the DPA is kept by the core table (described in Chapter 8).

The amount of real storage available to the DPA can be increased by installing a larger CPU. For SP users the size of real storage can be increased from 16MB to 64MB by migrating to HPO. For users of both SP and HPO a migration to XA SP offers up to 2GB of real storage.

Trace Table

The trace table is used by VM to record events that occur in the system. The information can be used for diagnostic purposes in the event of a system problem, to produce reports on system performance, and some non-IBM monitors use it as a source of monitoring data. Data is written into the trace table all the time in a wraparound manner like a flight recorder in an aircraft. This means that new data overwrites old data. To help in the identification of problems it is useful to know what the 'normal' contents of the trace table look like.

With SP and HPO, the default size for the trace table is set at 4 pages for every 1MB of real storage up to 16MB, and 1 page for every 1MB of real storage above 16MB. This results in 400K of real storage being allocated for trace tables on a machine running HPO with 64MB of real storage. With XA SP the default size for trace tables is one page for every 64K of real storage. With HPO release 5 and above the size of the trace tables can be specified by the SYSCOR TRACE= parameter in DMKSYS. With XA the size of the trace tables is specified by the TRACE option on the SYSSTORE macro of HCPSYS. The less space that is allocated to trace tables the more space can be made available for the DPA. Some sites work on the premise that a production system could run with as little as 16K allocated for trace tables. If a problem is experienced on the system, then an alternative nucleus with a full-size trace table is IPLed and used for diagnosing the problem. Unfortunately, it is not always possible to IPL a new system and then recreate the problem, so most sites tend to use a compromise value and specify a trace table size somewhere between 16K and the default value.

Free Storage Area

Part of real storage is allocated to the Free Storage Area (FSA). This area is used by the CP as a working storage area and contains various control blocks, eg virtual device blocks, spool file blocks and certain tables, eg segment, page and swap tables.

If the system runs out of space in the FSA it takes space from the DPA. With HPO, this space is always from the DPA below the 16MB line. The name given to this process is a free storage extend. With HPO a section of free storage is allocated as prime free storage. This consists of cache-aligned 128-byte blocks of storage. Prime areas are used by the system for some of its most common and dynamic control blocks, eg CPEXBLOK, SAVEAREA, IOBLOK. The default size for the prime area is 10 per cent of the FSA.

With XA, a free storage area is not specified at SYSGEN, but dynamically acquired from the DPA as required. Free storage is allocated based on the length of time a block of storage is required. Device blocks and spool blocks are usually long term and are acquired from chains of blocks. Storage for short duration blocks, eg IOBs and message blocks, is allocated from subpools.

With VM/XA, in addition to segment tables, page tables and state descriptions, there are two control blocks that reside in 4K page frames that are important for the maintenance of guest storage. These are:

- VMDBK — virtual machine description block (the XA equivalent to the VMBLOK);
- PGMBK — the paging management block.

With small CMS virtual machines (ie those requiring less than 32MB) it is wasteful of space to allocate a full page in the FSA for each segment table because only a few blocks are required. In this case it is possible for the segment table to be part of the VMDBK and the space to be saved.

FSA Contents

A large proportion of the FSA is taken up by page and swap tables, and it is estimated that 3000 bytes of free storage per megabyte of virtual storage are required for each logged-on user.

On older VM systems, spool-file blocks can be responsible for using large amounts of the FSA. 128 bytes are required for each spool file. There can frequently be large numbers of spool files on the machine, particularly with PROFS systems installed unless steps are taken to remove 'old' spool files. With VM release 5 and above this problem is resolved because spool-file control blocks are kept in a separate address space.

Every virtual machine that is logged on has a minimum of 6K of the FSA allocated to it. The actual value can be increased depending on the configuration of the virtual machine. Figure 7.7 gives an example of the typical set-up for a virtual machine that has 1M of storage allocated in its directory entry.

Virtual storage	
segment tables	64 bytes per MB
pagc tables	768 bytes per MB
swap tables	2176 bytes per MB
Virtual devices	
VDEVBLOK	720 bytes
VCTLUNIT	200 bytes
VCHANNEL	192 bytes
Miscellaneous	
retrieve buffer	160 bytes
PFK table	192 bytes
SSBLOK	320 bytes
SFBLOK	1280 bytes

Figure 7.7 Example Space Requirement for a User

This gives a minimum of 6072 bytes per user. A user with 8MB of storage, 30 virtual devices and 50 spool files would require 34,000 bytes.

Page, swap and segment tables in free storage are not only required up to the virtual machine size, but segment tables are needed for the full size of addressable storage. This is often forgotten and since release

5 was introduced IBM have moved the default location of CMS to the top end of storage, thereby also increasing segment-table allocation. The amount of storage used for page and swap tables can be calculated by multiplying TTSEGCNT (location X'404') by 192 bytes or, if FRETRAP is installed, by 208.

Most of these tables will be swapped out (starting when they occupy more than 12%). APAR VM29639 (PUT 88003) increases this support to include unshared page/swap tables that are part of a Named Saved System.

Reducing FSA Usage

To prevent the FSA extending into the DPA space and also to minimise the size of the FSA it can be useful to keep to a minimum the contents of the FSA (thereby ensuring that the maximum amount of space is available to the DPA). Unused page and swap tables can be migrated to paging devices. With HPO releases above 4.2 this is done automatically. For sites using earlier relases, the MIGRATE command can be used.

One easy way to reduce the number of spool file blocks is to PURGE the spool files. Ideally users would read in the files that are in their reader queues and then save them to mini-disk. Many sites run EXECs daily that delete spool files that are older than eight days (for example). Sites with PROFS often find spool-file blocks a real problem because of the ease with which PROFS users can create spool files but rarely seem to remove them.

As mentioned earlier, with SP release 5 and above spool-file blocks are kept in a separate address space in virtual storage, thereby reducing the amount of free storage utilised.

Any user who is not actively working should log off because this will free the 6K or more of FSA that they have allocated. Two methods can be used to accomplish this: either users can be educated to understand the importance of logging off when not performing work involving the processor, or alternatively an EXEC can be run that will FORCE off users who have been idle for a predetermined period of time, eg five minutes. The period of time selected must be long enough to allow plenty of thinking time for 'slow' users. Whatever length of time is selected it should be remembered that it is not worth creating a user-hostile environment. If there are PROFS users who log on in the morning and neither use the system after 9:30 nor log off, they will still be using up 6K of valuable storage. These users may be ideal candidates for forcing off, as a way of reducing the amount of FSA space used.

FSA Size

These is no point in allocating more FSA space than is required because it takes away space that could be used by the DPA. If the FSA is too small, it will take space away from the DPA to meet its requirements in a process called a free-storage extend. The space is always taken from the DPA below the 16 MB line. One consequence of the free-storage extend is that page-out activities may occur for pages that are in the DPA, resulting in a decrease in performance for those virtual machines. Free-storage extends also use CPU resources because the processor is in supervisor state rather than problem state when performing the extend, again degrading performance.

With non-XA systems, the amount of real storage to be allocated to the FSA is specified in DMKSYS at IPL time as FREE=nn, PRIME=nn. The method to adopt to find out if the value has been correctly specified is to display the two full words at DMKFRENP in real storage at regular intervals throughout a working day. Should the value of the first full word remain at, or near, zero all the time, this indicates that the allocated free-storage space is adequate for current usage. The amount of free-storage space should be increased if the value of the first full word is greater than 3E. The number of additional pages that are required can be calculated by subtracting the initial value of the second word displayed from the highest recorded value of the second word displayed. Because the value is in hex it will have to be converted to decimal. The DMKSYS FREE parameter value should be increased by the calculated amount. With HPO, free-storage space is requested using the DMKFREE macro and DMKFRET is used to release it. With XA the HCPFRE macro is used to manage free-storage requests.

SAVED SYSTEMS AND SEGMENTS

Saved systems and saved segments can be utilised as a way of using virtual storage more economically and efficiently. With non-XA systems they are identified to CP in DMKSNT. A description of each, and the way that they have been developed for XA, is given below.

Saved Systems

A saved system (also called Named Saved System — NSS) is a virtual operating system that may be stored in the PERM area on CP-owned DASD, and is IPLable by name instead of device address. A saved system is created by taking a snapshot of a virtual machine's storage, register contents and PSW at a single moment in time during processing, and writing that snapshot to disk.

Saved systems provide an efficient way of resuming execution without incurring the overheads associated with an IPL by device address. The area of virtual storage allocated when the saved system is loaded contains code that can be shared between a number of users. This means that the users do not each have their own copy and this reduces the amount of DPA space required by those users. There is also a saving in time because it is quicker to load the saved system once, rather than each user having to load the code from disk every time it is needed. Saved systems were introduced in the early 1970s as a way of improving system efficiency. CMS is an example of a saved system.

Discontiguous Saved Segments

A DisContiguous Saved Segment (DCSS) is similar to a saved system in that it can usually be shared by many users. This is because the code in a DCSS is usually re-entrant. When there is only one copy of the code there is a consequent saving in the amount of DPA space that will be used. DCSSs contain code that is loaded by CP function rather than by virtual I/O. All external references in the saved segment must be resolved, ie no code in the saved segment must call a subroutine that is not also located in the saved segment. It is necesary to allocate an area of virtual memory for each DCSS to process in and it is necessary to ensure that the spaces allocated for DCSSs do not overlap.

XA and Saved Segments

VM/XA uses a new architecture and new terms when dealing with DCSSs and Named Saved Segments (NSSs) compared to the older method used with VM/SP and HPO. With XA the DEFSEG and DEFSYS commands replace the DMKSNT module for defining DCSSs and NSSs. This means that saved segments are easier to manage without requiring a re-IPL of the system.

A *segment* is defined as a 1MB area that starts on a 1MB boundary. A saved segment is an area of virtual storage that is defined as holding saved data or software.

A *DCSS* is a saved segment that has been defined by the DEFSEG command without the SPACE operand. It must contain only a single data or software entity, and must start and end on a 1MB boundary.

A *saved-segment space* (DCSS-S) is a saved segment that has been defined by the DEFSEG command using the SPACE operand. It can contain multiple software and data entities, and it also must start and end on a 1MB boundary.

A *member saved segment* (DCSS-M) is a saved segment that belongs to as many as 64 saved-segment spaces, starting and ending on page boundaries and spanning megabyte boundaries.

In addition to the types of saved segments mentioned above there are NSSs, CPNSSs (CP system service NSSs), and CPDCSSs (CP system service DCSSs).

Information about DCSSs and NSSs is stored in a System Data File (SDF) in the spool. It identifies:

- memory ranges defined;
- usage;
- status (eg defined but not saved, or defined and saved).

CMS release 5.5 provides a SEGMENT macro and command that will allocate storage for a DCSS, load a DCSS and purge a DCSS. SEGMENT allows CMS to manage centrally all the DCSSs in a virtual machine, but it relies on application and vendor software cooperating by using it for DCSS manipulation instead of DIAGNOSE X'64' directly.

If there are only a few packages in saved segments and minimal simultaneous use of DCSSs it is recommended that the software is installed in DCSSs with each holding only a single entity. If there are a lot of saved segment packages and a complex and perhaps unpredictable interaction between packages, software should be packed into segment spaces (DCSS-S) or installed in overlaid DCSSs.

Software that is unable to exploit XA facilities must be placed below the 16MB line. If single-occupancy DCSSs are used then this space (perhaps 13 one-MB segments) will soon be used up. Additional problems arise from the fact that each segment must be completely shared or unshared.

CPDCSSs are used to store monitor data with XA.

MAXIMISING DPA SPACE

The following are suggested ways of minimising the real storage constraint for users and maximising DPA space:

— The size of the FSA should be kept to a minimum. This can be achieved in the following ways:

- For HPO users of releases below 4.2 the MIGRATE command can be used to migrate unused page and swap tables to DASD.
- For users of releases below 5 the number of spool-file blocks can be reduced by purging spool files.
- The amount of space taken up by virtual machine control blocks can be reduced by ensuring that idle users log off.
- Unnecessary devices can be eliminated from user-directory entries. This reduces the number of control blocks used for each virtual machine.
- Virtual device addresses should be numbered consecutively to minimise the number of virtual channel and virtual control unit blocks.

— The size of the trace table with release 5 and above or XA should be reduced by using the TRACE option of the SYSCOR macro in DMKSYS or the TRACE option of the SYSSTORE macro in HCPSYS.

— The size of resident nucleus area should be minimised. This can be achieved in the following ways:

- Unwanted devices can be removed from DMKRIO.
- Unwanted modules that will not be used can be removed from the LOADLIST.

— DCSSs should be used wherever possible in the DPA to reduce the amount of duplicated code.

— More main memory can be installed:

- up to 16MB for SP;
- up to 64MB for HPO;
- up to 2GB for XA/SP.

— The version of VM installed can be upgraded, eg migrate from SP to HPO or from HPO to XA SP.

— The number of monitor buffers can be reduced using the BUFFS option of the SYSCOR macro. (If this is done it is important to watch for monitor suspension records.)

— The SET RESERVE and LOCK commands should be used sparingly.

8 Paging

Paging is the name given to the process by which pages from virtual machines are copied from auxiliary storage to real storage (a page-in) and from real storage to auxiliary storage (a page-out). The process is necessary to facilitate the apparently concurrent execution of a number of separate virtual machines which may need to occupy more space than is available in real storage. Only the instructions that are within a page of a virtual machine in the Dynamic Paging Area (DPA) can be processed. Paging can be a major performance bottleneck when the right pages are not in the right place at the right time. Although paging works in a similar manner with all VM systems, the detail of how it works is different for VM/SP, VM/SP HPO and VM/XA SP systems.

PAGE FRAMES

Within the DPA are predefined 4K-size areas called page frames. Into these page frames are copied the pages of virtual machines. When the virtual machine is no longer active it is necessary to copy out the contents of the page frame to a page slot in auxiliary storage. When this has been done the page frame is free for use by the next page that needs to be brought into real storage. The process is slightly simpler than this because, if the contents of the page in real storage have not been altered, there is no need to copy them out to auxiliary storage because the version already on auxiliary storage will be the same. To ensure that performance is good it is necessary to ensure that there are always page frames available for pages of active virtual machines to be paged in to. This is where complications to the simple model described above occur. With HPO an additional feature called swapping was introduced as a way improving (complicating) the paging process. With XA a similar process is used, but it is called block paging.

SWAPPING

Swapping is the name given to the process by which blocks of pages, called swap sets, are moved from real storage to auxiliary storage (swap-out) or from auxiliary storage to real storage (swap-in). The process was introduced with HPO as a way of improving performance. The areas of auxiliary storage that are used are on CP-owned devices and are defined as SWAP areas. Swap tables are used to describe the location on auxiliary storage of the swap sets for each user. The system maintains swap queues for interactive (Q1) and non-interactive (Q2) users. Users on a swap queue may have their swap set swapped out. A swap set has the referenced working-set pages of a user put in it at queue drop time. If the pages were unreferenced they are put on the flushlist. If the number of pages in a swap set is less than the minimum working set size value specified using the SET MINWS command, unreferenced pages are added to make up the number. After the swap set is placed on the swap queue, any remaining unreferenced pages for that particular user are called the trim set. In a process called trimming all the entries for the trim set are placed on the flushlist. If a page fault occurs for a swapped-out page, all the pages in the swap set will be read in togcther. The number of swap sets that can be paged in concurrently is specified by the SET SRM MINNUMSS command. The value specified should be equal to the number of swap devices installed in order to allow concurrent I/O from each. The size of the swap set depends on the device type that is used for swapping. For 3380s a value of 9 or 19 is used. The value is specified in the SYSPAG macro, eg

```
SYSPAG . . .,TYPE=SW,SWSIZE=19.
```

TABLES

In addition to segment and page tables used for paging there is a page-frame table called the core table which contains information about every page frame. There is also a swap table that keeps track of the SWAP areas so that free page slots can be identified and the location of the swap sets is known.

Core Table

The core table contains an entry for every page frame and contains such information as whether the frame is in use and by whom. With SP, the core table contains two lists of linked pointers called the freelist and the flushlist. With HPO, there is an additional component called the swap queue.

Freelist

Within the core table is the freelist. This contains references to all the page frames that are free for use. After an IPL the majority of the page frames will have an entry in the freelist, but as the system becomes busier more of the available page frames will become utilised. It is necessary throughout the day to ensure that there are always enough page frames available to allow for free storage extends and for page-ins or swap-ins.

With SP, the number of page frames that must be listed in the freelist is equal to the number of in-queue users plus one. This allows every user to experience a page fault and leaves one page available for a free storage extend.

With HPO, the number of page frames in the freelist is equal to the value for SP, plus an additional amount to allow every page in a swap set to be copied in from every SWAP device. The additional number of page frames required is equal to the MINNUMSS (minimum number of swap sets) multiplied by the swap-set size.

Flushlist

The page frames referenced by the flushlist belong to virtual machines that are not ready to use the CPU. The page frames could be given to the freelist.

Swap Queues

The page frames referenced by swap queues contain pages that make up swap sets. There are two logical queues, one for interactive users (Q1) and one for non-interactive users (Q2).

MAINTAINING FREELIST PAGES

Page frames must be available to allow pages of processing virtual machine to page in to. They must be available for free storage extends, and with HPO to allow pages from swap sets to be swapped in. The freelist keeps a list of available page frames. If there are not enough available page frames in the freelist CP must add page frames to this list. With SP a simple process is adopted; with HPO the DMKSEL (select) routine goes through a five-stage process to increase the number of page frames on the freelist.

DMKSEL Routine

The DMKSEL routine is a five-stage process that places in the freelist pointers to page frames that are free for use. The stages in this process are described below.

Stage 1

At four-second intervals a garbage-collector routine searches one-eighth of the DPA looking for any miscellaneous page frames that could be added to the freelist. Miscellaneous pages include:

- pages belonging to out of queue users referenced by CP;
- spool buffer pages;
- transient system address space pages (unreferenced);
- virtual machine pseudo segments.

Stage 2

In stage 2 users are moved from the interactive to the non-interactive swap queue and pages from the non-interactive queue are swapped out. Not all the pages in a user's working set are swapped out. Only enough pages to replenish the freelist are taken.

With HPO releases below 5, the length of time a user spends on each queue can be specified using the SET SRM SWPQTIME command. The default value for the interactive queue is 20 seconds, and many users do not change this default value. The default value for the non-interactive queue is 100 seconds, and most sites reduce this value to around 5 seconds in order to encourage swapping rather than paging. The value may be reduced even further if demand paging rates are high. The swap queue times can be displayed using the QUERY SRM SWPQTIME command.

When there is no contention for storage space the time spent on queues will be longer than the values specified.

Stage 3

Pages that were put on the flushlist by the garbage-collector routine and by trimming (described earlier) are placed on the freelist. If the contents of any of these pages has changed since it was paged in, the page must be paged out first. Users in Q1 are slightly more favoured than users in Q2.

Stage 4

If stage four is reached the system is experiencing storage problems. Use of the QUERY QTIME command will gain more information from the system.

Users are swapped out even if their swap-queue time has not expired. This is carried out in two stages. In stage one, non-interactive users are swapped out. In stage two, interactive users are swapped out. Virtual machines are swapped one at a time in age order, ie first in first out (FIFO).

Stage 5

Although SP has only the following method as a way of replenishing its freelist page frames, with HPO it is a sign of severe paging problems. The core table is scanned and the reference bit for each page frame is checked. If the reference bit is off (ie the page has not been referenced), the frame is added to the freelist. If there are no unreferenced pages, CP selects pages that are unchanged. In this case the contents of the page will have been referenced but will not have been altered in any way, ie its contents are identical to the copy of the page on auxiliary storage. During this first pass the reference bits are reset to zero.

If there are still not enough page frames for the freelist the table is scanned for a second time. Any pages belonging to in-core users that have not been referenced between the two passes are stolen. If the contents of the page to be stolen have been changed (ie the change bit is set on) a copy of the contents must first be paged out to auxiliary storage. Any page that has been refenced between the two scanning operations will have had its reference bit changed from zero to one and will, therefore, not be selected. When enough page frames have been found a pointer is kept. The subsequent core-table scan starts from that point. This process does tend to favour in-queue users.

With SP, the time taken for one complete pass of the core table is a good performance indicator. It indicates the length of time that a page can remain in storage without being referenced. The longer the time the better the performance because CP is not involved in moving pages in and out of storage. On average out-of-queue users remain in storage for half of the scan time, ie they will be picked by the scan's first pass. The average time for in-queue users is one and a half times the core-scan time, ie they will be picked up on the scan's second pass. With SP the optimum scan time is large enough for the majority of an interactive user's pages to be still in storage when that user rejoins the queue. The scan time must, therefore, be longer than the user's 'think' time. A typical value would be around 10 seconds.

If stage five is regularly reached with HPO this can lead to thrashing, a sure indication that something is wrong. The solutions are to provide more DPA space or to reduce the amount of concurrent work. Suggestions are given in Chapter 7 of ways to maximise the dynamic paging area. The exact method adopted is very site dependent.

HARDWARE CONSIDERATIONS

The only virtual machine instructions that can be executed are in pages in the DPA in real storage. Real storage is located in the processor, which is hardware. Auxiliary storage exists on DASD. DASD are hardware. The connections between the DASD and the processor are also hardware. There are several hardware considerations that can affect performance.

Real Storage

With sites running SP the size of real storage can be up to 16MB. If 16 megabytes are not installed the extra could be added to make more page frames available to the DPA. If 16MB are installed it may be necessary to upgrade to HPO, which can use up to 64MB of real storage. If the 64MB ceiling is reached with HPO, it may be necessary to upgrade the software to XA, which allows up to 2GB of real storage. This theoretically sounds fine. In real life there would be the cost to consider of the increase in real storage, probably involving the purchase of a new processor. There is also the cost of the new software. It is only worth increasing the amount of real storage if it is constraining the performance of the system. If the main bottleneck is I/O, no amount of extra real storage will improve performance because I/O will still be a bottleneck. If paging I/O is the main problem, the use of expanded storage could help reduce this.

DASD Considerations

Auxiliary storage is usually on disk, although it could also be on solid-state devices or expanded storage. Areas of disk space are allocated for auxiliary storage. With SP, the SYSOWN macro of the DMKSYS module is used to tell CP about TEMP and PAGE allocation on packs. The TEMP area is used for spooling and can be used for paging if the PAGE area is full. With HPO, the SWAP area can, additionally, be defined to CP. PAGE and SWAP areas are identified to CP using the SYSPAG macro.

SP

With SP, page-out operations take place to the fastest device available. If all the devices are the same speed it performs one page-out operation, in turn, to each device, in the order that they are specified in the SYSOWN macro. The available page slot that is nearest to the centre of the device is used. If PAGE areas are specified on packs that are on different channels, the packs should be specified in the SYSOWN macro so that the channels alternate. In fact, page areas should be allocated across as many channels and control units as possible so as to avoid contention. Page areas should be relatively small so as to reduce seek times, eg about 80 cylinders on a 3380, and there should be only one area per actuator placed near the middle of the pack. Because the centre of the pack is address 0, if the PAGE area is spread across the centre it increases seek times. A yardstick to use when calculating how many PAGE areas are required is to allocate one (per 3380 actuator) for every 15 pages per second required.

HPO

With HPO there is a hierarchy of paging areas. These are shown below:

- SW swap area;

- PP preferred paging;
- PG general paging;
- PM paging migration;
- PS spooling (this is used as an overflow only).

Swapping takes place to SW areas. If these SW areas are unavailable the next paging area in the hierarchy is used, and so on down to PS. Paging will take place to PP devices. If they are full the next device in the hierarchy is used down to spooling areas (PS). Page migration can occur and pages are moved from one device to another lower in the hierarchy. This occurs when the device is getting full. The percentage can be specified using the SET SRM PGULL command. Page migration should only be allowed to occur from expanded-storage or solid-state devices, although even this incurs some performance penalty. Several page-outs can occur to a single device before the next device is moved on to. This allows block page-outs to occur. The number of pages in the block depends on the device type. The values used are summarised in Figure 8.1.

Block size	Device type
8	3330
3	3340
8	3350
3	3370
8	3375
10	3380
1	3880-1
1	Expanded storage

Figure 8.1 Number of Pages per Block

A moving cursor algorithm is used to select page slots. This means that a cursor moves forward from one end of a paging area to the other end then back again. This method is used to ensure that contiguous space is found for block paging or swap sets. The technique utilises all the paging area. Therefore paging areas should be small to prevent excessive head movements and a consequent deterioration in performance. PAGE and SWAP areas should be allocated near the middle of a pack and should be relatively small, 60 cylinders for PAGE, 120 cylinders for SWAP, to reduce seek times.

XA

With XA, the SYSCPVOL macro in HCPSYS is used to specify the volumes that are to be used for paging in the required path rotation order. There is no swapping with XA, which uses block paging. Blocks are placed on a device until 75 per cent of the space behind the 'moving wave' is empty. New blocks are placed from the beginning again. All the pages in a working set are paged to disk together, even if they are unchanged. This preserves locality of reference. It also means that higher than expected paging rates are observable. Pages are placed on devices with the fastest service time. It is recommended that paging take place to dedicated devices or, if that is not possible, to devices that have relatively inactive data on them.

GUEST-OPERATING SYSTEM PAGING

If guest-operating systems are run under VM they will expect to page from their auxiliary storage to their real storage. How this is actually handled in the VM environment can have a significant impact on the performance of that guest-operating system.

A typical guest system will have 'virtual' auxiliary storage and 'virtual' real storage, an arrangement illustrated in Figure 8.2. VM itself has a similar arrangement. If VM and the guest are combined, ie the guest-operating system is run under VM, the result would look like Figure 8.3. This would involve a page moving from the guest's auxiliary storage to the guest's 'real storage', which would, in fact, be part of the auxiliary storage for VM. VM would then page it from its auxiliary storage into its real storage. This set-up is called double paging and is obviously inefficient. To overcome this difficulty IBM introduced handshaking. The two handshaking techniques, non-paging mode

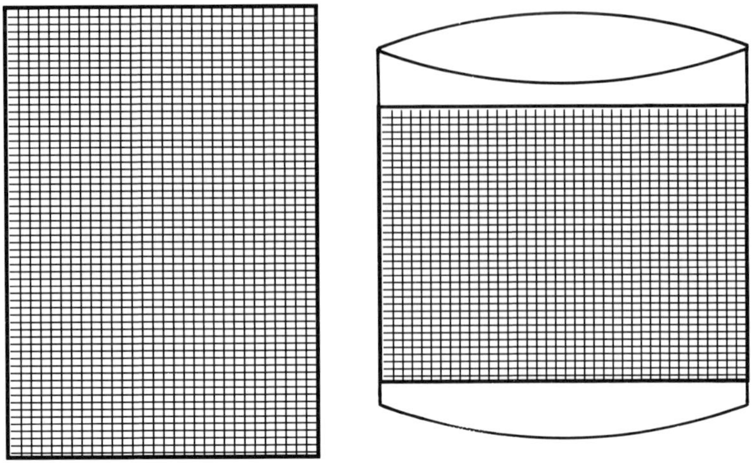

Guest-operating system's real storage

Guest-operating system's auxiliary storage

Figure 8.2 Guest System's Virtual Storage Layout

VM

Guest system

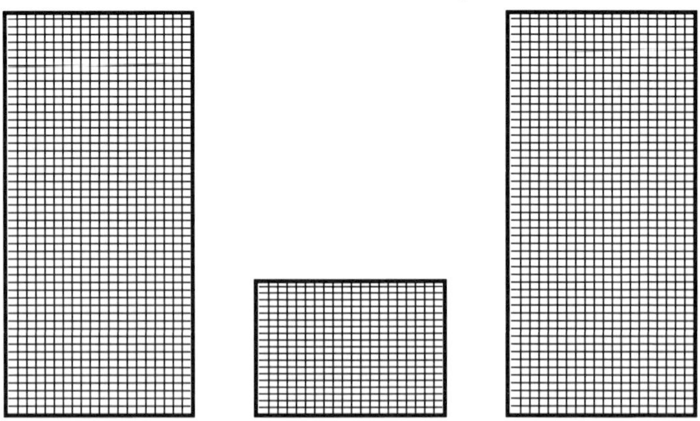

VM's real storage

Guest's 'real storage'

Guest's auxiliary storage

Figure 8.3 Double Paging

and pseudo page faults, were used as ways of giving a one-to-one match of guest real and guest virtual storage. Performance of the guest is improved because the VM overhead is reduced.

Non-paging Mode

It is possible to run a guest system in virtual storage such that its virtual address space is equal to its virtual machine size. This is illustrated in Figure 8.4. The guest-operating system, eg VSE, does not have to move pages from its auxiliary storage to its real storage. Therefore only single paging occurs as pages are moved from auxiliary storage into real storage for VM to process them. VSE is told that it is in non-paging mode by using MODE=VM. This also stops CCW translation taking place.

Pseudo Page Fault

When a page fault occurs for a partition within a guest system VM will issue a pseudo page fault. This allows the guest-operating system to despatch another partition. If a pseudo page fault were not issued by VM the guest system itself would be suspended until after the page fault was resolved. This again improves the performance of the guest-operating system. Pseudo page fault handling is turned on using the SET PAGEX ON command.

V=R Guests

It is possible to run a guest-operating system (eg MVS) in real storage. This is described as running V=R, ie Virtual equals Real. This is illustrated in Figure 8.5. This offers the advantage that the guest system can be despatched using its own segment and page tables. It also means that VM does not need to build shadow page tables. VM can be made to avoid this by using the SET STBYPASS command. Channel program translation can also be bypassed in this situation by using the SET NOTRANS ON command. VSE with the VAE facility can run V=R. In this case MODE=370 is set. This also prevents CCW translation from taking place. In 370 mode, VSE will not IPL unless page datasets are defined.

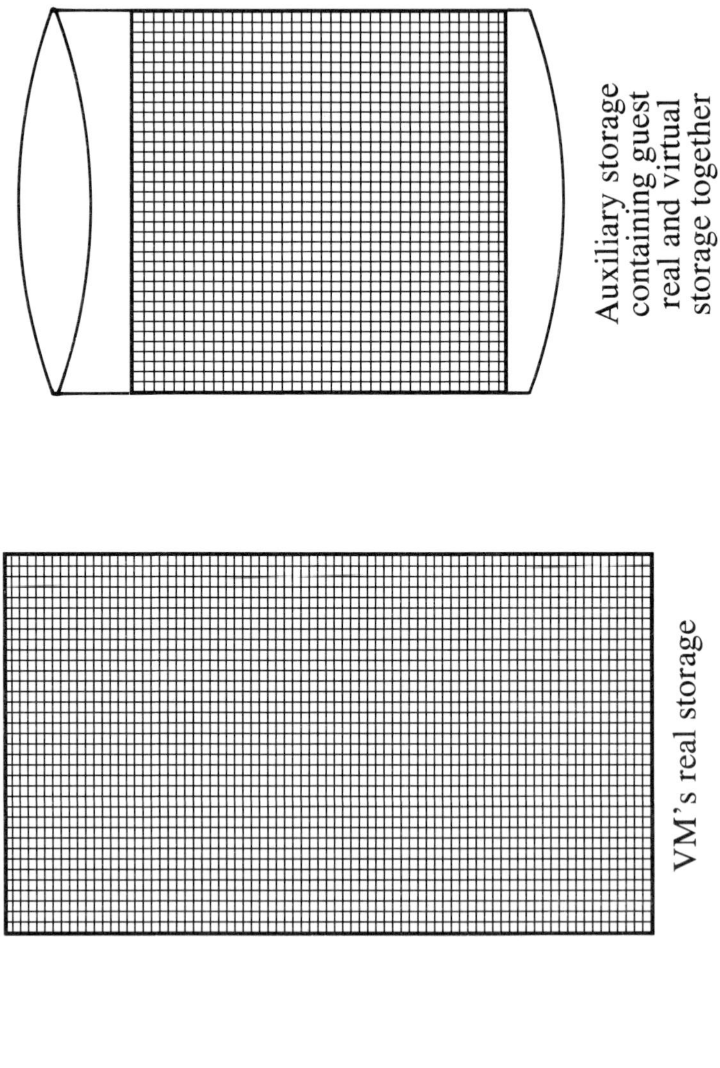

Figure 8.4 Non-paging Mode

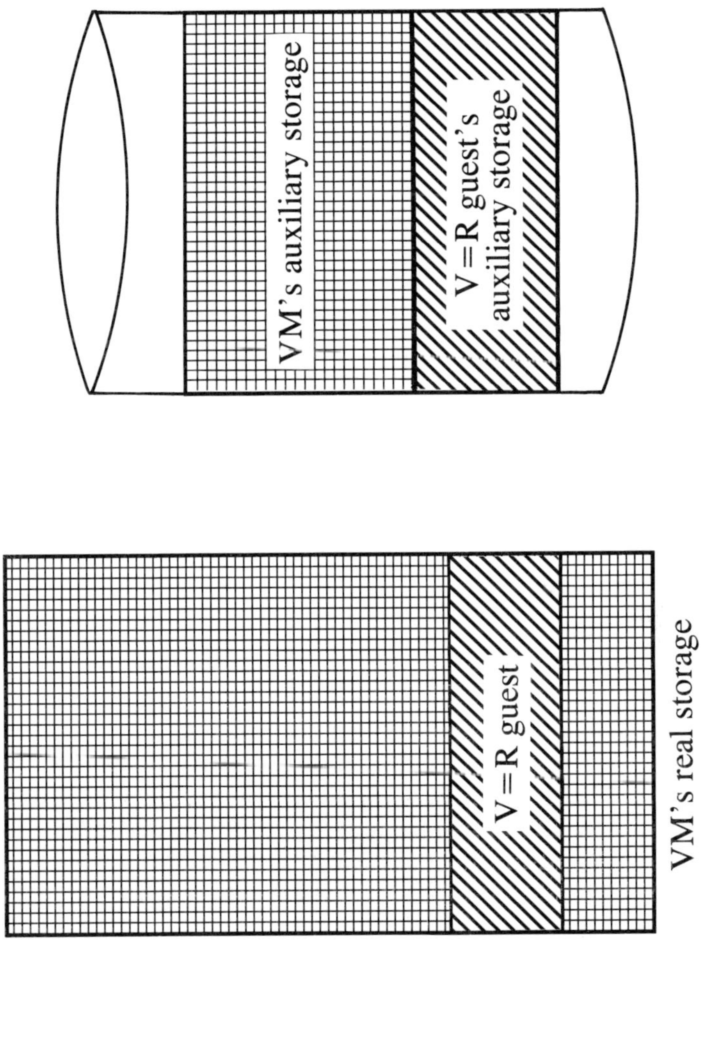

Figure 8.5 Non-paging Mode

Shadow Page Tables

In order to map from guest virtual addresses to real addresses for guest-operating systems, SP and HPO systems use shadow page tables. Their use involves a high performance overhead. Shadow page tables are created entry by entry as page faults occur for a guest system. When pages are stolen from the guest system, the shadow page table entries no longer match the contents of storage, CP does not know which entry in the table to invalidate, and the whole of the shadow page table is thus invalidated. When the guest system is next despatched the entries in the shadow page table are revalidated individually as page faults occur. The microcode VMA is able to identify those potential page faults that are caused by the shadow page table being invalidated even though the page is still in real storage. VMA turns off the invalid bit in the shadow page table and so a page-in is not required, and execution can continue. This consequently improves performance.

If MVS is run as a guest system in virtual storage rather than in real storage the SET STBYPASS nnK command can be used to improve performance. With MVS some of the code in an address space is shared by all address spaces. There is no point in creating new shadow page tables for a new address space that is being despatched when part of the new table is identical to part of the old table. It is more economical to retain from the old table that part that will be the samc in the new table. This can be done by specifying any high value. VM will reject the value and give the appropriate value to use. This value can then be keyed in.

The number of shadow page tables that can be retained in storage at any one time can be specified. There is a trade-off in that the more tables that are in real storage the less space that is available. However, the access to address space pages is quicker if the shadow page tables are in real storage. The default value is 3. Usually the maximum value of 16 is used. This can be specified using the SET STMULTI nn command. Because the common area of an MVS address space is common to all address spaces it is possible to use this command to specify the size of the common area in segments and prevent tables for that area from having to be built repeatedly.

XA does not build shadow page tables because it does allow two-level address translation. The removal of this particular overhead results in a performance improvement by running a guest under XA rather than SP or HPO.

XA Guests

XA allows one guest system to be run V=R (Virtual equals Real) and up to five to be run V=F (Virtual equals Fixed). All six guests are in real storage. This makes use of the Multiple High Performance Guest (MHPG) feature. MHPG and PR/SM (Processor Resource/System Manager) both make use of the SIE (Start Interpretive Execution) assist available on some of the newer processors. The guest systems use their own segment and page tables to handle 'virtual' to 'real' address translations, and XA uses its segment and page tables to handle guest 'real' to host real address translation.

SECTION IV

CMS and CMS Facilities

This section examines CMS, the Conversational Monitor System which is a major component of a VM system and is the component that the majority of users of VM come into contact with. The section also looks at the major components that run under CMS, eg PROFS.

9 CMS

Most people who come into contact with VM actually make use of CMS (Conversational Monitor System). CMS is an interactive single-user operating system that is available only in a VM environment. Associated with the operating system are a number of operator commands. Many of these commands are available to any user, eg Q DISK, which will display information about all the mini-disks in use by that user.

With XA SP bi-modal CMS is available. This will support both the older 370-mode operation and the new XA-mode of operation for CMS users.

CMS ENVIRONMENT

Each CMS user makes use of a single copy of the CMS operating system code. Sharing the code uses less virtual storage space than if every CMS user had his/her own copy loaded in all the time. Each user who logs on to CMS has his or her own virtual machine. This means that the terminal is the console of the virtual machine and all the other components of a mainframe system will appear to be available and dedicated to that one system. In addition to the console there will appear to be virtual storage space. This is the address space that can be utilised to execute commands and programs, etc. There will also appear to be unit record devices. Unit record devices are printers, card readers and card punches. Although real card readers and card punches tend to be a thing of the past they are still in use in the CMS virtual system and often used as a way of sending a file from one CMS user to another. The virtual printer can be used to send a hardcopy of a file to a real printer. Each user requires somewhere to store files, whether they are data files or program files or whatever. These files are stored on virtual disks. To make this physically possible, real disks are formatted into small areas called mini-disks. These mini-disks are allocated to each CMS user. This is illustrated in Figure 9.1. In addition to any mini-disks that have been allocated to a user it is possible to make use of mini-disks that have been allocated to another user. This is achieved by using the LINK command. The format of the command is:

```
LINK MAINT 190 191 RR
```

This example allows the user to link to a mini-disk owned by another user called MAINT. The virtual address of MAINT's mini-disk is 190 and it will be addressed by the user at 191. The letters RR indicate that the link is to be read only. This means that the user cannot write to MAINT's mini-disk. Figure 1.1 illustrates a user's virtual machine.

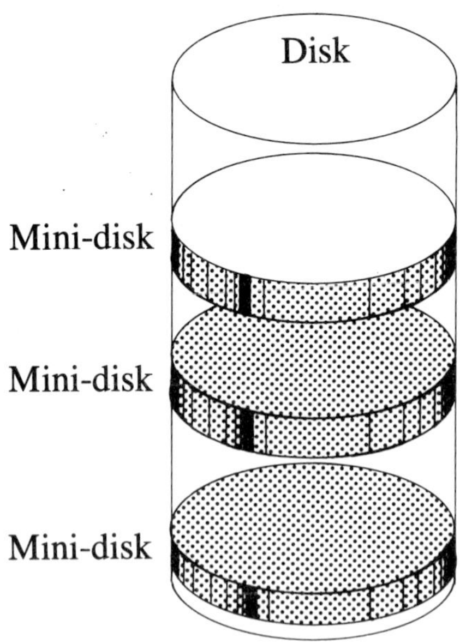

Figure 9.1 Real Disk Formatted into Mini-disks

Directory

The configuration of a user's virtual machine is defined to the system by entries in a directory. Each user must have an entry to be able to log on. An example of a typical directory entry for a CMS user is given in Figure 9.2.

```
USER TREVOR PWORD 1M 2M ABCDEG
    IPL CMS
    CONSOLE 009 3270
    SPOOL OOC 2540 READER *
    SPOOL OOD 2540 PUNCH A
    SPOOL OOE 1403 A
    LINK MAINT 190 190 RR
    LINK MAINT 19E 193 RR
    MDISK 191 3380 010 005 VMS001 MR
    MDISK 192 3380 060 003 VMS002 MR
```

Figure 9.2 Example Directory Entry

Figure 9.2 specifies that the user is call TREVOR and will log on using that user-id. The password to be entered at log-on time is PWORD. For security reasons no user should have a password as simplistic as the one in the example, and he or she should change it regularly. The value 1M specifies that one megabyte of virtual storage is to be made available when the user logs on. If the user requires more storage space then the two megabytes (the second value) will be allocated. The values ABCDEG specify the command classes that can be used. The other entries specify the virtual machine configuration by identifying the virtual console, the virtual reader and the virtual punch. The mini-disks associated with the virtual machine are specified and any other user's mini-disks that can be used.

Command Classes

At one stage there were only seven command classes available. With current versions (release 4 and above) of VM there are thirty-two command classes. To restrict users to certain commands only, commands were grouped together into command classes and command classes were allocated to particular types of users. So, for example, the general user was given command class G commands to use. If the user tried to use any command that was not in this group the command would not be accepted. Class A commands contained many more powerful commands that could be used to alter the VM environment. Class A commands were assigned to the system operator. Some commands were placed in more than one command class. A full list of the old command classes is given in Figure 9.3. At many sites the command classes that are assigned are still largely based on this old system.

Class	**User group**
A	System operator
B	System resource operator
C	System programmer
D	Spooling operator
E	System analyst
F	Service representative
G	General user
H	Reserved by IBM
any	Any user

Figure 9.3 Command Classes

Starting CMS

Because the majority of users want to work with CMS, most users' directory entries contain the command IPL CMS. This will automatically start the CMS environment for them. An alternative to this is for the line to be omitted from the directory and the users to enter the command themselves once their virtual machines have been established. This is possible because CMS is a saved system. Another alternative is to specify a virtual address from which CMS is to be loaded. At IPL time the operator will enter

I 190

This command will load the CMS code. This method can be used for any operating system (eg MVS).

Console

The console for the system will usually be 3270-type device, ie screen and keyboard. The virtual console will usually have a virtual address of 009. Because the device that is being used is a real device it will also have an address. The address of the terminal is very unlikely to be 009 and for all communication to and from the virtual console software will have to translate the virtual address to the real address so that messages are sent to the right screen.

Unit Record Devices

The unit record devices specified are a printer, a card reader and a card punch. In the course of a working day the real unit record devices are seldom required, but the virtual devices are used frequently. The VM control program intercepts any I/O requests that use the unit record devices and carries them out by either reading or writing data to disk. This process is called spooling and the files that are involved are called spool files. If jobs are to be submitted from CMS to a guest-operating system they will be submitted by routeing the output from the virtual punch of the CMS machine to the virtual reader of the guest system. Spool files are allocated in the TEMP area of CP-owned DASD.

Disks

Each virtual machine has a number of disks associated with it. In most cases (the usual exception is a guest-operating system) although the disks will appear to be whole disks and also be given a virtual address, they will typically be only part of a disk and are referred to as mini-disks.

The entry for each MDISK in the directory specifies the virtual address to be used for the mini-disk, the device type that is being used (ie 3380) and the volume serial number of the disk being used, eg VMS001. The values 010 and 005 specify the starting cylinder on the real disk for the mini-disk (ie 10) and the size of the mini-disk (ie 5 cylinders). The last entry specifies the access type. Figure 9.4 gives a full list of access types.

The mini-disks referenced in the LINK statement belong to another user and their contents can be read by the user. Typically, every CMS user will have a read only link to MAINT's 190 and 19E disks. MAINT's 190 contains all the files that are needed for running CMS in a virtual machine. Sharing the files avoids duplication and saves on disk space required and ultimately saves on cost. 19E usually contains the other files that are required by most of the users of CMS but these files are not an integral part of CMS.

Associated with each mini-disk at a particular virtual address is a filemode. The filemode is usually written as a single letter. A user's A disk has a virtual address of 191 and contains data files, EXECs or programs for that user. Frequently a user will have a D disk which may also contain data, EXECs or programs. This usually has the address 192. The other two disks that all CMS users have are the S disk and the Y disk. These disks are owned by user-id MAINT, but all other CMS users are linked to them. The S disk has a virtual address of 190 and contains the CMS programs. CMS is stored on reserved disk space at the end of the CMS S disk. When the S disk is formatted the RECOMP option of format is used to reserve space at the end of the mini-disk. Usually multiple nuclei are kept for live and test versions etc. The Y disk has a virtual address of 19E and contains extensions to the operating system.

CMS MEMORY ALLOCATION

Figure 9.5 illustrates a map of the memory layout for a CMS release 5.5 virtual machine. The nucleus constant area (NUCON) is a control block that resides between address zero and X'A000' within the CMS address space. It is used by CMS and contains data about the current CMS session. The transient area is 8K in size and is located at address X'E000'. It is used to load and run commands and applications in support of commands and applications in the user area. A program loaded in the transient area will stay there until another program is loaded. This is useful for frequently used commands. The user area in a CMS

Code	**Access**
R	Read only access provided no other user has access
W	Read/write access provided no other user has access
M	Read/write access provided no other user has read/write access
RR	Read only access no matter how many other users have access
WR	Read/write access if sole user; read only if other users have access
MR	Read/write access if no other user has read/write access, otherwise read only access
MW	Read/write access if sole user and if other users have access

Figure 9.4 Access Types

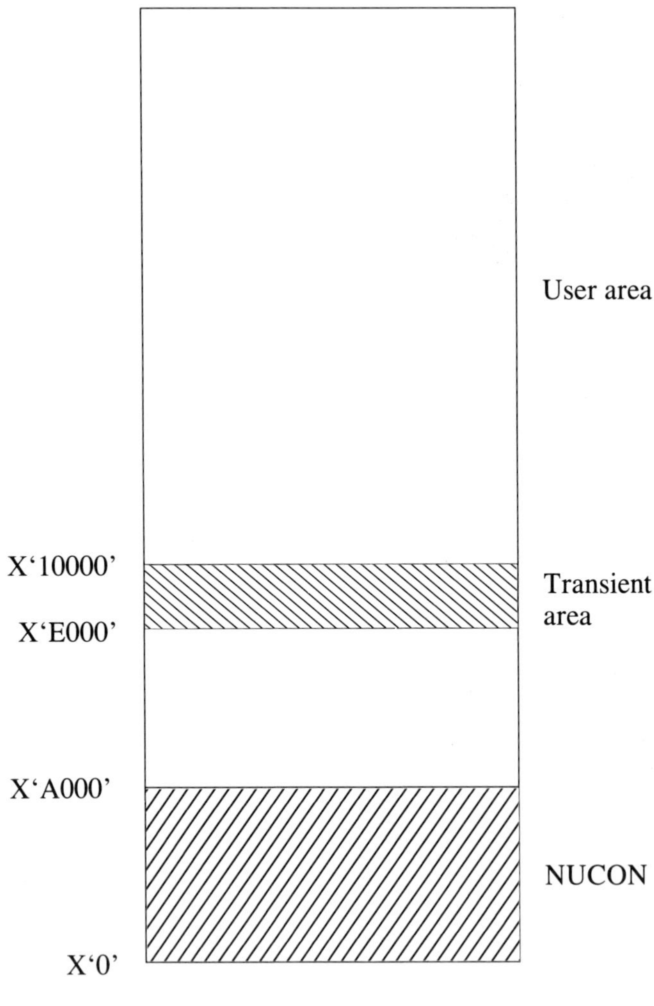

Figure 9.5 CMS 5.5 Memory Map

virtual machine is divided into two parts which are separated by the transient area. It is the area used by most applications to load and run from.

Applications generated with the CMS GENMOD command have fixed execution addresses. These, typically, run in either the transient area or the user area. Subpools are areas of memory that can be treated as a single unit and have names that are up to eight bytes in length. Subpools can be shared, private or global. In environments where application programs call application programs, subpools can be used to determine which application program is to use storage. Private subpools have the memory allocated to them and deallocated when the application or function terminates. Shared subpools allow called routines to allocate storage from the same subpool as the caller in order that data can be passed back to the calling program. Global subpools allow applications (nucleus extensions) to allocate memory that remains allocated after the application terminates.

CMS releases 5.5 and above make use of the new CMSSTOR and SUBPOOL macros in order to manage the allocation and deallocation of storage.

CMS commands can be enhanced or modified using nucleus extensions or NUCEXTs. A nucleus extension is a program that is added to the CMS nucleus for a specific user rather than for all users. New commands or applications can be stored in a user's address space for improved performance.

Some programs running under CMS contain ACONS. ACONS stands for address constant. This is a specific memory reference in a program that does not change when the program is loaded into various memory addresses.

ACCESSING CMS

The way that most people gain access to CMS is by logging on. This is done by finding a terminal that is displaying the VM logo. With non-XA systems, the actual design may change from site to site because it can be specified by using the DMKBOX module. The next step is to press the enter key, which will clear the logo from the screen.

It may at this stage be necessary to use the DIAL command (see Chapter 12) or to just enter:

LOGON TREVOR

where TREVOR is the user-id. The system responds by:

ENTER PASSWORD

The password must then be keyed in, but it will not be displayed on the screen. This is a security measure to prevent unauthorised people from obtaining passwords. If the password is incorrect the system will respond with a message to that effect. Depending on the security package installed, if any, it may be possible to re-key the password correctly and continue, or it may be necessary to start again, or it may be necessary to contact the on-site security administrator to have the log-on-id and password reinstated. It is possible to enter the log-on command, the user-id and password all on one line. However, this will be visible on screen and is a security risk.

Assuming that the log-on-id and password match those in the directory, the user will be connected to a virtual machine. If the command IPL CMS was part of the directory entry for that user then CMS will have been invoked automatically. If for any reason a user did not want CMS to start automatically the command NOIPL should be put at the end of the log-on command.

Terminal Status

A terminal status message is always displayed at the bottom right-hand corner of the screen. The messages either refer to terminal input or terminal output. The six messages are:

- CP READ;
- VM READ;
- RUNNING;
- NOT ACCEPTED;
- MORE...;
- HOLDING.

CP READ

The CP READ message indicates that the control program is expecting some data to be input at the terminal. It is present on the screen after the logo is cleared during the log-on procedure.

VM READ

The VM READ message indicates that a program running from the terminal expects some data to be input. The program could be CMS (it usually is) or an application program.

RUNNING

The RUNNING message indicates either that CMS is carrying out the last command that was entered, or it is waiting for the next command to be entered. If a new command is entered and the previous command has not been completed, the new command will not be carried out immediately.

NOT ACCEPTED

In the event that VM is unable to handle a command or data that has been entered at a terminal it will display the message NOT ACCEPTED. If this happens the best plan is to wait until it completes its current operation and then to try again.

MORE...

Sometimes the response to a command contains more bytes of data than can be displayed on a single page on the screen of the terminal. To indicate that there is more than this single page of data the message MORE... is displayed. If no action is taken the next page will be displayed after 60 seconds. Pressing the clear key or the PA2 key will display the second page immediately. Pressing the enter key will hold the first page on screen indefinitely.

HOLDING

The message HOLDING indicates that the current page of output will be held on screen indefinitely as a result of the enter key having been pressed. When the user no longer requires the page to be held, pressing clear or PA2 returns to the previous status (MORE...).

FILES

Under CMS all files follow a particular naming convention. That is, each file has a three-part identifier made up of a filename (fn), a filetype (ft) and a filemode (fm). The filename cannot be more than eight characters long and can be made up of letters, digits and special characters. The special characters used are @, # , $, +, :, -, _. The filetype is also restricted to a maximum of eight characters and can be made up of letters, digits and special characters (as for filename). There are a number of reserved filetypes that can be used. These not only give a better indication of the type of file, but also have the added advantage of creating the file with the appropriate size records. The reserved filetypes in common use are given in Figure 9.6. The filemode used is either a single letter or a letter and a number. The letter indicates on which mini-disk the file is stored. The majority of a user's files will be on their A disk (191) and will have a filemode of A. The filemode number indicates the kind of processing that can be performed on that file. The filemode numbers that can be used are in the range 0 to 6 inclusive. A full list of the filemode numbers and their meaning is given in Figure 9.7. Typically, for most files, users do not code a filemode number, but let the system default to 1, which allows read/write access.

VSAM FILES

CMS users can access VSAM (Virtual Storage Access Method) files. In fact CMS users make use of VSE VSAM. VSAM has three file organisations — key sequenced (KSDS), relative record (RRDS) and entry sequenced (ESDS).

The AMS program commands are executed using the CMS AMSERV command. The command format is:

AMSERV filename

where filename is the name of the file containing the AMS commands. This file must be created first and must have a filetype of AMSERV.

Before CMS users can access VSAM files in the catalog they must key in:

SET DOS ON (VSAM

They also need to code DLBLs (Disk LaBeLs).

Filetype	Usual contents
AMSERV	VSAM AMS control statements
ASSEMBLE	Assembler source code
BASIC	BASIC source code
COBOL	COBOL source code
EXEC	Command procedure language statements
FORTRAN	FORTRAN source code
HELP..	Part of CMS HELP facility
LISTING	Output from a language processor
LOADLIB	A number of executable modules created by the link editor
MACLIB	A library of macro definitions or copy files
MACRO	A macro definition
MEMO	Text — memo
MODULE	An executable program
NAMES	A list of the names of other users used for communication
NOTE	Text sent between terminal users
NOTEBOOK	A collection of notes sent between terminal users
PASCAL	Pascal source code
PLI	PL/I source code
PLIOPT	PL/I source code
SCRIPT	Text to be processed by SCRIPT
SYNONYM	A table of synonyms for CMS commands and EXEC and MODULE files
TEXT	Object code
TXTLIB	A library of object code programs
VSBASIC	VS BASIC source code
XEDIT	XEDIT macro definitions

Figure 9.6 Reserved filetypes

Filemode number	Meaning
0	This indicates that the file is private. Only users with read/write access to the mini-disk can access the file
1	This is the default value. It indicates that the file can be read and written to
2	Has the same effect as 1. It is often used for files that are shared by users who link to a common mini-disk
3	This indicates a temporary file, ie deleted after it has been read
4	This indicates that the file is in simulated OS format
5	Has the same effect as 1. It is often used to group a number of logically related files
6	This indicates that the file can be updated in place

Figure 9.7 Filemode Numbers

All VSAM entities, which include datasets (or clusters), dataspaces and catalogs, must have an entry in a VSAM catalog. Each VSAM file or cluster is stored in logical units called Control Intervals. These in turn are grouped together to form a logical entity called a Control Area. A Control Interval is the smallest unit of data that may be physically transferred between disk and core storage. For a given file all data Control Intervals are the same unchangeable size.

VSAM files may be defined as:

- unique — one cluster per dataspace, both allocated at the same time.
- suballocated — more than one cluster in the dataspace. The dataspace is defined first, and clusters are added later.
- dynamic — the cluster is defined first, space is allocated by the system when the file is opened and used. The parameters NOALLOCATION and REUSE arc coded.

Entry Sequenced Datasets

Data records may be fixed or variable in length and are stored in the dataset one after the other in order of arrival.

Relative Record Datasets

Fixed-length records can be entered into a file in assigned slots. The slot position is determined by the relative record number supplied by the application program, typically from unique data within the record itself, eg part numbers or customer numbers. Records are written to each Control Interval as appropriate during the creation and update process in such a way that I/O operation will take place only as necessary. This is achieved by the VSAM buffering routines.

Key Sequenced Datasets

Either fixed- or variable-length records may be stored in a KSDS. Records are stored on ascending key, which means that any record will have a key value higher than the record preceding it and a key value lower than any record following it within the Control Interval. KSDSs are divided into two parts, a data and an index part.

USING THE SPOOL

Each CMS virtual machine has a virtual printer, a virtual punch and a virtual card reader associated with it. These virtual devices allow users to make use of the spool.

Spool

When the VM system is set up, space is allocated on CP-owned DASD for the spool area. This spool area is used to contain print and punch files. Print files that users want to have a hard copy of can be printed on the real printer. The reason that the files are stored in the spool area on DASD is so that the real printer(s) can be controlled by CP and shared between the many users who want to utilise it.

Each spool file that is created is given a unique four-digit spool-id (in the range 0001 to 9900). An example of the output that is produced when a list of the files queued to the printer is requested is given in Figure 9.8. Many users treat the spool as a mini-disk overflow area. This should not be encouraged. In Figure 9.8, ORIGINID is the user-id of the user who placed the file in the queue; FILE refers to the unique spool-id; CLAS gives the printer class; RECRDS specifies how large the file is; CO indicates how many copies will be printed; HLD indicates whether the file is to be held on the spool or printed on the real printer; ROUTE identifies a printer; DATA and TIME specify when the file was placed on the queue; NAME gives the filename; TYPE gives the filetype; and DIST is the distribution code.

ORIGINID	FILE	CLAS	RECRDS	CO	HLD	ROUTE	DATE	TIME	NAME	TYPE	DIST
TUSER	0379	A PR	000007	01	USR	PRT02	09/12	10:35	TESTA	DATA	ABCD
TUSER	0452	A PR	000013	01	USR	PRT02	09/12	10:48	TESTB	DATA	ABCD

Figure 9.8 Example Output from Query PRinTer Command

Printing

Movement of a file from a virtual machine to a real printer is illustrated in Figure 9.9. The file is printed using the virtual printer as a mechanism to move it from the virtual machine to the spool. Once on the spool the file will be printed by the real printer subject to the usual criteria of class, number of other print files waiting, size of other print files, etc.

The default class of the print files produced by a virtual machine depends on the value specified in the directory entry for that user. For example if the entry reads:

SPOOL 00E 1403 A

this means that the default print class is A. Print classes are used as a way of grouping output that is to be routed to a particular printer, eg a remote printer or one loaded with special stationery (eg 4-inch invoices).

To create a print file a user would enter:

PRINT filename filetype filemode

This would send a spool file to spool to await printing.

To find out what files are waiting to be printed the user can enter:

Q V UR

which will give information for all the virtual unit record devices. Alternatively, if the user wanted to know how many files were queued the following command could be entered:

Q F

which queries how many files are on the spool. The third alternative is to type:

CP Q PRT ALL

which will list all files queued to the printer.

Using the CP SPOOL command it is possible to alter the class of the output, the number of copies of the print file to be produced, the form type to be used (it defaults to STANDARD) and whether it is to be held or not. The characteristics of print files can also be modified using the CHANGE command. The format of the command to change the class of a print file from A to T is:

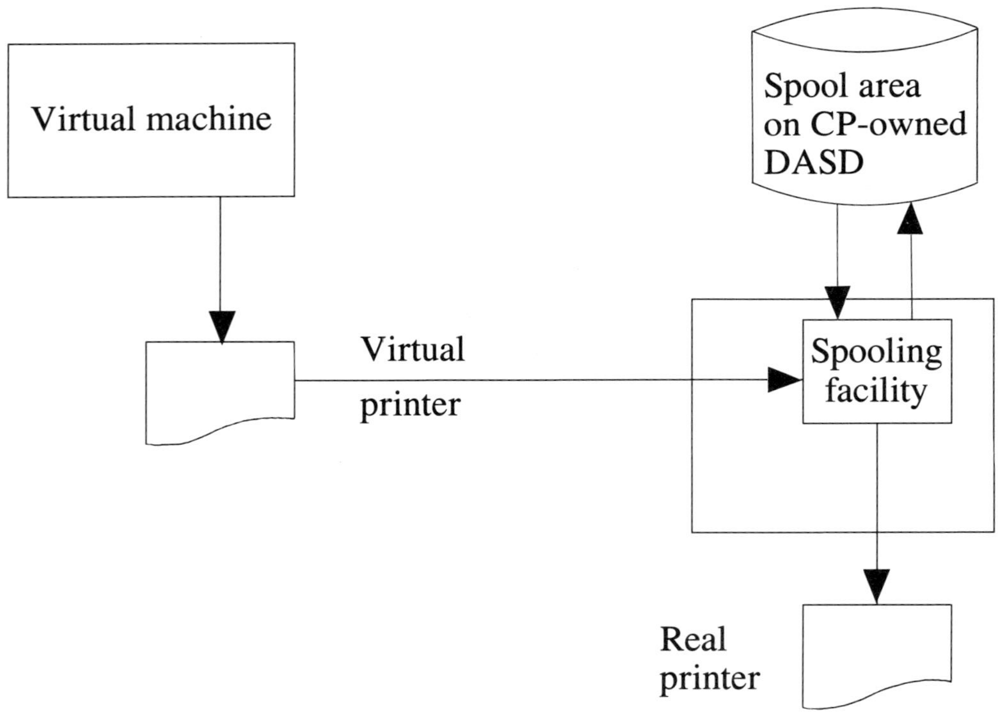

Figurer 9.9 Spooling from a Virtual Machine to a Real Printer

CP CHANGE PRINTER A T

Other characteristics that can be changed are the number of copies (up to a maximum of 255) and the hold status.

To remove an unwanted print file from the queue the PURGE command is used. Its usual format is:

PURGE PRINTER spool-id

Punching

The punch commands are very similar to the print commands. The command to create a punch file is:

PUNCH filename filetype filemode

This generates a header card at the front of the virtual card deck which has the format:

:READ filename filetype filemode origin date-created time-created

If a header card is not required (NOH can be put at the end of the punch command. The file to be punched must fit on a card. This means that it cannot contain records that are longer than 80 characters.

The command CP QUERY PUNCH ALL will display information about all the punch files for that user in the spool.

Sometimes it is useful to move spool files from one user or queue to another. The format of the command to move punch files from one user to the reader queue of another user is:

CP TRANSFER PUNCH ALL TO newuser READER

If only one file is to be transferred the spool-id can be used instead of ALL.

Reading

The commands to use the reader are similar to those for printing and punching. The usual entry in the directory for a reader is

SPOOL 00C 2540 READER *

The asterisk (*) indicates that any class file can be read.

The reader is frequently used as a method of loading a new CMS file. This is achieved by using the RECEIVE command. The command format is:

RECEIVE spool-id filename filetype filemode

The filename filetype filemode are the file identifiers for the new file. If a file with that name exists already, there is a (REPLACE option that can be put at the end of the RECEIVE command. If the file that is being received has a punch header card on it, the file identifier can be omitted and it will use information from that card. If there is no header card the file will take the default name of READCARD CMSUT1. If the file identifier and spool-id are omitted the next spool file on the virtual reader will be read in.

CMS COMMANDS

A CMS user can issue both CP and CMS commands. The commands that can be carried out depend on the command classes that are assigned to that user. Most CMS users can use the commands in command class G.

CP commands can be entered by three different methods. The first method is to prefix the command by CP. The command would look like:

#CP QUERY FILES

This puts the user in direct communication with the control program.

The second method is to prefix the command with CP. The command would look like:

CP QUERY PRINTER

This instructs CMS to pass the command to the control program to be executed. Once the command has been executed the CMS READY (R;) message appears on the screen. If only CP is entered the CP READ message will appear in the bottom right-hand corner of the screen. CP commands can be entered. To terminate CP READ mode the user must enter the command:

BEGIN

The third method of entering CP commands is simply to enter the command. This is grossly inefficient and should be discouraged, but does work. The implied CP function (IMPCP) must be turned on for it to work. CMS sees whether the command is a CMS command; if not, it sees whether it is a CP command. If it is, it will be executed.

When a command is entered, the search sequence illustrated in Figure 9.10 may be carried out.

In no way is the following section meant as a replacement for the IBM manuals that list and explain all the CMS commands that are available. However, it is the intention to include some of the more frequently used commands with an explanation of their use.

New files can be created using the XEDIT command:

XEDIT fn ft fm

The same command can be used to edit existing files.

To access a file on another user's mini-disk and copy it the following steps need to be taken. First the second user must be linked to:

CP LINK nuser 191 199 R

This will link to the 191 disk of a user called nuser. The disk will become the 199 disk of the linking user. The R indicates that the link is to be read only.

ACCESS 199 T

The above command will access the mini-disk at virtual address 199 with a filemode of T.

To copy a file from the mini-disk, the COPY command is used, eg

COPY fn ft T = = A

This will copy a file called fn ft on T and put the copy with the same name on the A disk. After the copy is complete the disk must be released by:

RELEASE T

This should be done straight away because it reduces the number of disks to be searched and will therefore improve performance.

To disconnect the user from the mini-disk:

CP DETACH 199

To change the file identifier from ofn oft ofm to nfm nft nfm:

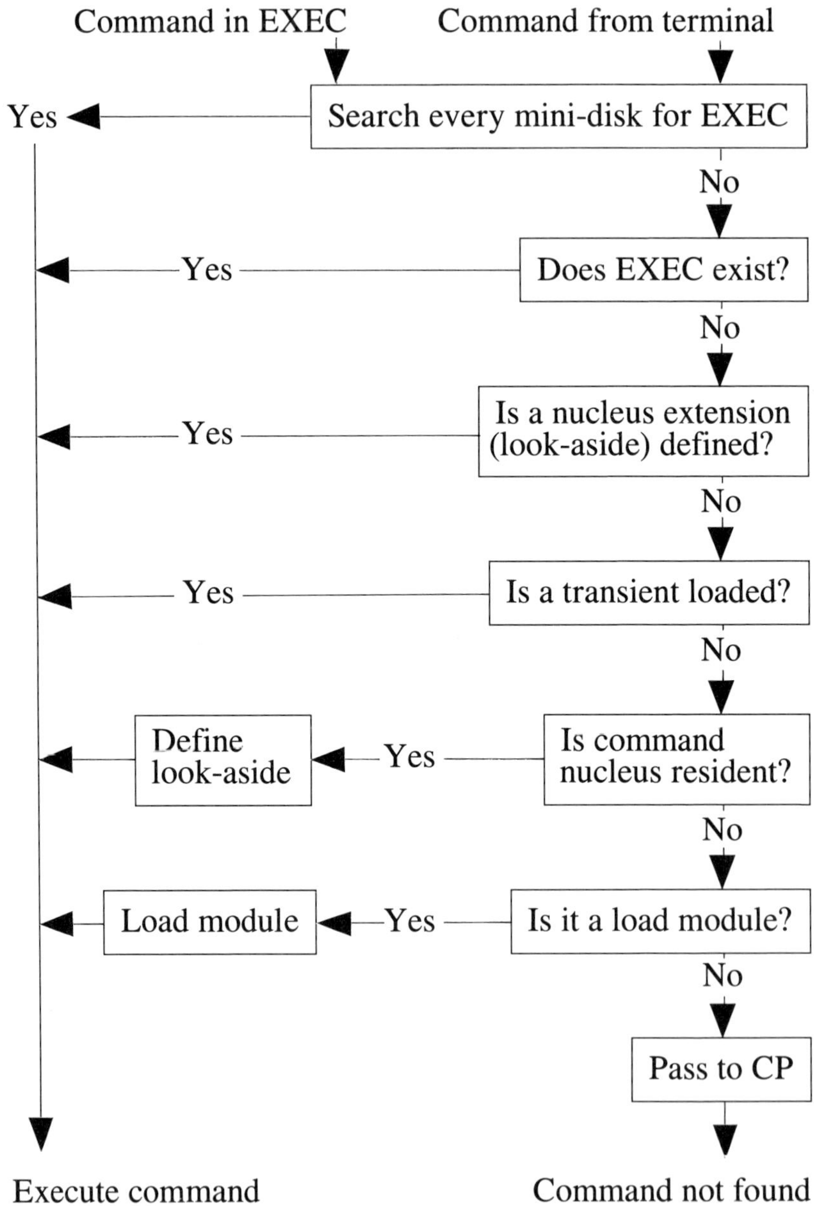

Figure 9.10 CMS Command Resolution

RENAME ofn oft ofm nfn nft nfm

To display the contents of a file on screen:

TYPE fn ft fm

If the display needs to be terminated this can be done using the HT (Hold Typing) command.

To allocate a command to a specified PF key:

CP SET PF1 IMMED command

When the PF key is pressed the command will be entered. If the command is not to be entered immediately so that additions may be made (eg a filename put at the end) the IMMED part of the command must be omitted.

The following commands can be used to query what real or virtual disks are associated with the user:

CP Q DASD

Q DISK

If more disk space is required temporarily by a user, TDSK space can be allocated using the DEFine command.

CP DEF T3380 199 2

This says that a temporary disk is to be put on a 3380 disk pack, it is to have a 3-digit virtual address specified as 199 in the example and it is to be 2 cylinders in size.

The disk must be formatted by:

FORMAT 199 T

This allocates the filemode of T to the disk at virtual address 199. The system also asks if all files on the disk are to be initialised. The correct response is:

YES

A six-character disk label is also required.

When the disk is no longer required it can be released using the REL command, ie:

REL 199

The other way to release it is to log off.

One way to improve performance is to have the EXEC that is to be used already loaded into storage, eg:

EXECLOAD fn ft

To remove a loaded EXEC the EXECDROP command is used, ie:

EXECDROP fn ft

To display or stack information from a user's NAMES file the NAMEFind command can be used.

To display or stack information about user-id, node-id, RSCS-id, etc the IDentify command is used.

When writing EXECs people often make use of the FILEDEF and GLOBALV commands. FILEDEF simulates the MVS DD statement when specifying files to be used. GLOBALV can be used to set, maintain and retrieve named variables.

From time to time a user will need to send a message to the operator. This can be done by entering:

CP MSG OP message text

If the message is to be sent to another user the user-id must be keyed in in place of OP. Electronic mail can be sent using the NOTE command, eg

NOTE fred

This would put the user in XEDIT mode so that the text of the note could be written. When complete it would be sent to Fred. User Fred can read mail from the NOTE command or SENDFile command (used to send existing files) by using the PEEK command, eg:

PEEK spool-id

The spool-id is the notes spool number. To move a note from a reader and put it on a mini-disk the RECEIVE command is used, eg:

RECEIVE spool-id

To start an EXEC file the following command is entered:

EXEC fn ft fm

EXEC files usually contain EXEC or REXX instructions.

To see if a file exists the LISTfile command can be used, eg:

L fn ft fm

It is possible to use the wildcard character, eg:

L * ft

This will display all the files with a particular filetype on the default A disk.

If a file is to be deleted this can be performed using the ERASE command, eg:

ERASE fn ft fm

If a user does not require any of the files queued to the reader they can all be erased using the PURge command, ie:

PUR RDR

Rather than using commands when manipulating files most people find it easier to use the FILEList command and modify the display on screen using the command (CMD) column. FILEL will list all the files associated with a user. An example is given in Figure 9.11. The following commands are typically entered in the command column:

DISCARD

ERASE

PRINT

TYPE

XEDIT

RENAME

CMS COMMAND USAGE

By monitoring the frequency of CMS commands entered by the user population at a site, performance improvements can be obtained. Usually found amongst the ten most frequently used IBM distributed CMS commands are:

```
                TREVOR  FILELIST  AO  V  108     TRUNC=108     SIZE=4  LINE=-1     COL=1     ALT=0
CMD  FILENAME   FILETYPE   FM   FORMAT  LRECL  RECORDS  BLOCKS  DATE       TIME

     + TEST     AMSERV     A1   F       80     7        1       09/29/89   01:28:44
       PRINT    EXEC       A1   F       80     33       5       09/14/89   10:15:09
       INFO     SCRIPT     A1   F       80     196      12      10/08/89   09:58:31
       LIST     LISTING    A1   F       133    297      27      08/06/89   16:37:21



1 = HELP  2 = REFRESH  3 = QUIT  4 = SORT (TYPE)  5 = SORT (DATE)  6 = SORT (SIZE)
7 = BACKWARD  8 = FORWARD  9 = FL /N  10 = #  11 = XEDIT  12 = CURSOR
```

Figure 9.11 FILEL Output

- ACCESS;
- EXECDROP;
- EXECLOAD;
- FILEDEF;
- GLOBALV;
- IDENTIFY;
- LISTFILE;
- NAMEFIND;
- SET;
- XEDIT.

MAXIMISING CMS PERFORMANCE

Some suggestions are given below for improving the performance experienced by CMS users:

- Frequently used EXECs could be recoded as command MODULEs.
- Frequently used groups of commands could be combined into an EXEC as a way of improving the performance of an individual user.
- Frequently used EXECs could be EXECLOADed.
- With SP release 5 and above frequently used EXECs can be placed in the installation DCSS (CMSINST). The segment is rebuilt using DCSSGEN. EXECs can be shared in read-only mode by all users. This saves both time and storage.
- The use of NUCXLOAD command will also save program loads.
- Judicious placement of files is a technique that can be used to minimise I/O waits for disk resident commands.
- Because disks without any .MODULE, .EXEC or .XEDIT macros on them are omitted from the CMS file search, the CMS file search can be speeded up by keeping data files separate from MODULE, EXEC and XEDIT files.
- Files on the A disk should be stored contiguously and in the order of frequency of use, with the most frequently used ones first to reduce access times.

- The SAVEFD (save file directory) command available with SP release 5 and above can be used to place file directories of commonly used CMS mini-disks in a DCSS. Users who require read-only access save I/O and storage. If the disks are updated the SAVEFD SAVE command must be reissued.
- With XA SP release 2 CMS mini-disks and the user directory can be cached in expanded storage, again reducing access times.
- Mini-disks that are not currently in use should be RELeased and DETached to reduce the number of disks searched during command resolution.
- COMMAND or MACRO should be used as the filetype for XEDIT macros.
- 'Address COMMAND' should be used to speed up CMS command processing.
- GLOBALV should be used rather than utility files to remember things across EXECs.
- Faster alternatives to SORT and COPYFILE should be used wherever possible.
- Time can be saved by using the short ready message (R;) instead of READY. This can be achieved by using the SET READYMSG SMSG command.
- To make CMS more flexible the CMS saved system should be defined without the VSYSRES= and SYSCYL= parameters. The S disks can then be swapped by simply swapping directory entries, one for CMS test and one the production CMS system.

10 CMS Facilities

Apart from the basic CMS environment which was described in the previous chapter, users will come into contact with the large number of facilities that are available for running under it including XEDIT, REXX, ISPF, CICS, SQL/DS, PROFS and SFS. This chapter starts by examining how the user's CMS environment is defined using the PROFILE EXEC facility.

PROFILE EXEC

Whenever CMS is IPLed, either automatically from the directory entry or explicitly by the user, it executes a file called PROFILE EXEC as part of its initialisation process. The PROFILE EXEC can be used to tailor the user's environment to suit the particular requirements of that user. Entries might include:

- setting PF key definitions;
- specifying SET commands;
- accessing any libraries that will be needed for programming;
- accessing any other disks, not specified in the directory;
- establishing distribution and routeing information for a virtual printer.

An example of a PROFILE EXEC is given in Figure 10.1. Similar to a PROFILE EXEC is a PROFILE XEDIT file (see below).

USING XEDIT

XEDIT is the name given to the latest editor for VM. The first was

```
'CP SPOOL CONSOLE DIST ABC100'
'CP SPOOL PRINTER ROUTE ABC123 DIST ABC100'
'CP SPOOL PUNCH DIST ABC123'
GLOBAL MACLIB CMSLIB
GLOBAL TXTLIB PLILIB
```

Figure 10.1 Example PROFILE EXEC

called EDIT and the second was called EDGAR. XEDIT can be used to create and modify files. A file may be created or modified by entering:

X fn ft fm

Alternatively the edit environment may be entered by putting XEDIT in the command column next to a file identifier displayed by the FILEL command.

XEDIT Profile

The XEDIT environment can be tailored to suit a user's particular requirements. This is achieved by using a file called PROFILE XEDIT that is automatically executed when the XEDIT environment is entered. An example PROFILE XEDIT file is given in Figure 10.2. It illustrates how the environment can be tailored to suit the user's wishes.

XEDIT Commands

An example of the sort of display produced by the use of XEDIT is given in Figure 10.3. Commands may be entered on the command line, which is at the bottom left-hand corner. If a new file has been created the first command to be entered there is:

INPUT

This puts the editor in input mode and allows lines of data, code or text to be keyed in. When no more lines are to be entered input mode is terminated by pressing the enter key twice. This changes the mode to edit mode.

```
/* my XEDIT profile */
set autosave 10
set cmdline top
set nulls on
set msgmode on
set scale off
set trunc 73
set case mixed
set tofeof off
set curline on 4
set pf3 FILE
```

Figure 10.2 Example PROFILE XEDIT

To change small amounts of the file the simplest method is to move the cursor to where the change is to be made and overtype the wrong data with the correct data. If data is to be deleted there is a delete key on the keyboard. If more data is to be added there is an insert key placed next to the delete key to allow this. It may first be necessary to place the cursor at the end of the line and press PA2. This removes trailing characters. After an insert it is necessary to press the RESET key.

Files may be edited using the '= = = = =' area on the left of the text. What are called prefix commands can be placed here. The general rules are that a single letter will perform a command once. A letter followed by a digit will perform the command the number of times indicated by the value of the digit. Double letters indicate that a block of text is being edited. For example D would delete a line; A3 would add three blank lines immediately after the indicated line; and DD would indicate the start or end of a block of text to be deleted. A summary of the more regularly used commands is given in Figure 10.4.

```
TREVOR              AO  F  80  TRUNC=72   SIZE=46   LINE=2   COL=1   ALT=4

=====     * * * TOP OF FILE * * *
=====     NEW LINE
=====     EXTRA LINE
          |...+....1....+....2....+....3....+....4....+....5....+....6....+....7...
=====     MORE TEXT
=====     ANOTHER LINE
=====     * * * END OF FILE * * *



====>  -                                                          XEDIT 1 FILE
```

Figure 10.3 Example XEDIT Display

Command	Meaning
A	Add one blank line after indicated line
D	Delete indicated line
' '	Duplicate indicated line
C	Copy indicated line
M	Move indicated line
F	Place selected text on line following indicated line
P	Place selected text on line immediately previous to the indicated line
/	Inserted data to be placed after indicated line

Figure 10.4 Summary of Prefix Commands

New data may be entered after the line indicated by a / in the prefix area provided that the INPUT subcommand is used.

To save a copy of the edited file including the updates that have been made the SAVE command can be used. The user types SAVE on the command line.

To finish the XEDIT session the commands FILE, QUIT and QQUIT can be used. FILE will take a copy of the changes made to a file and save them to disk. If QUIT is entered the system will ask for confirmation. At this stage FILE can be entered. If no changes are to be saved QQUIT can be entered at this time.

To scroll up and down the commands UP *x* or DOWN *x* can be used, where *x* is a number of lines. Alternatively PF7 and PF8 can be used with the same result. Getting to the beginning or end of a file can be achieved using the commands TOP and Bottom.

To change a character string the Change command can be used.

C /me/you/ **

This will change every occurrence of *me* to *you*. If the ** is omitted only the first occurrence will be changed.

To avoid updates to a file being lost the AUTOSAVE command can be used. The format for this handy little command is:

SET AUTOSAVE 10

This says that after every ten changes have been made to the file the changes will be automatically saved to a new file with a numeric filename and AUTOSAVE as its filetype.

To copy an existing file into one that is being edited the GET command is used:

GET fn ft fm

This will put a copy of the specified file as part of the current file. If only 25 lines are required starting with line 100 the command would look like:

GET fn ft fm 100 25

To carry out split-screen editing the command format is:

SET SCR 2

REXX

The REstructured eXtended eXecutor (REXX) is an interpreted language which means that no compilation is necessary. It is a free format language, which makes writing it very easy, but can lead to slow, badly written programs being produced. It has very little by way of punctuation requirements (; as an optional line delimiter). REXX programs are processed by the System Product Interpreter.

The future of REXX is assured as IBM now include it as part of SAA (Systems Application Architecture) which means that the VM REXX, or a subset of it, will be available for MVS users. This also means that REXX EXECs written under CMS should run when executed under MVS.

Before REXX became available there were two other similar, but less powerful interpreted languages available for CMS. They were called EXEC and EXEC 2. EXEC, EXEC 2 and REXX files are all created with a filetype of EXEC. So that the correct interpreter is used when the file is executed, all REXX files must begin with a comment, ie:

```
/*          */
```

EXEC 2 files usually begin with &TRACE, and EXEC files can begin with anything, usually &CONTROL. EXEC and EXEC 2 will not be covered because they are largely superseded by REXX. However, there are many existing EXEC files that have been written using these older languages.

REXX makes use of variables, ie symbols or names whose values may be altered during the execution of the program. The variable names used must not start with a digit or contain a full stop. With REXX, as with BASIC, the variables are not declared before use, and until a value is assigned to them have the value of their own name (not zero).

REXX uses a number of arithmetic operators. These are summarised in Figure 10.5.

Operator	Action
+	Add
−	Subtract
*	Multiply
/	Divided by
%	Divide by and return integer portion only
//	Divide by and return remainder
**	Exponentiation

Figure 10.5 REXX Arithmetic Operators

To write from an EXEC to the terminal the SAY command is used, eg:

SAY 'message to user'

To read any response from the terminal user and include it in the program the ARG or PULL commands can be used. An example would be:

ARG v1 v2 v3

This would read three values keyed in from the terminal and assign them in order to the variables v1, v2 and v3 respectively.

It is possible to concatenate two values using the concatenate symbol ||. An example of this is given below:

SAY 'Dr Livingstone' || 'I presume'

This would print on the screen as

Dr LivingstoneI presume

REXX is quite sophisticated in that it allows the use of Boolean operators (and, or, etc). These are illustrated in Figure 10.6.

Symbol	Logical operation	Effect
&	AND	Returns 1 if both terms are true
|	OR	Returns 1 if either term is true
&&	EXCLUSIVE	Returns 1 if either (but not both) terms are true
¬	NOT	Returns 1 for 0 and 0 for 1

Figure 10.6 Boolean Operators

REXX is similar to BASIC in that it allows IF . . . THEN . . . ELSE statements. It also uses DO statements which can be used to set up repetitive loops. DO is followed by one of the following words: BY, FOR, FOREVER, TO, UNTIL, WHILE and END. An example would be:

```
DO FOREVER
  SAY 'type your name'
  PULL input
  IF input ¬=' ' THEN LEAVE
  SAY 'come on'
END
```

The SELECT statement allows an expression to be evaluated and the first true (ie with a value of 1) expression encountered will be evaluated. An example is given below:

```
SAY 'are you Trevor?'
PULL input .

SELECT
  WHEN input ='YES' THEN SAY 'Please proceed'
  WHEN input ='NO' THEN SAY 'go away'
  OTHERWISE
              DO SAY 'answer the question'
              END
```

The CALL statement can be used to pass control to a named instruction, eg

```
CALL end_para
........
end_para:
    ......
    ......
```

Other ways in which the flow within an EXEC can be changed are by using EXIT, ITERATE, LEAVE, RETURN or SIGNAL. The effects of these commands are given in Figure 10.7.

REXX is capable of string handling (ie text) and as a general rule all statements that are not REXX or are not to be interpreted should be put in quotation marks.

REXX also has the capability to handle arrays. This it does by

Command	Meaning
EXIT	Leaves procedure and optionally returns a return code
ITERATE	Control passes from the current statement in a DO loop to the bottom of the loop
LEAVE	Control passes from the current statement in a DO loop to the statement following the loop
RETURN	Control passes from a program or subroutine back to its calling point
SIGNAL	Used as a GOTO instruction

Figure 10.7 Flow Control Instructions

using compound symbols. A compound symbol has characters on either side of a full stop. Characters in front of the full stop are called the stem.

VM and CMS commands can be included in REXX EXECs as a way of tailoring or extending the command. When CMS receives a command from an EXEC or from a terminal, it goes through a process to determine the nature of the command (see Figure 9.10). The first step is to search (potentially) the directories of all ACCESSed disks to see whether any one of them contains an EXEC whose name matches the name of the command to be executed. If many disks are ACCESSed, this can be somewhat time consuming. Since most commands executed by EXECs are CMS commands (not other EXECs), this is generally a needless overhead, and it is repeated each time the EXEC issues a command.

CMS provides a simpler inteface (using SVC 202), which does not go through the complicated search process. This interface may be invoked by using the REXX statement 'address COMMAND'. If placed at the front of the EXEC, this one statement will cause the default environment for all commands to be changed from CMS to COMMAND. As a result of this all commands passed to CMS must be true CMS commands. CP commands and EXECs are not considered to be true CMS commands according to this definition, so EXEC names must be preceded by the word 'EXEC', and CP commands must be preceded by the word 'CP'. The 'CP' command itself is documented in the *CMS Command Reference* manual, not in the *CP Command Reference* manual, because it is a CMS command. This is true even if the EXEC is written by IBM; some examples are FILELIST, PEEK, RECEIVE and SENDFILE.

REXX EXECs are executed by entering the filename. The filetype default is EXEC and the default filemode is A.

Maximising REXX Performance

Performance improvements can be achieved with REXX if the following guidelines are followed:

- Use upper and lower case as appropriate. REXX is optimised for mixed case work.
- EXECUPDT should be used to remove blanks and comments from EXECs, and CMPREXX for REXX. They can then be invoked much faster.
- Appropriate items should be enclosed in quotes.
- 'ADDRESS command' should be used as this saves the interpreter having to perform synonym resolution or searching for EXECs of the same name before invoking a CMS command.
- Store files using RECFM=V.
- To avoid a lot of unnecessary variables in large programs DROP should be used.
- Internal subroutine calls are more economic than external ones.

ISPF

The Interactive System Productivity Facility (ISPF) is available with CMS and with MVS's TSO and VSE's ICCF. It is basically a facility that allows an application developer to create what are called dialogs using ISPF. These will present users with a new set of menus in a meaningful order that will allow them to carry out a particular piece of work. These can be developed very quickly using ISPF.

The ISPF dialog manager can be invoked from programs using the CALL command. The services available are given in Figure 10.8. Creating a dialog involves four stages. These are:

- dialog functions — ie the programs;
- dialog panels — ie the screen display definition;
- dialog messages — ie the messages for the user;
- file tailoring skeletons — these are dynamically tailored and can be used, for instance, to create batch jobs that are submitted.

ISPF/PDF (Interactive System Productivity Facility/Program Development Facility) is a full-screen menu-driven facility that allows users to perform certain tasks easily. This includes facilities that allow programs to be designed, debugged and tested easily, and facilitates the editing of files. It also allows users to issue CMS commands and provides explanatory HELP menus. An example of the Primary Option Panel is shown in Figure 10.9, although it should be remembered that this can be modified at each site. Alternative menus can be obtained by entering the menu selection number on the command line.

ISPF is considered by many to be a poor substitute for DMS (Display Management System), which was available with earlier releases of VM/SP. This also provided an easy method of defining full-screen displays.

VM BATCH

It is possible for CMS users to despatch work in batch mode using the VM Batch Facility, a service virtual machine which typically has the user-id of CMSBATCH. The use of the batch facility means that users' terminals are free for them to carry out other work and they do not have to wait for the batch job to complete. The VM Batch Facility includes a scheduling system. Jobs (a punch file) are submitted to the batch CMS-id. CMSBATCH reads the punch file, notifies the submitter, executes the commands and directs output to wherever specified. Users are informed about the status of their batch jobs both when they enquire directly, and automatically. It is possible to set the system up such that batch jobs are automatically cancelled if certain parameter

Service	Function
Display	Allows full screen presentation of data and full screen input entry
Variable	Allows variables to be associated with values
Message	Allows context-sensitive and information messages to be sent to users
Table	Allows data to be stored in two-dimensional tables
File tailoring	Allows variables to be substituted into a skeleton
Library access	Allows management of files managed through ISPF
Miscellaneous	Various facilities provided by ISPF — includes log file, split screening, access to editor programs, etc

Figure 10.8 ISPF Services

```
-------------------------ISPF/PDF PRIMARY OPTION PANEL ----------------------------
SELECT OPTION  ===>                                          USERID     -XEPHON
Ø   ISPF PARMS    - SPECIFY TERMINAL AND USER PARAMETERS     TIME       -12:47
1   BROWSE        - DISPLAY SOURCE DATA OR OUTPUT LISTINGS   TERMINAL   -3278
2   EDIT          - CREATE OR CHANGE SOURCE DATA             PF KEYS    -12
3   UTILITIES     - PERFORM UTILITY FUNCTIONS
4   FOREGROUND    - INVOKE LANGUAGE PROCESSORS
5   BATCH         - SUBMIT TO BATCH FOR LANGUAGE PROCESSING
6   COMMAND       - ENTER CMS COMMAND OR EXEC
7   DIALOG TEST   - PERFORM DIALOG TESTING
T   TUTORIAL      - DISPLAY INFORMATION ABOUT SPF
X   EXIT          - TERMINATE ISPF USING LIST/LOG DEFAULTS

PRESS END KEY TO TERMINATE ISPF
```

Figure 10.9 ISPF/PDF Primary Option Menu

values are exceeded, eg CPU usage, SIOs and number of print lines.

PROFS

Many CMS users make use of PROFS (PRofessional OFfice System), an office automation product. PROFS is a derivative of IBM's own internal product called NOSS. It is estimated that there are around 3500 PROFS systems supporting approximately 700,000 users worldwide.

PROFS is loaded as a DCSS and uses various CMS facilities such as XEDIT and ISPF. PROFS offers the following four facilities:

- various time-management facilities (these cover such things as diary facilities, calendars and reminder notes);
- electronic mail facilities (these allow document distribution using RSCS Networking to mail boxes on different PROFS systems);
- search and retrieval facilities (these allow documents to be located using specific search terms that were entered when the document was created or modified);
- a word-processing facility called DW/370, which is replacing the Document Composition Facility (DCF).

PROFS is used primarily for its electronic mail facilities. Each PROFS user is provided with a mail box and can send:

- messages — short notes to another logged-on PROFS user;
- notes — informal communications that are stored in the recipient's mail box;
- documents — formal communications that are stored in a central filing system, and logged.

The latest version of PROFS is 2.2, but in addition a user requires PASF, which is the PROFS Application Support Feature. PASF is a set of extensions to PROFS which provides task-oriented menus for access to PROFS, to Application System (AS — an integrated decision support tool) and to Query Management Facility (QMF — used to access SQL/DS). It also provides PC to host communication. SolutionPac Office Series, VM Edition contains both PROFS and PASF plus the additional software they require to function fully. This package is marketed as an easy-to-install, quick-to-get-running solution to the problem faced by many sites when installing new products. PROFS with PASF and DW/370 and AS (Application System — an application development system) is now being marketed by IBM as a product called Office Vision/VM (OV/VM).

Although PROFS is generally well regarded users have experienced some problems with it. These include the following:

- It is difficult to delete old or unwanted documents from the document database. Users find it harder to use documents than notes, but documents provide a permanent audit trail and are therefore preferred by management.
- Many users have found DCF hard to use, and consider it to be more like a programming language. DW/370 goes some way towards helping to overcome this problem.
- It is necessary to purchase third-party software in order to send faxes or telexes or even link into other electronic mail systems (eg Telecom Gold). PROFS itself does not provide this facility.
- A general lack of advanced features.

Users sending notes can have an enormous impact on system performance. Notes are kept on the spool and cannot be backed up to tape. The spool space that is available for ordinary spool files is reduced and it may cause the spool area to fill up and crash the system. All the notes would be lost in the event of a VM cold start. With releases of VM below 5, 128K of Free Storage Area (FSA) is taken up by each spool-file control block, and typical PROFS users generate a lot of spool files, ie notes. PROFS users who log on use up 6K of the free storage area. If they do no work while logged on they are taking away valuable free storage space.

Maximising PROFS Performance

Some suggestions for improving the performance of PROFS are given below.

- Users should learn why they need to read and remove notes regularly, and why they should not stay logged on when they are inactive.
- To improve I/O performance PROFS mini-disks should be given

dedicated actuators wherever possible. PROFS shared code should not be put on the same actuator as VMSRES.

- Daily REORGS should be performed.
- Increase the PROFS timer interval (up to 999 seconds). Although it affects reminders, it improves performance by increasing the number of users who are considered to be inactive and eligible for migration and therefore reducing the amount of paging and swapping performed.
- The interval timer may be disabled for all machines except those that have an OFS $remind file at log-on or who use the reminder function. This reduces page and swap activity and also free storage requirements.

SQL/DS

SQL/DS (Structured Query Language/Data System) is a relational database that runs under CMS. The VM version of SQL/DS is almost identical to the VSE version and is also very similar to the MVS DB2 (DataBase 2) system. A database is defined as a structured collection of related data, and a distinction can usually be drawn between the 'logical' and 'physical' view of the data. SQL/DS is installed at more VM sites than any other relational database. Each SQL/DS virtual machine is referred to as a server. SQL/DS supports most of the requirements of a database, for example data independence, recovery and restart, etc. Unfortunately, it does not support referential integrity and this is left to the user. SQL/DS uses the SQL language. This allows tables to be defined and maintained and allows data within the tables to be created, queried, updated and deleted. SQL/DS performs particularly well for 'query only'-type databases, where the data is imported from another system and remains stable and non-volatile, rather than operational-type databases.

Multiple SQL/DS databases are usually maintained; each database is a separate virtual machine with its own mini-disks. No attempt should be made to use SQL/DS mini-disks as CMS mini-disks. SQL/DS uses the mini-disks for three purposes:

- to contain the directory — this is a single mini-disk which is used as a 'bit map' to locate data.

- To contain data — these DBEXTENTS exist on one or more mini-disks. The data is stored within the tables.
- To log changes — this mini-disk(s) contains the SQL/DS log of all changes in case of failure.

A virtual machine can be connected to only one database machine at any one time. Therefore it is impossible to support distributed processing, ie where applications share data from one or more tables residing in one or more databases. Virtual machines communicate with a database machine using IUCV. Each server machine can own many database extents and a single CMS user can therefore access multiple DBSPACES within any one server machine.

An SQL server can be connected to more than one virtual machine. This is possible because SQL/DS has multi-tasking code and uses VM Block I/O. Multiple CMS users use IUCV to send their requests to the SQL/DS server machine. This then uses IUCV and the *BLOCK-IO CP service to access the database.

The maximum number of concurrent requesting machines is restricted by the number of 'real agents', which are defined to SQL/DS. Theoretically, SQL/DS could handle a much higher number of requesting machines in terms of connections; however, a real agent needs 200K of virtual storage to support it. A real agent is used while a logical unit of work (LUW) is running. An LUW will last from the start of the first SQL statement executed and includes all subsequent SQL statements until the user issues a commit work statement. For performance reasons it is best to ensure that LUWs are kept as short as possible, otherwise the number of real agents needed is higher. This increases the demands on virtual storage. For screen-based applications it is generally thought best never to let an LUW run over a terminal I/O. However, products like ISQL do not always obey this condition.

In addition to real agents, SQL/DS affects VM paging by using virtual storage buffers to hold frequently referenced data. The size of these buffers can be controlled by the systems programmers. If large buffers are used less real DASD I/O is required. However, if the buffers are too large this increases the VM paging rate and causes a degradation in both VM and SQL/DS performance. If SQL/DS is paged by VM, the whole database and all connected users will stop processing.

Data access paths that are used are chosen by a component of SQL/DS called the optimiser. They are not chosen by the user and this may affect performance. The optimiser uses statistics to select the 'best' data access path. If out-of-date statistics are used by the optimiser a data path giving poor performance may be chosen. The statistics used by the optimiser are gathered by running a batch job. However, running the job may lock out users, causing even worse performance.

Maximising SQL/DS Performance

Some performance suggestions on the installation and use of SQL are given below:

- A DCSS should be used with multiple SQL/DS server machines.
- Multiple SQL/DS databases should be installed in separate virtual machines, each with its own databases initially. This is easier than trying to split usage later.
- The following modules should be made nucleus resident:

  DMKIUA;
  DMKIUE;
  DMKIUL;
  DMKBIO.
- The SET QDROP dbname OFF USERS command should be used to enhance performance.
- Once SQL is up and running the SET RESERVE command should be used.
- SQL should be restricted to query-only activities because it does this best.
- All LUWs should be small, thereby reducing the amount of virtual storage required.
- The use of storage buffers should be maximised.
- SQL-managed mini-disks should never be used as CMS mini-disks.
- Volatile data should be unloaded and reloaded frequently.
- The clustered index option should be used.
- The number of indexes used should be kept to a minimum.

- Pool usage should be monitored to ensure that it does not fill up causing a database abend.
- Statistics used by the optimiser should be kept up to date.

CICS

With the introduction of CICS/VM it is now possible to run CICS under CMS. CICS (Customer Information Control System) is an interactive or on-line system which allows users to access a database from a terminal. A user need not be aware of the difference between the CMS and CICS environments. The user only logs on once, to the CMS user-id. There is no need to re-enter a user-id and password to enter the CICS environment. This is achieved by entering a CMS command or from a menu. The user may either select an option from a menu or type in a four-character transaction identifier. This will call a program which will perform the desired activity.

The type of work performed generally falls into one of the following three categories:

- on-line enquiry;
- on-line enquiry with update;
- on-line data entry.

CICS is madc up of four components:

- managements, or control programs;
- tables;
- Control Areas;
- application programs.

Each set of managements or control programs is responsible for one specific component of the CICS system. For example, terminal management looks after I/O to and from terminals, and file management looks after file I/O.

The tables specify what items are available to that CICS environment. For example, any programs that are to be used must have an entry in the Program Processing Table (PPT) and any file that can be used must have an entry in the File Control Table (FCT). If an item is not in a table it is unavailable.

Control Areas are used by CICS to keep track of what is happening while it is executing. When any event occurs the information or pointers within a control area will be updated.

The application programs perform the work that the user wants done. These programs may be specifically written on site or bought as a package. They are invoked by the user either by entering a transaction identifier or by selecting an item from a menu. The other CICS components are a necessary overhead to allow these application programs to execute. The programs are usually re-entrant, which means that they can be used repeatedly and no changes (eg bit settings) occur in the code while they are in use. Application programs running in CICS can issue CICS commands.

The performance of the CICS system can be affected by the location, size and arrangement of the files it uses, in particular VSAM key sequenced file's data and index components.

File access is achieved through the use of server machines, either VSAM or SQL/DS. If the CICS system uses Transient Data or Temporary Storage, SQL/DS is a prerequisite because these functions are implemented by SQL/DS. Additionally, it will only allow access to data held at a remote site if that data is managed by a CICS system.

CICS systems have long been running under VSE and MVS and the VM version is really only a subset of these two. Its maximum transaction rate is in the range of 50 to 60 per minute compared to a typical maximum in excess of 200 per minute with the MVS or VSE versions. Unfortunately, with CICS/VM there is no support for older macro-level systems which run in CICS systems under MVS and VSE. This might prevent VSE or MVS CICS users throwing away their guest systems and running all CICS applications under CICS/VM.

CICS/VM is maintained by panel definitions rather than by the use of tables as with VSE and MVS versions and the whole process is, therefore, much simpler.

SHARED FILE SYSTEM

The Shared File System (SFS), which is available with VM/SP release 6, allows CMS users to store files in a file pool rather than on minidisks, and allows files to be accessed through a directory. This makes life easier for data administrators and users alike. It also makes file sharing much easier. It has been suggested that this is VM's first step in the direction of MVS's System Managed Storage (SMS).

SFS is implemented as a two-part subsystem:

- A CMS-based service machine provides centralised storage and management of file data.
- An interface to CMS is provided by a set of Callable Service Library (CSL) routines.

The SFS service machine is a file server that declares itself as an APPC/VM (Advanced Program to Program Communication/Virtual Machine) global resource. The service machine owns mini-disks assigned to hold SFS-resident data and runs a CMS-based application through which that data is managed and accessed. End users use CSL routines and APPC/VM to communicate with the SFS virtual machine.

The mini-disks managed by the SFS machine are known as a file pool. They can be subdivided into storage groups. The first of these is reserved for SFS control and contains space management and file directory information. Additional file pools can be established by defining more SFS server machines. A user can use the file pool only after registration in it. This involves defining file space for a user in a storage group and initialising the user's high-level directory. A limit is set on the amount of space in the storage group that can be used by the specified user. A user can be enrolled in more than one file pool. Space from the pool is allocated to the user as required.

Subdirectories may be specified within a directory, and subdirectories within that, giving a maximum nesting depth of eight levels, ie filepool-id:user-id.dir1.dir2...dir8. Alternatively, an SFS directory can be accessed like a mini-disk by allocating a letter to it.

Although SFS allows concurrent access to a file by more than one user, only one user can be writing to the file at a time, while any number can be reading it. This is achieved by using file locking.

DFSMS/VM

The concept of the software controlling the placement of files rather than a person is one that is fairly new to IBM operating systems. Data Facility System Managed Storage has been available to MVS users for a couple of years, but has only now been announced for VM. DFSMS/VM is available for all the latest VM releases, including XA. Its function is to make the migration of mini-disks from existing real disks to new real disks simpler and faster.

The main feature of DFSMS/VM is the Interactive Storage Management Facility (ISMF). Movement of mini-disks between FBA and FBA devices, and between CKD and CKD devices is performed by high speed data mover. When mini-disks are moved from FBA to CKD devices the COPYfile command is used.

ISMF has a user interface, on-line help facilities and consists of the following three applications:

- ISMF Profile
- Mini-disk
- List.

ISMF Profile is used to select the level of error information to log.

Mini-disk is used to create, tailor and save lists of mini-disks that meet particular criteria. It can be used to perform operations against selected mini-disks in a list.

List is used to manage and use saved mini-disk lists. Users may create lists of mini-disks by specifying any combination of device type, volume serial number, virtual address, owner-id, size and starting address on volume.

The DFSMS COPY command can be used to copy SFS and SQL/DS mini-disks. The DFSMS CHECK command can be used to check that the internal structure of a mini-disk is intact.

SECTION V

I/O and DASD, and Communication

The performance of the processor is important in the overall performance of a VM system. However, a lot of time and effort is spent in moving files to and from DASD and moving data between the processor and a user's terminal. The next two chapters examine these aspects of how a VM system performs.

11 I/O and DASD

The movement of data or programs in and out of the processor makes use of the I/O (Input/Output) subsystem. The request for I/O comes from programs that are being executed within the processor. The I/O subsystem can often be a major bottleneck and an understanding of how it works can be important in optimising the performance of the VM system. A large percentage of I/O activity is between DASD (where files are stored) and the processor. (The rest is usually to unit record devices and FEPs.)

DISKS

The majority of DASD at most sites are disks (eg 3380s). When a new disk is installed the DMKFMT module is run. It writes a label record on cylinder zero and writes zeros over the rest of the disk. The format of the labelling command is:

FORMAT 481,3380,volser,LABEL

where volser is the volume serial number of the pack being labelled. DMKFMT then allocates space. Details of what is allocated and where are stored in a record called the volume allocation map (ALOCBLOK), which is stored on real cylinder zero of the disk.

The disks may be CP-owned volumes (and put in the sysowned list during SYSGEN) or CP-system volumes. The CP-owned volumes contain the DRCT, PERM, TDSK and TEMP areas. The CP-system volumes contain the user mini-disks. DMKFMT can be used to allocate the DRCT, PERM, TDSK and TEMP areas. Any space on a CP-owned disk that is not allocated becomes TEMP space. The more detailed allocation of the PERM space is done by the DMKSYS macros (eg SYSNUC,

SYSERR, SYSWRM, SYSCKP and SYSPAG) at SYSGEN. Also at SYSGEN time the DMKSNT macro allocates NAMESYS, NAMENCP, NAME3800, NAMELANG.

Mini-disks on CP-system volumes are allocated using the directory entry for the user. To format a disk for use by CMS the command to use is:

FORMAT cuu mode nocyl/noblk blksize 4K

After new DASD are installed and formatted their real addresses are added to DMKRIO. After a SYSGEN and re-IPL they can be used. Data collection software (accounting, monitor, etc) must also be informed about the new disk.

MINI-DISKS

The majority of I/O operations that take place are between the processor and mini-disks. A real disk may be formatted into one or more mini-disks. Mini-disks are made available to a virtual machine by being included in the directory entry for that virtual machine. If mini-disks are to be shared the directory entry must have a password associated with the mini-disk. CMS users usually have an A disk at address 191 which contains the EXECs and data files of that CMS user. They also have read-only access to an S disk (the system disk), and a Y disk. The S and the Y disks are maintained by the MAINT user-id.

Associated with each mini-disk are control blocks that are stored in the FSA (Free Storage Area). These are used by CP to translate the virtual address into a real address so that the request for access can go to the correct real disk.

A directory at the front of each mini-disk contains pointers to all the files on the mini-disk. When a change is made to the mini-disk a new directory is created reflecting this change. It is this second directory that is accessed to find the location of any file. When the next change is made the original directory is made to reflect the change and becomes the live directory. The two directories flip-flop back and forth as each change is made. In the event of a user inadvertently deleting a file it is possible to recover it if action is taken quickly enough. A deleted file is not, in fact, deleted; all that happens is that the pointers to it are removed from the directory. In order to recover the file it is necessary to flip back from the current directory to the previous directory which contained the pointers to the file. A method and program to do this was written by David Raines of Darchem in the UK.

Recovery Procedure

Assuming a file called fn ft fm has been erased from the 191 A disk, the procedure for its recovery is given below:

1 A temporary disk of the same size (and type) as the 191 must be defined at address 59E.

2 A copy of the 191 disk must be DDRed to the 59E disk.

3 The program given below (or similar) must be run.

4 The recovered file must be copied back from the 59E to the 191.

5 CMS must be re-IPLed because the program unfortunately leaves the CMS file system in the virtual machine in an unpredictable state.

The program works only for FBA devices because it uses DIAGNOSE X'20' (general I/O). It could run on CKD device types if DIAGNOSE X'18' (standard DASD I/O) was used instead.

Obviously the procedure only works if the last change made to the problem mini-disk was the deletion of the file that is to be recovered. If any other changes have been made this will have flipped the directory over again, hence making the file irrecoverable. The program is given in Figure 11.1 and is reproduced from *VM Update* by kind permission of Xephon Technology Transfer.

Temporary Mini-disks

If more space is required than is currently available for a temporary file the user can allocate a temporary mini-disk. The space used is taken from the TDSK area on CP-owned volumes (see Chapter 3). To allocate temporary disk space a user must (1) DEFine what type of disk pack the temporary disk is to be on, the virtual address to be used for the temporary disk, and how many cylinders of space the temporary disk is to occupy; (2) FORMAT the temporary disk at the virtual address and allocate a letter or filemode to it; (3) respond to a prompt by confirming that the FORMAT is to take place; (4) give the volume serial number of the real disk on which the temporary mini-disk is to be put.

```
* Description:  This module will flip the DASD directory of a CMS
*               mini-disk. This module will only flip a disk with
*               the address of '59E'. The coded CCW will only work
*               on FBA disks. The sequence of events before this
*               module is run should be:
*                  (i) A temporary FBA mdisk should be defined as 59E.
*                 (ii) The problem disk should be DDR copied to this
*                      disk.
*                (iii) This module should be run.
*                 (iv) The tdisk should be accessed and the file to be
*                      RECOVERED copied back to the problem disk.
*                  (v) The TDISK should be detached.
* Register Usage:-
*
* R1- Not used             R5- CCW address          R9- Not used
* R2- Base for PARML       R6- Not used             R10- Not used
* R3- Not used             R7- Not used             R11- Not used
* R4- Disk address         R8- Not used             R12- Base Register.
RECOVERM CSECT
         PRINT  NOGEN
         USING  *,R12                    ESTABLISH ADDRESSABILITY
         ST     R14, SAVERET             STORE RETURN ADDRESS
         LR     R12,R15
         LA     R15,0
         LM     R4,R5,=A(X'59E',CCWAD1)  LOAD TEMP DISK ADDR + READ CCW
         DC     X'83',X'45',X'0020'      EXECUTE IT.
         LTR    R15,R15                  IS THE RETURN CODE 0 ?
         BNE    ERM1                     NO.. GO WRITE ERROR MESSAGE 1
         CLI    DATA+19,X'05'            ARE WE ON FIVE
         BE     FIVE                     YES.. GO FLIP TO 4
         MVI    DATA+19,X'05'            NO.. FLIP TO 5
         B      PUT                      GO FLIP
FIVE     MVI    DATA+19,X'04'            FLIP TO 4
PUT      MVC    DATA+32(4), DATA+28      COPY OLD POINTER
         L      R5,=A(CCWAD)             LOAD WRITE CCW
         DC     X'83',X'45',X'0020'      EXECUTE IT.
         C      R15,=A(X'00')            IS THE RETURN CODE 0 ?
         BNE    ERM1                     NO.. GO WRITE ERROR MESSAGE 1
         LA     R15,0                     LOAD ZERO RETURN CODE
GOHOME   L      R14,SAVERET               LOAD RETURN ADDRESS
         BR     R14                          GO HOME!
*     E R R O R     M E S S A G E .
ERM1     ST     R15,REG15
         ST     R5,REG5
         LINEDIT  TEXT='.. Error. Invalid return code from Diagnose 20.
                RC=.. ..',
                SUB=(CHARA,HI,DECA, REG15,CHARA, LOW), DOT=NO,RENT=NO
```

```
         CLI     REG15+3,X'0D'             IS THE RETURN CODE 13 ?
         BNE     ERMSKIP                   NO.. NO POINT IN SENSE
         LINEDIT TEXT='..          Sense Bytes are as follows:   ',DOT=NO,
                 COMP=NO,SUB=(CHARA,HI)
         LINEDIT TEXT='                    .........' ,DOT=NO,
                 SUB=(HEXA,REG5),COMP=NO
         LINEDIT TEXT='                    s2s3s0s1  ..' ,
                 DOT=NO,COMP=NO,SUB=(CHARA,LOW)
ERMSKIP  L       R15,REG15
         B       GOHOME
*  C H A N N E L   C O M M A N D   W O R D S.
         DS      0D
CCWAD1   CCW     X'63',SEEKAD,SILI+CC,16   SET-UP EXTENTS
SRCH1    CCW     X'43',SEERAD,SILI+CC,8    LOCATE
READ     CCW     X'42',DATA,SILI,512       READ FIRST BLOCK
         DS      0D
CCWAD    CCW     X'63',SEEKAD,SILI+CC,16   SET-UP EXTENTS
SRCH     CCW     X'43',SEEWAD,SILI+CC,8    LOCATE
WRITE    CCW     X'41',DATA,SILI,512       WRITE FIRST BLOCK
         DS      0D
SEEKAD   DC      X'00'                     MASK
         DC      X'000000'                 RESERVED
         DC      F'0'                      MAJOR OFFSET
         DC      F'0'                      FIRST BLOCK OFFSET
         DC      F'2'                      LAST BLOCK OFFSET
SEERAD   DC      X'06'                     OPERATION (FBA READ FLAG 06)
         DC      X'00'                     AUX BYTE
         DC      H'1'                      NUMBER OF BLOCKS
         DC      F'1'                      BLOCK OFFSET
         DS      0D
SEEWAD   DC      X'01'                     OPERATION (FBA WRITE FLAG 01)
         DC      X'00'                     AUX BYTE
         DC      H'1'                      NUMBER OF BLOCKS
         DC      F'1'                      BLOCK OFFSET
         DS      0D
*  C o n s t a n t s .
DATA     DC      512CL1' '                 OUR DATA
         DS      0D
SAVERET  S       F                         DEFINE SAVERET FULLWORD
REG15    DS      F                         DEFINE REG15    FULLWORD
REG5     DS      F                         DEFINE REG5     FULLWORD
HI       DC      X'1DE8'                   3270 HI INTENSITY
LOW      DC      X'1D60'                   3270 LOW INTENSITY
SILI     EQU     X'20'                     CODE TO TURN OFF INVALID LENGTH
CC       EQU     X'40'                     CODE TO CHAIN COMMANDS
         REGEQU
         END
```

Figure 11.1 RECOVERM Assemble

The commands are shown in Figure 11.2.

```
CP DEFINE T3380 295 4
FORMAT 295 H
YES
VMS003
```

where

295	is virtual address
4	is number of cylinders to be allocated
H	is the filemode to be used
VMS003	is the volser of the disk

Figure 11.2 Commands to Create a New Temporary Mini-disk

The temporary mini-disk is deleted when the user logs off. Temporary mini-disks cannot be retained between sessions.

Accessing Mini-disks

Because the CMS users at a site often need to share files there is a command that allows one user to access dynamically the files on a mini-disk belonging to another user. A user's mini-disk can only be accessed by someone else provided that the directory entry for that mini-disk has a password associated with it. The process requires two steps. First a user must LINK to the other user's disk using the LINK command. The user must also specify the other user's user-id, the virtual address of the mini-disk on the other user's machine, and the virtual address of his own mini-disk. Next the user can gain access using the ACCess command, specifying the virtual address and filemode to be used. An example of a typical sequence of commands to LINK and copy a file is given in Figure 11.3. To free another user's mini-disk after a LINK it must be released and detached. This is also shown in Figure 11.3.

```
LINK altuser 191 291 R
ACCESS 291 J
        LIST * * J
        COPYFILE fn ft J = = A
REL J
DET 199
```

Where
  altuser is another virtual machine
  191 is the virtual address of the required mini-disk
  291 is the virtual address of the user's mini-disk
  R gives read-only access
  J is the filemode for the user.

Figure 11.3 Command Sequence used to LINK to another Mini-disk

FILES

CMS users can access files on their mini-disks. These can either be accessed using filename filetype filemode, or by using SFS (Shared File System) access method. These are described in full in Chapters 9 and 10. They can also access VSAM files using VSE VSAM. VSAM catalogs can be put on any mini-disk, but the catalogs cannot share the mini-disk with CMS files because the disk must have CP not CMS formatting. The catalog is set up using AMS (Access Method Services).

I/O PATH

I/O path refers to the route taken by data moving from disk or tape to the processor, or from the processor to either disk or tape. Disk and tape are the two most frequently used media for storing data, although solid-state DASD are also sometimes used. At the processor end is a channel, or with XA a subchannel system. These exist as part of the

EXternal Data Controller (EXDC) on 3080s and 3090s. The EXDC is connected by cable to a control unit which in turn is connected to individual disks, or tapes. With 3380 disks there is a 3880 controller referred to as a storage director. With SP and HPO a response to a request for data must travel along the same path as the request itself. With XA dynamic path reconnect allows the response to return using any available path back to the processor. An I/O path is illustrated in Figure 11.4.

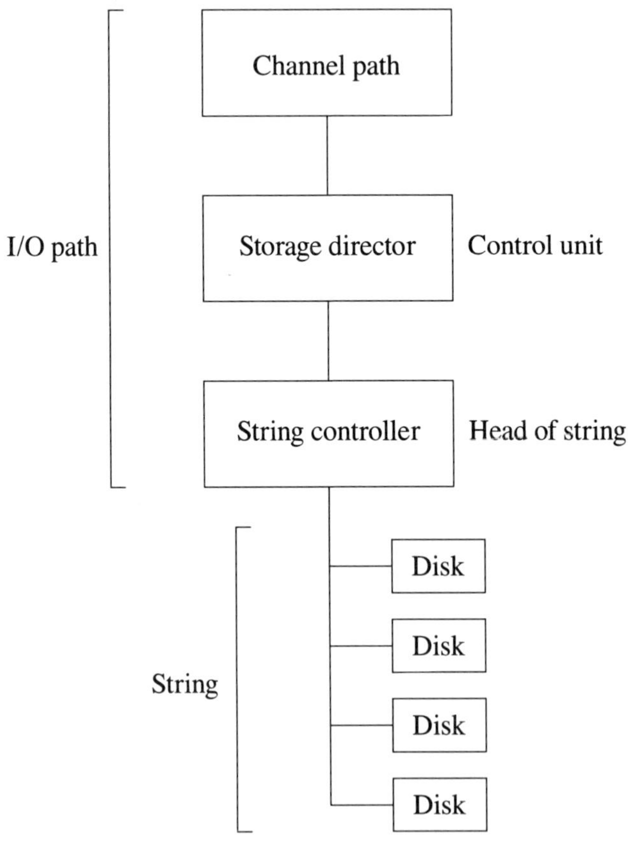

Figure 11.4 Diagram of an I/O Path

CHANNEL

A channel is a processor in its own right that controls I/O to control units attached to it. The channel is given instructions by a Channel Command Word (CCW) which comes from the processsor. CCWs are doublewords, ie 8 bytes, and contain instructions such as:

- read count key data;
- read sector;
- search;
- seek;
- set sector.

The maximum loading on a channel is usually considered to be around 30 per cent. Once values above that are reached serious performance degradation can occur. However, when XA is using Dynamic Path Reconnect and 3380s it is possible to raise this maximum to around 40 per cent. If a well-tuned DASD controller is installed the value could go up to as high as 50 per cent, and if solid-state devices are used values of around 70 per cent could be used.

SP can support up to 16 channels, HPO can support up to 32 channels and XA has a maximum of 256 subchannels. XA allows the use of Dynamic Path Selection, which means that the subchannel system attempts to find a path to a device. If the first path is busy it dynamically tries any alternatives.

I/O SEQUENCE OF EVENTS

During an I/O operation (3380 device) a series of software and hardware events takes place. These can be summarised as:

- Queue time;
- Seeking;
- Connect time;
- Protocol.

Queue Time

Queue time is further subdivided into two stages, which are wait for device, and wait for path.

Wait for Device

A virtual machine has to wait for a device if that device is currently in use by another virtual machine. The only way the time spent waiting for a device can be reduced is by reducing the length of time that a device is busy.

Wait for Path

Once the I/O operation has been started, the I/O may have to wait in the channel subsystem for a path to the device to become available. If the path is available (ie channel, control unit, head of string and internal data path are free), the system can attempt to access the device, unless it is in use by another system (shared DASD).

Seeking

The seeking stage is further divided into three substages which are called seek, latency and RPS reconnect delay.

Seek

If the device and the path arc free, the I/O operation can be started. The I/O operation is usually started by a seek command initiated by the control unit. Time spent processing the seek CCW and the set sector CCW are ignored. As soon as the device receives the seek information the I/O path (ie the channel, control unit and string controller) is released and the component parts are free to process other I/O requests. The time needed for the arm to move to the cylinder and to select the correct track head is referred to as seek time. Seek times for the 3380 device are:

- minimum 3 msec;
- average 16 msec;
- maximum 30 msec;

It is estimated that about 30 per cent of DASD I/O requests result in non-zero seeks. Therefore, the average time for an I/O request can be calculated as 16 msec × 0.33 = 5.3 msec. Because seeking activity for a disk depends on the way that files are referenced, the average time taken for an I/O request can be reduced by controlling the location of files on the disk.

Latency

There is no way of knowing the current position of a rotating disk relative to the position of the required sector. On average, half a rotation, the so-called latency, must elapse before the correct sector position is reached.

RPS (Rotational Position Sensing) Reconnect Delay

Once the correct sector position is reached, the device will try to reconnect to the path. The time available to do this is very limited because the disk is spinning at 3600 rpm. If the attempt is unsuccessful the actuator must try again during the next revolution. When this happens, an RPS delay of one full revolution (16.7 msec) occurs. The RPS reconnect delay depends on the path being busy due to the activity of other actuators on the same path. With SP and HPO the data must return to the channel that initiated the I/O operation. As channel utilisations increase, the chances of the channels being busy increase exponentially. With XA any I/O path can be used for reconnection. This makes the probability of finding an available path much higher, and so the impact of RPS misses is much less under XA. RPS misses can be seen by any monitor as high service times. RPS delay can be reduced by reducing path busy time.

Connect Time

The connect time stage is further subdivided into two substages which are called search and data transfer.

Search

Data can be read or written until after the requested record location has been verified using a search ID or search on KEY command. This search time is usually very short (1 msec).

Data Transfer
Data transfer can begin at device speed when the required block (record) is found. The length of time taken for a data transfer can be calculated by dividing the block size by the data transfer speed of the device (eg 4K block divided by 3MB/sec for the 3380 yields 1.36 msec).

Protocol

In the control unit (eg 3880) a finite amount of time must be spent in the initiation and completion of each command. During this time the path is busy because the control unit is part of the path to the device. Another part of the processing overlaps with device activity. The value of the protocol time depends on the 3880 micro-code level and is variable ($\pm$1.6 msec).

START I/O

To initiate an I/O activity a virtual machine can issue a Start I/O (SIO) instruction or a Start I/O Fast instruction. Older operating systems typically issued SIOs and newer ones issue SIOF instructions. When a guest-operating system issues a Start I/O instruction the guest's execution is suspended until the corresponding real SIO can be performed, ie it is put in an IOWAIT state. Therefore it cannot continue to process work or despatch any of its partitions. CP queues the I/O until the path is free and then the I/O is started. If any part of the path is busy the I/O is requeued and CP will retry it later using a FIFO algorithm (First In First Out). When the I/O is successfully issued CP reflects the appropriate condition code to the guest-operating system and starts running it again.

Example condition codes include:

- device busy;
- device not operational;
- successful.

The guest system will remain suspended until CP knows which condition code to present to it.

If the guest-operating system uses the SIOF instruction it can be redespatched immediately after issuing an SIOF because the SIOF instruction allows for deferred condition codes to be presented later if the I/O is not successfully intitiated. This reduces IOWAITs and so improves performance. If the SIOF instruction is used it does require additional programming support. If more modern guest-operating systems are run on older processors that do not implement the SIOF instruction, the instruction is treated as an SIO. All current versions of MVS, VSE and VM use the SIOF instruction.

Some processors (eg some 4381s) have an SIOFQing (Start I/O Fast Queuing) facility available. Although it is sometimes recommended that this be turned off, it is usually beneficial, in terms of overall performance, to utilise the facility.

CMS virtual machines use the DIAGNOSE instruction interface to perform most of their I/O. The virtual machine is suspended until the I/O operation completes because DIAGNOSE instructions are processed synchronously.

CP schedules most I/O activity using a FIFO algorithm. The exception to this rule is paging because it is so important in terms of performance. All paging I/O is handled in preference to normal I/O activity.

PATH SELECTION

On the more modern processors (eg 3080s and 3090s), if a path to a device is busy the I/O request is queued in the channel, and the channel will be responsible for reissuing the SIOF instruction rather than CP. On the plus side, this saves CP from having to keep processing I/O instructions and it can therefore be performing other work. On the negative side, CP never sees a busy condition and, therefore, never invokes its alternate path logic. This results in all I/O going down the primary path and never trying the alternate path, if one has been specified.

One method of reducing the problem of one channel being overutilised is to alternate the definition of which is the primary path in the DMKRIO macro. Reducing the contention on the path should improve I/O performance. An example of part of the macro is given in Figure 11.5. SP and HPO systems always re-drive the I/O via the alternate channel (ALTCH in DMKRIO) if present, before using the alternate control unit (ALTCU in DMKRIO). If there is only one control unit on the channel it is likely to still be busy and the I/O will fail again.

Another solution to the problem that is available with HPO is to make a modification to the DMKIOQ macro (DMKIOS for HPO release 3 users) which can be used to make CP flip-flop between channels. This modification is given in Figure 11.6.

```
RDEVICE ADDRESS=120, DEVTYPE=3350, ALTCU=220
RDEVICE ADDRESS=122, DEVTYPE=3350, ALTCU=220

RDEVICE ADDRESS=221, DEVTYPE=3350, ALTCU=120
RDEVICE ADDRESS=223, DEVTYPE=3350, ALTCU=120
```

Or

```
RDEVICE ADDRESS=(120,4), DEVTYPE=3350, ALTCU=220
RDEVICE ADDRESS=(224,4), DEVTYPE=3350, ALTCU=120
```

Figure 11.5 DMKRIO Macro

```
./ ★ FLIP-FLOP PATHS TO BALANCE CHANNELS TO REDUCE
./ ★ QUEUING IN 3083 CHANNELS
./ I 18670000 £ 18670010 10                      (for DMKIOS on HPO 3.0)
./ I 04300000 £ 04300010 10                      (for DMKIOQ on HPO 3.4)
          NC     RDEVCUB, RDEVCUB         IF NO ALTERNATE CU
          BZ     NOFLIP                   DO NOT FLIP-FLOP
          TM     RDEVPTHS, RDEVAOF        NO FLIP-FLOP
          BO     NOFLIP                   IF
          TM     RDEVPTHS, REDVBOF        EITHER CU
          BO     NOFLIP                   HAS ALL PATHS OFFLINE
          TM     RDEVOFF, X'FF'           NO FLIP-FLOP IF PATH
          BNZ    NOFLIP                   OFFLINE AT THE MOMENT
          L      R0, RDEVCUB              FLIP-FLOP PATHS TO BALANCE
          MVC    RDEVCUB, RDEVCUA         3083 CHANNELS, SINCE
          ST     R0, RDEVCUA              THEY WILL Q INTERNALLY
★                FLIP-FLOP OFFLINE        SWITCHES FOR CONTROL UNITS
          PACK   RDEVPTHS, RDEVPTHS       REVERSE BYTE
NOFLIP    EQU    ★
```

Figure 11.6 Alternate Channel Modification

If a site has SLU406 or above this mod should be applied after label FXPTH rather than 04300000.

With VM/XA lack of path rotation is not a problem because rotation is performed automatically by the channel subsystem. The IOCP (Input Output Configuration Program) must accurately match the hardware configuration, otherwise channels etc may not be used. Each device must be defined by only one IODEVICE macro.

Because XA uses never-ending channel programs (suspend resume) the reports from monitors can be particularly confusing when they look at paging packs. Paging packs will always appear to be around 95 per cent busy.

RESOURCE CONSUMPTION

Because VM uses virtual addresses these must be converted to real addresses for any I/O activity to take place. This conversion uses processor resources. I/O commands must be translated from virtual addresses to real addresses, and I/O buffers from virtual to real storage addresses. I/Os to mini-disks require virtual to real cylinder address translation. With XA, 370 SIO commands must be translated to XA SSCH (Start SubCHannel) commands.

An I/O request from a virtual machine uses up CPU cycles and storage when it is interpreted. CP has to translate the channel program so that it references the correct pages, accommodates mini-disk relocation and honours read-only device status. A copy of the channel program is made by CP and the addresses and control words are relocated appropriately. Reducing the CP overhead by reducing the number of I/Os makes more of the CP available for productive work. Dedicated DASD reduce the amount of translation work.

MAXIMISING I/O PERFORMANCE

The following are some suggested ways of improving I/O performance at a site.

- The biggest improvement in I/O performance can be achieved by reducing the number of I/O operations that take place. Some suggestions of how this can be achieved are given below.
- Before the contents of disks are moved or modified in any way an

analysis of seek activity on the DASD must be carried out. This can indicate highly used areas, and a map of the allocated areas of the volume will show which virtual machines are responsible for activity against each area. Disk access analysis should be carried out at different times of the day because there may be a wide variation in the pattern of access. There is no point in tuning for only one of several different access patterns.

- I/O activity should be balanced across devices, control units and channels wherever possible.
- System mini-disks should not be all put on one actuator; the load should be spread.
- Page and data contention on the same channel should be avoided. This is because paging has priority over other I/O activity.
- If 3380s are not formatted into 4K blocks, space is used for Inter-Block Gaps (IBG) and this space is wasted. No other number divides so exactly into the track size of a 3380 as 4K blocks do. 4K is also the optimum size for other disks.
- The only time when 4K block size would not be used would be for mini-disks that contain very small EXECs.
- CMS release 5 has a read-ahead facility for disk access. This will get two blocks during an I/O operation rather than just one. If 4K blocks are used, this means that 8K will be transferred. If the next block is to be read it is already in storage and I/O operation is not required.
- If the RECFM V parameter is coded it saves space but RECFM F is faster.
- If heavily used software is placed on a separate disk there are two advantages. There is an improvement in performance because contention is reduced. It is possible to audit the use of that software (by utilising VM accounting data).
- If the number of active users to a disk exceeds 50 it is worth considering duplicating the disk. An example would be the S disk. The duplicate should be from a DDR back-up so that all copies use the same shared S-STATs. The duplicate copy should be put on a different disk pack to avoid contention. For the Y disk it must have the same Y-stats. An alternative to duplicating heavily used mini-

disks is to cache them. Because the files will be continuously accessed they will stay in cache storage and so better performance will be achieved.

- If the previous method is not adopted access times can be reduced if the files on frequently accessed mini-disks are placed in order of frequency of use. The most heavily used files should go first.
- Access times for frequently used mini-disks can be reduced if they are placed near the centre of the pack and placed next to each other. This reduces the amount of head movement required to access them. Wherever possible the minimum number of heavily used mini-disks should be placed on any one pack.
- The SAVEFD command can be used to make file directories of common mini-disks shared. This saves on I/O and storage.
- If cache is used, all the items on the DASD should be cached, not just some. If some are not, I/O takes place at normal DASD speed for those items. When I/O completes, cache speed I/O can take place. If some items are not cached, all the advantages of caching are lost.
- If dedicated DASD are used this reduces the amount of translation work required by CP.
- Actuators should be dedicated to PROFS DASD, ie they should not be shared with active data.
- Terminals should never be put on the same channels as paging packs. The services to the terminals will always wait until disk I/O is complete.
- The heavy use of temporary disks can have an impact on I/O performance. Formatting is I/O intensive and can slow down other I/O activity.
- Optimum performance can be achieved if the busiest DASD volumes are placed at the end of a string. This is because, when a volume on a string is ready to be serviced, a flag is set at the volume. These flags are ORed together at the head of string. When the head of string detects a service-request flag it starts a sequential search of the string, checking to see which device requires service. When a flag is found the controller services the volume and resets the flag. The controller will then return to the beginning.

If the service-request flag is still set it begins the search again. If a heavily used pack is placed at the beginning of string it will tend to hog the service cycles and so lock out the trailing volumes which will be waiting for service. If less heavily used volumes are placed at the start of the string they will be serviced more quickly and will be out of the path when the next scan is done.

- The 3380 models A and D store large amounts of data. Unfortunately, there is only one path available for the whole string. As the disks get busier so the likelihood of a busy head of string occuring increases. It is recommended that only one box (ie four addresses) on a string is used and that a maximum of three is not exceeded.
- With 3380 models E, J and K there are four paths to service a maximum of sixteen volumes on each string. Busy volumes should always be placed at the end of each substring, otherwise they will lock out the less busy volumes.
- Because 3380 models A04, AA04 and AD04 have only one path to service up to 16 volumes those volumes must be placed in the correct order in the string.
- With 3380 models AE04, AJ04 and AK04 there are four paths to each unit servicing four units in the string. Heavily used volumes should be placed at the end of the string.
- For similar reasons heavily used strings should be placed lower on controllers and heavily used controllers should be placed further down channels.
- Virtual addresses should be allocated in a similar way because of the way the RDEVBLOKs are processed. Therefore terminals should be on lower addresses than tape drives.
- With XA, part of expanded storage can be used as a mini-disk cache area. When this is used, performance improvements can result.

12 Communication

With the increase in the number of users working from remote terminals and the growth in distributed processing, an understanding of the role of communication at a VM site, and also the software required for this communication to take place, is becoming more and more important.

SOFTWARE OVERVIEW

Throughout the history of VM there has been software for communication. However, the development of this software has not always been in parallel with the development in communication software for other IBM-operating systems. This has resulted in the large amount of software and the confusing overlap that exist now.

Terminals

Initially, VM offered ASCII support for teletype terminals (and, in fact, still does). ASCII terminals usually work in line-by-line mode, which makes any full screen applications run inefficiently. Local terminals were first supported and later remote point-to-point terminal support was added. When IBM introduced the 3270 family of terminals, support for local and remote (EBCDIC) terminals was needed. ASCII-to-3270 protocol (EBCDIC) conversion products were used to overcome the difficulties. There are software converters and hardware converters. An example of the latter is the 7171, which looks like a PC with an expansion cabinet. The Logical Device Support Facility (LDSF) allowed users to log on to a remote VM system as though it was the local system. It was introduced with the first VM/SP systems. VM/XA offers support for local non-SNA 3270 systems only.

On a modern terminal in VM mode the screen has the last two rows as command-input area. In application mode (eg CICS or XEDIT) the screen is in full-screen mode. To simplify the interface between terminals and CP, generic CCWs (Channel Command Words) are defined for virtual screen I/O operations. These are later converted into the appropriate CCWs for the actual terminal being used.

For non-SNA working, up to 256 3270 clusters may be attached with up to 32 terminals in a cluster. CP can be used to poll the terminals but this is inefficient. To avoid this it is necessary to use Passthrough release 3, or VTAM. With SNA multidrop connections are allowed.

Passthrough

Passthrough runs in non-SNA networks. It allows users to log on to remote terminals as though they were local terminals. The Passthrough Virtual Machine (PVM) controls multitasking. By offering 3274 emulation facilities, Passthrough allows VM, VSE and MVS machines to be connected in a BSC network. Passthrough also introduced multi-point BSC 3270 support and switched point-to-point support.

Passthrough has three line drivers:

- DVMBSC VM to VM via BSC (Binary Synchronous Communication) lines;
- DVMCTC VM to VM via CTCA (Channel To Channel Adaptor);
- DVMSIM VM appearing as a remote 3274 BSC controller to a host.

The DIAL command was introduced with VM/SP release 2. Users were able to DIAL from remote terminals to gain access to the Passthrough virtual machine. The process was simple: a user cleared the VM logo from the screen and entered DIAL PVM. The Passthrough menu appeared and the user selected the system or application he wished to connect to. Access from Passthrough to the local VM system was achieved by using the Logical Device Support Facility (LDSF). The introduction of the DIAL command allowed CICS (running in a guest-operating system) and CMS users to use the same terminal. It did not solve the problem of *returning* to CMS from CICS.

The current version of PVM no longer has a 256-line limit and can use multi-drop lines.

RSCS

RSCS (Remote Spooling Communication Subsystem) uses the store and forward spool handling concept. RSCS version 1 supports BSC communication and CTCA links. Version 2 additionally supports SDLC (Synchronous Data Link Control) links and requires VTAM.

Files are placed on the spool and identified by a CP TAG command. This names the remote destination and sometimes a user-id, eg

```
CP TAG DEV PUNCH site-id user-id
CP SPOOL PUNCH TO RSCS
PUNCH fn ft
```

If the user sending the file has a NAMES file containing the following entry:

```
:nick.TREVOR
:name.Trevor Eddolls
:node.XEPHON
:user.SYSPROG
```

the command could then be:

```
SENDFILE fn ft TO TREVOR
```

All direct-link remote names, indirect remote names and local system names are listed in RSCS DIRECT on the RSCS 191 disk. Other information in the directory includes link address, driver type and a spooling class.

RSCS version 1 is an operating system that is IPLed from its 191 disk. Line drivers are dynamically loaded by name for greater flexibility. Examples of common line drivers are:

- DMTVMB VM to VM via a BSC line;
- DMTVMC VM to VM via a CTCA;
- DMTNJI VM to JES;
- DMTPOW VM to VSE/POWER.

RSCS can be controlled from its own console or from the operator console.

Both RSCS and Passthrough are BSC-based protocols which allow multiple CPUs to be part of a network. The main drawbacks associated with BSC protocols are:

- The CPU rather than the FEP (Front End Processor) controls the basic communications functions. This results in a performance overhead.
- Because BSC is a point-to-point protocol there is an extra overhead if it is networked.
- Because it is a non-SDLC protocol it cannot be part of an SNA (Systems Network Architecture) network.

RSCS version 2 runs under GCS and does not IPL its own operating system. The VTAM virtual machine performs all the real I/O. Therefore the line drivers are run under VTAM not RSCS in the form of the MSNF (Multi System Networking Facility). RSCS version 2 enhanced VM connectivity by allowing VM spool files to be sent to or from:

- a VSE system running POWER Networking via a CTCA or BSC line;
- an MVS system using JES via a CTCA or a BSC line;
- another VM system running RSCS via a CTCA or a BSC line;
- an RJE station or host using HASP or ASP protocols via a BSC linc;
- a 2780 or 3780 Remote Job Entry (RJE) terminal via a BSC line;
- non-SNA 3270 printers for printing.

It is also possible to use RSCS as an intermediate node for forwarding spool files to a third or subsequent node.

VTAM RSCS Network Application (VRNA) was a set of add-ons to RSCS release 2. It allowed data to be routed to the VRNA application running in a VSE or VS1 guest system. It did not offer MVS support.

VTAM

VTAM (Virtual Telecommunications Access Method) was originally a rewrite of BTAM with the interfaces simplified. VTAM is basically a network management product. Line management is moved from the application (as in BTAM) and a special application to manage all the communication facilities is provided. The access method is a set of subroutines designed to transfer data to and from the management application. It was used originally on MVS and VSE systems. VTAM is part of IBM's Systems Network Architecture (SNA) and is the main program running in a mainframe that controls the movement of messages in a network. The other main component of SNA is the Network Control Program (NCP) which runs in the Front End Processor (FEP), eg 3745 etc.

VTAM and NCP are responsible for controlling most of the devices that use subsystems, eg 3270-type printers and screens, distributed processors and SNA/RJE workstations. VTAM controls data transfer to and from 'local' devices, ie attached to channels and to programs. NCP controls data transfer to and from 'remote' devices, ie devices that are attached to the FEP. By letting the NCP perform a lot of the work involved in communications the processor is free to perform other work and does not have to use up CPU cycles etc controlling the network.

VTAM manages session establishment and data flow between terminals and application programs. It also supports the execution of concurrent multiple teleprocessing applications, giving each application a logically direct connection to terminals.

VTAM has the capacity to:

- control the allocation of network resources;
- establish, terminate and control connections between application programs and terminals;
- transfer data between application programs and terminals;
- allow the sharing of telecommunications equipment;
- allow FEPs and cluster controllers to perform some network functions;
- allow network operation to be monitored;
- allow the network configuration to be modified while the network is in use.

VTAM provides operator commands to control the environment. Using the commands the operator can:

- modify the network in response to changes in requirements;

- help to increase the efficiency of the network;
- minimise the impact on the network if part of the network fails.

The actual commands allow the operator to:

- activate and deactivate terminals;
- initiate requests for connections between terminals and application programs;
- modify network configuration dynamically;
- halt telecommunications activities in an orderly manner;
- monitor the network;
- control some debugging programs;
- monitor the status of application programs and each program's usage of network resources.

The operator can start (S) VTAM and stop (Z) it. Display (D) will show the status of specified applications programs, terminals, FEPs, paths, etc. Modify (F) allows the network operator to dynamically change the way VTAM operates, eg start and stop VTAM trace facility; dump the NCP; control on-line testing programs; change polling delay, negative response to polling, session limit, device transmission limit on lines. Vary (V) allows: the network to be changed, ie activating or deactivating terminals, FEPs, lines or application programs; the loading and deactivating of NCPs; a log-on request to an application program for a terminal to be made.

VTAM is started after each IPL. The default name for VTAM is NET. The utility program that is used to load the NCP is called and the NCP is loaded into the FEP. The programs to run VTAM are loaded. Modules beginning USSnnnn, and MODEnnn are loaded in. These are user-created tables that are used for Unformatted System Services (USS) and for session parameters to be used when devices are logging on to application programs (MODETAB). A configuration file and a list are loaded which define the VTAM environment.

Minor nodes are grouped together to form major nodes by defining them in one part of the list file. A minor node is a resource definition for a line, a program, a cluster controller, a terminal, a printer, etc.

Before VTAM can allow data and commands to move between two resources they must both be 'active'. The VTAM component SSCP

(Systems Services Control Point) must establish a session with each resource. For example, if a major node for an SNA controller is activated VTAM starts a session between its SSCP and the Physical Unit (PU) component of the microcode running in the FEP. Next VTAM starts a session between the SSCP and the Logical Unit (LU) component that is part of the FEP microcode for each device. These are referred to as SSCP-PU sessions and SSCP-LU sessions.

When a request to be connected to a VTAM application is sent from a terminal it is passed to the SSCP in the VTAM that controls the terminal. The SSCP replaces the request sent by a standard log-on command using the USSTAB that was defined for the device. When the request is sent by VTAM to the application it includes some session parameters from an entry called DLOGMOD from the log-on mode table MODETAB that was defined for the device.

While a user is working from a terminal and logged on to an application the LU component of that terminal is in session with the LU component of the program. This is called an LU-LU session. A Logical Unit (LU) refers to the point at which a user can join an SNA network. LU1 is a high-performance print stream; LU2 is a 3270 data stream; LU3 is a 3270 print data stream. LU6 is a Logical Unit to allow host-to-host data exchange.

An RU (Request/Response Unit) is an SNA term for message units within the network.

A Single Node Control Point (SNCP) is a network control element within a type 2.1 node. It provides some SSCP-type functions for 2.1 peer-to-peer coupled sessions.

The System Services Control Point (SSCP) is software within VTAM which handles network name/address conversion, device configuration, network diagnostics and recovery. The SSCP is an NAU located on a host node in the network and typically provides support for LUs and PUs with less capability.

A Physical Unit (PU) or Node Type (NT) within an SNA network is an SNA node that controls the node's communication hardware.

System Network Interconnection (SNI) is SNA software in NCP and VTAM which enables dissimilar SNA networks to exchange information. Within an SNA network are Network Addressable Units (NAUs), eg SSCPs, PUs, LUs. These can send or receive requests and responses. An SNA network is made up of NAUs and the underlying path control network. Extended Network Addressing (ENA) is part of SNA (ACF/VTAM and ACF/NCP) that allows extremely large (up to 8 million LUs and 255 sub-areas) networks to be set up.

VTAM commands can be sent from the system console or any authorised application program.

VTAM with VM has always been less than straightforward. The first attempt at linking VM and VTAM was the introduction of Virtual Communication Network Application (VCNA). It allowed a remote terminal entry into any system (VM, VSE, MVS). It had a prerequisite of a VSE or VS1 (not MVS) guest-operating system. VCNA executes under VTAM in the guest-operating system. VCNA communicates with the CCS (Console Communications Services) and CCS interfaces with the usual VM routines. In this way CMS appears to be communicating with an ordinary terminal.

VM/SP release 4 offered VTAM support without the need for a guest-operating system. ACF/VTAM release 3 runs under GCS (Group Control System). GCS (which is described in more detail later) provides recovery facilities for failing machines. VTAM runs under GCS in a VTAM service machine (VSM).

GCS uses VSCS (VM SNA Console Support), which is an updated version of VCNA. VSCS is an application that runs alongside VTAM in the VSM. VTAM controls I/O and, therefore, bypasses the VM I/O routines. VTAM handles terminals, CTCAs and FEPs. VTAM will route data to another node, which can be either VTAM in a guest-operating system, or VSCS. VSCS passes data to CCS. CCS then passes the data to the appropriate virtual machine to which the user is logged on. The relationship between VTAM and VM is illustrated in Figure 12.1.

Using VM/VTAM it is possible to link VM to X.25 packet switched networks, eg TELENET, using asynchronous communication.

VM/SP release 5 introduced TSAF (Transparent Services Access Facility) as a vehicle for LU6.2 connections or APPC/VM (Advanced Program-to-Program Communication). APPC support uses APIs (Application Program Interfaces) through the Common Programming Interface (CPI) which is part of SAA (Systems Application Architecture). Processors can be linked and, provided each has a TSAF service

<table>
<tr><td colspan="4">VM/SP 4</td></tr>
<tr><td colspan="3">VM/GCS</td><td rowspan="2"></td></tr>
<tr><td>VTAM with VSCS</td><td>NetView</td><td>RSCS</td></tr>
</table>

Figure 12.1 Relationship between VTAM and VM

machine, they can communicate using BSC protocols, through a CTCA or a LAN. TSAF emulates SNA over BSC lines. LU6.2 is designed to allow mid-range processors to talk to each other without needing a mainframe. LU6.2 also supports asynchronous (store-and-forward) networking. LU6.2 is a device independent process-to-process protocol and acts as the session manager within SAA.

AVS (APPC/VM VTAM Support) is the VTAM version of TSAF which became available with VM/SP release 6. It allows device communication through an SNA link.

The only VM user allowed to send commands to the VTAM service machine for execution is the user specified as the secondary user-id in the directory for the VTAM service machine, and this is usually the VM operator. A difficulty can arise if it is ever necessary to enter VTAM commands from somewhere other than the console.

VM/SP does not offer a method of enqueue to preserve CMS files when edited in 'multiple-write' (MW) mode. However, if VTAM files (VTAMLST, USS and logmode tables, etc) are to be maintained while VTAM is up, there is no choice but to open these files on an MW-linked disk. Disk corruption occurs if two users (ie VTAM and MAINT) both attempt to write at the same time.

IBM suggests that the various VTAM files are kept on the MAINT 298 disk and the VTAM directory entry links to this disk as its own 191.

Capturing the VTAM Tuning File

VTAM will write pseudo-SMF records to a CMS file on its 191 A disk if the start-up parameter for tuning statistics (TUNSTAT) is turned on. This file is opened at VTAM start-up with a file name of FILE TUNSTATS A and is specified in the PROFILE GCS for the VTAM machine with the FILEDEF label TUNSTATS. The file is readable only when the file is closed, and the file is closed only when VTAM is shut down properly (ie Z NET). If VTAM shut-down occurs near midnight the file can be captured without requiring operator intervention and can be reviewed later during normal working hours by adopting the following procedure:

- The following line

  datea = DATE(SORTED)

  can be added to the PROFILE GCS for VTAM. DATE(SORTED) is a REXX function and datea is a variable.

- The FILEDEF statement can be changed to

  'FILEDEF TUNSTATS DISK FILE' datea 'A1'

  The variable datea contains the current date in CCYYMMDD order (eg 19900215) and the CMS filename for the FILEDEF TUNSTATS is FILE 19900215 A1 (using the date in the example). The result of this is that every time VTAM is started it opens a file with a different filetype. The previous file is, therefore, available for review at any time.

This method has two drawbacks. They are:

- The VTAM disk will start to fill up after a period of time. If VTAM tries to write a tuning record and the disk is full, it will crash. Therefore at regular intervals it is necessary to IPL CMS in the VTAM machine and erase the old files. To prevent VTAM from crashing the mini-disk must also be fairly large.

- If VTAM is started twice in the same day the data from the first start-up is lost. This is a rare occurrence and the data lost should be minimal.

IUCV

IUCV (Inter User Communication Vehicle) manages communication among programs, either between virtual machines (on the same processor) or between virtual machines and CP. System services are a special form of IUCV that provide communication between CP and virtual machines. The module DMKIUC contains a table of system services and module DMKIUB lists the modules that support system services. The names of system services are prefixed by an asterisk (*). The system services are listed in Figure 12.2.

VMCF

VMCF (Virtual Machine Communication Facility) allows virtual machines to send and receive data to and from other virtual machines. It is similar to IUCV in function but older.

NetView

NetView is an SNA network management tool that runs under GCS. It is meant to be the centre of future networks and is also meant to act as the basis of future automated and remote operations. It was initially a collection of management software that already existed, including NCCF (Network Communications Control Facility), NLDM (Network Logical Data Management), NPDA (Network Problem Determination Application) and others.

The Network Communications Control Facility (NCCF) runs as a VTAM application and provides network operator control facilities in SNA (and BSC) networks. NCCF is required in order to use other products such as NPDA, NLDM, etc. It is now part of NetView.

Network Logical Data Manager (NLDM) is an NCCF application that collects SNA session-related information and makes it available to NCCF operators. It is used to detect network faults not explicitly picked up by other network management tools. It is now part of NetView.

Network Problem Determination Application (NPDA) runs under NCCF and provides network error analysis. It collects errors reported by communications controllers, modems, lines, cluster controllers, control units and terminals, and organises and displays error statistics. NPDA is now part of NetView.

The Operator Communications Control Facility (OCCF) runs under NCCF and allows one or more remote systems to be operated from a host system over an SNA network. It redirects console messages from the remote site to the controlling site.

*BLOCKIO	provides device-independent access to mini-disks with support for multiple concurrent pending I/O requests
*CCS	uses a VTAM service machine to provide VM console capabilities to SNA terminals
*CRM	allows an authorised virtual that connects to CRM (the Collection Resource Management system service) to become the TSAF virtual machine
*IDENT	allows authorised TSAF virtual machines to revoke resource ownership
*LOGREC	allows an authorised user to receive a copy of error records written to the error-recording area of CP-owned DASD
*MONITOR	is available with XA and places performance measurement data in a service virtual machine
*MSG	allows messages and responses from CP to be read by a program (rather than having them displayed at a terminal)
*MSGALL	receives incoming messages in classes not directed to the *MSG system service
*RPI	is used by many of the access control programs to allow user access to be permitted or denied
*SIGNAL	allows members of a machine group to signal each other
*SPL	allows an authorised virtual machine to handle logical printer functions

Figure 12.2 IUCV System Services

The Communications Network Management Interface (CNMI) is an access method interface which allows an NCCF command processor to request and receive network management information from the network.

The Network Performance and Reporting System (NETPARS) is a mainframe batch program that is used to analyse performance data collected by NPA or NPM (NetView Performance Monitor).

NetView Distribution Manager (NetView DM) is a replacement for the older DSX product. It allows centralised control of software distribution among processors in an SNA network.

The Distributed Systems Executive (DSX) runs in a central host connected to mid-range systems (8100, Series/1 and System/36) connected in an SNA network. DSX on the host communicates with DSNX on a distributed node. The combination of DSX and DSNX is also known as DM. DSX was replaced by NetView Distribution Manager.

The Distributed Systems Node Executive (DSNX) is software which sits in a distributed machine (typically AS/400 or S/370 with VM) to support unmanned data distribution across a network. The machine with DSNX communicates with a host machine running the DSX software. The combination of DSX and DSNX is known as DM.

SNA File Services (SNA/FS) is a subsystem within NetView/DM which supports the movement of files across a network. It works on a store-and-forward principle allowing the receiver and transmitter to be on-line at different times.

The NetView File Transfer Protocol is a high-performance utility for bulk data transfer among S/370s in an SNA network.

NetView (was network) Performance Monitor (NPM) monitors the performance (data flow, response times, etc) of SNA networks. Data is transferred to the mainframe for analysis. It replaces NPA.

TeleProcessing Network Simulator (TPNS) is a package for simulating networks of terminals, mainframes, FEPs, etc. It is used in conjunction with NPM. It supports TRN connection.

The VTAM Node Control Application (VNCA) is network management software whose functions are now part of NetView.

TCP/IP

The Transmission Control Protocol/Internet Protocol (TCP/IP) is a set of communication protocols that were not originally devised by IBM. IP defines a way of linking computers and workstations together. TCP defines how the data can be used. TCP/IP can be used for LANs (Local Area Networks) (in particular Ethernet). A user-id of TCPIP manages all TCP/IP activity. The user-id FTP manages file transfer requests from remote users on other systems. ARP (Address Resolution Program) assists TCPIP in resolving complex network addressing, for example when one LAN bridges to another. PCs attached to a token ring network (TRN) can also link to TCPIP.

Communications Controller

Communications controllers, eg 37x5, are also known as Front End Processors (FEPs). A communications controller may run EP (Emulation Program) which will support asynchronous ASCII terminals and BSC lines for RSCS, and remote 3270 clusters. The EP is stored in a DCSS (DisContiguous Saved Segment) and is loaded into the 37x5 by the command CP NET LOAD.EP. It is not part of SNA. If SNA is used, VTAM controls the 37x5 and therefore the NET LOAD command is not used. The Network Control Program (NCP) is loaded. NCP off-loads certain line protocol and routeing functions from the host CPU. Under SNA polling is carried out from the 37x5.

The Network Routeing Facility (NRF) is an NCP facility that allows LUs (Logical Units) in different nodes to communicate through an FEP without a host node LU being involved.

Non-SNA Interconnection (NSI) is software that runs in an FEP allowing BSC terminals to work over an SNA network.

The Network Terminal Option (NTO) runs under NCP and is an SNA and ASCII protocol converter.

PU Passthrough is a protocol converter that allows a TRN (Token Ring Network) terminal to talk across an SNA network to a host VTAM despite the incompatibility of the SNA and TRN protocols. It is implemented in FEPs, cluster controllers (3174) and host communications adaptors (9370 and 4361).

LANs

Local Area Networks (LANs) allow separate processors to be connected. For Local Area Networks, VM supports two controllers, the now defunct 7171 Device Attachment Control Unit (DACU), still found at some sites, and the newer 8232 LAN Channel Station (LCS).

GROUP CONTROL SYSTEM

The Group Control System (GCS) is like a cross between MVS and CMS and is considered by many to be a subset of MVS. GCS has only a subset of CP commands and no CMS commands. It is a saved system and can be IPLed by name. It can process REXX EXECs and has its own PROFILE. GCS and its applications run in what is called a Virtual Machine Group (VMGroup) and use CP Signal System Services to communicate, as well as for cross-machine synchronisation. VMGroup and Signal System Services are described in more detail later. The Group Control System is a VMGroup NSS (Named Saved System) common supervisor called GCS.

The VM logo is replaced in GCS by an Unformatted System Services (USS) message. USS messages are defined in USS tables, stored in the VTAM main library (SYS1.VTAMLIB).

GCS Facilities

GCS offers the following facilities:

- Storage management;
- Program management;
- I/O (data) management;
- Recovery.

Storage Management

GCS supports three different types of storage:

- shared read/write;
- shared read-only;
- private.

These three storage areas must not overlap. GCS provides controlled read and write access to its own storage for data sharing between virtual machines in its group. This shared read/write storage also contains the re-entrant code that makes up the GCS supervisor, the GCS trace table, common free storage and control blocks, etc.

There is a synchronised lock facility for both common and local storage. The shared (common) read/write storage can be within a virtual machine and this is recommended for both the VTAM and the GCS recovery virtual machine.

Shared read-only storage is re-entrant code contained in a DisContiguous Saved Segment (DCSS), which resides wholly outside any virtual machine that will use it. The DCSS can contain any GCS-specific code or CMS/GCS code. An example of this is VSAM. The same code can be used in both CMS and GCS. GCS also supports shared read-only storage for application code. This code can have multiple entry points (CSECTs). The entry points are defined using the CONTENTS macro and are stored in a directory module. The directory module is first loaded into the DCSS. The CONTENTS macro defines both program name and entry point. All the program names in the DCSS must be unique.

Private storage can be accessed only by the virtual machine it exists in. This storage is used for data areas and by applications as well as containing the non-shared code of GCS.

Protection of the GCS common storage is achieved by:

- program authorisation;
- use of storage protect keys;
- store and fetch protection.

A GCS application can use the GETMAIN and FREEMAIN macros to allocate storage by subpool. A number of subpool types are available and their allocation is controlled by PSW key for GETMAIN.

The LOCKWD and VALIDATE macros allow authorised programs to use PSW key 0 to access common storage but it is worth remembering that an entire virtual machine can go into a wait state while waiting for a common storage lock! The LOCKWD macro is also used to release any storage locks that have been acquired by the application.

Program Management

Except for programs that are executed from a DCSS all programs are loaded from a CMS LOADLIB. The GLOBAL LOADLIB command is used to specify which libraries are to be searched. The maximum is 8 with SP release 4 and 63 with release 5.

The OSRUN command is used to effect both the LOAD and START of a program. When OSRUN loads an application the application is ATTACHed as a GCS subtask.

GCS uses a subset of MVS macros to implement program management. To load a module an application can use:

- LOAD to load a module into storage;
- LINK to load a module into storage and call it;
- XCTL to load a module into storage and transfer control to it.

GCS also provides the following macros to help control this:

- BLDL creates a directory list of module names and attributes.
- CALL calls a program and passes control to an entry point in the same or another CSECT.
- DELETE frees a module from control of its caller; also deletes from storage.
- IDENTIFY creates a new entry point for a load module.
- RETURN returns control.
- SAVE saves register contents.
- SYNCH calls another program synchronously.

When a subtask terminates, GCS can clean up storage, files, locks, etc if OSRUN or ATTACH are used. A number of other possibilities exist.

I/O Management

GCS provides the GENIO macro, which is the basis for the VM/GCS General I/O Service. General I/O functions usually run unauthorised and support for specific devices, device queuing and device error recovery are all handled at channel program level within the application.

The GENIO macro provides the following functions:

- Device characteristics — GCS uses DIAG X'24'.
- Open device — DASD not supported, program must provide exit to handle interrupts.
- Close device.
- Start I/O — EXCP to an OPEN device; may be queued if busy; uses Start I/O Fast (SIOF).
- Real I/O — must be authorised; requires PGLOCK and STARTR operand on GENIO; uses DIAG X'98'; bypasses CP channel translation.
- Halt I/O.
- Modify — active channel program modified; uses DIAG X'28'.

The FILEDEF command must be used to identify CMS files and CP spool files which can be processed using the MVS/SP 1.3.1 macros: DCB, DCBD, OPEN, POINT, READ, PUT, CHECK, GET, WRITE, NOTE and PUT.

When processing CP spool files the CP commands DEFINE, SPOOL, TAG and DETACH all apply as normal.

All the usual CMS rules seem to apply to GCS support for disk sharing.

Although it is also possible to use any CP DIAGNOSE there is no GCS equivalent of HNDEXT or HNDINT to allow detection of interrupts that occur after the diagnose instruction has been executed.

VSAM support comes with the same problems inherent in using it with CMS: it must use separate ICKDSF formatted disks, and there is no native back-up and restore. Supported macros are: ACB, CHECK, CLOSE, ENDREQ, ERASE, EXLST, RPL, GENCB, GET, MODCB, OPEN, POINT, PUT, SHOWCB and TESTCB. Use of OPEN, CLOSE, GET and PUT will cause a switch from OS to VSE format ACB, RPL and EXLIST.

Recovery

In the event of a member of a VMGroup abending, each of the other members will be able to take appropriate recovery action when receiving the SIGNAL-OUT.

The first virtual machine to join a VMGroup is the recovery machine for that group. If the recovery machine leaves the group, a GCS-supplied termination exit must be taken by all remaining members of that group. The group can be recovered by first restarting the group's recovery machine.

When any other member of a group terminates, GCS automatically schedules the recovery machine to clean up the resources held by that virtual machine. This could involve closing files, freeing locks and cleaning up any blocks in common free storage.

Exits are provided to allow application recovery from a number of situations. A task can intercept and recover using an MVS-like ESTAE macro. An ESTAE is not invoked if termination is the result of a Halt eXecution (HX) command.

The SCHEDEX macro is for cross-machine task scheduling, the task exit returning to the calling member. The TASKEXIT macro allows an authorised virtual machine to intercept task termination in any other virtual machine. The MACHEXIT macro allows an authorised virtual machine to intercept the termination of another virtual machine.

GCS Components

The two main components of GCS are the Virtual Machine Group (VMGroup) and the Signal System Services.

The Virtual Machine Group

A Virtual Machine Group (VMGroup) is one or more virtual machine(s) that have loaded a particular Named Saved System (NSS). The NSS must be defined in DMKSNT as VMGROUP=YES (this forces PROTECT=OFF). Its other characteristics are summarised below:

- It can be loaded only by using an IPL command; DIAG X'64' Loadsys does not work for a VMGroup NSS.
- It cannot be IPLed by device; ie IPL 590.
- The VMGroup NSS is unprotected, ie changes are seen by all members of the VMGroup.
- VMGroup membership gives authorisation to use CP Signal System Services.

CP Signal System Services

Signal System Services is a version of the Inter-User Communication Vehicle (IUCV), and contains an 8-byte message facility. Each virtual machine that connects to the Signal System Service is assigned a unique 16-bit SIGNAL-ID for that group. SIGNAL-IDs are unique only within each group, and if more than one group exists the same SIGNAL-ID may be present in each group.

When using Signal System Services a VMGroup member can:

- receive notification when a new virtual machine joins the group (SIGNAL-IN);
- receive notification of a virtual machine leaving the group (SIGNAL-OUT);
- signal any (or all) members of the group with an 8-byte message;
- receive a signal from any other group member.

In order to use Signal System Services a user must first join a VMGroup and then issue an IUCV DECLARE BUFFER followed by an IUCV CONNECT specifying USERID=*SIGNAL and PRMDATA=YES. The IPUSER data field in the IUCV CONNECT must contain 8 bytes of signal data, a 1-byte signal flag and a 2-byte SIGNAL-ID (SIGNAL-IN). On successful completion of the IUCV CONNECT the IPUSER field in the IUCV external interrupt buffer contains the same signal data and flag as the connect and, if the user specified via the connect flags, the CP-assigned unique SIGNAL-ID.

Leaving a CP Signal System Service (SIGNAL-OUT) is achieved by issuing either an IUCV SEVER or an IUCV RETRIEVE BUFFER. CP will issue a SIGNAL-OUT on behalf of a virtual machine that issues any of the following commands:

- IPL;
- SYSTEM RESTART;
- SYSTEM CLEAR;
- DEFINE STORAGE;
- DEFINE CHANNELS;
- SET ECMODE;

- LOGOFF.

If a (virtual) machine check occurs the SIGNAL-OUT is presented to all remaining members of the group.

Problems with GCS

There are a number of unforeseen problems associated with GCS, and some of these are described below.

- The commands CP ADSTOP and CPTRACE should not be used to trace execution through a GCS segment. The reason for this is that the two commands store special dummy instructions in the machine's virtual storage, and other machines in the group will come across these and will abend. The solution is to use CP PER.
- The directory entry for an autologged GCS machine must contain:

  PARM AUTOLOG

  Otherwise the virtual console will be locked when an attempt is made to reconnect to it. If the problem does occur

  #CP ATTN

  can be entered to overcome it.
- GCS treats filemode 4 files in the same manner as filemode 1 and 2 files. The effect of this is that a mode 4 file created by CMS or GCS cannot be read by the other. No attempt should be made to do this.
- VMDUMP can be skipped without modifying GCS code by setting a PER trap at the instruction before the X'83890094' instruction. This can be found by

  #CP D PSW

  while the dump is in progress. CMD BEGIN xxxx is the PER instruction, eg

  PER INSTR RANGE 417C4 RUN CMD B 417CE
- In the event of GCS becoming corrupted and it needing to be refreshed more needs to be done than simply re-IPLing the recovery machine. Although this procedure kills any GCS machines still running, it does not delete the GCS segment from the group. This is

because CP will hook the virtual machine into the existing segment if it is currently part of any virtual machine's virtual storage. It is only when no virtual machine has it that a new copy of GCS is brought from DASD storage. Therefore, to refresh GCS, all machines must do SYSTEM CLEAR, IPL, or a LOGOFF before the recovery machine is IPLed.

- If either the EXTR or ECB operands are used with the ATTACH command the task block and initial state block for the task are kept until DETACHed by the parent task. If the parent task exits without issuing the DETACH command an A03 abend occurs.
- 005 system abends can occur when I/O is performed to RECFM VB files. With variable block length files, records and Record Descriptor Words (RDWs) are packed into a buffer with a block descriptor word prefix. For an I/O call, GCS calculates the buffer length based on the maximum buffer size in the DCB. This ignores the prefix at the head of the buffer. If a GETMAIN is performed to obtain a buffer for a record that is smaller than the maximum block size, GCS checks the user's buffer for the maximum block length. The consequence of this is that GCS looks beyond the buffer, and may look into an adjacent page which has a different storage key.
- When a GETMAIN VC instruction is issued a minimum and maximum amount of storage are specified. If GCS cannot allocate the maximum amount specified, it will allocate the minimum. With CMS, if the maximum is unavailable the system will try to get the largest amount possible. This difference can cause users problems.
- The JSTCB=YES parameter of the ATTACH macro makes a subtask independent. This option works only from the COMMAND task.

ERRORS

When I/O problems occur under VM, it can be useful to examine the trace table as this keeps a record of I/Os that have taken place. In the trace table X'0B' codes trace SIOs, X'18' lists SIOFs, X'05' is an interrupt code indicating that an I/O request is complete. To get trace table information either the system must be abended to force a dump or the user must be very quick to get the information before it is overwritten. CPTRAP will write a spool file record for some user-ids.

CCWTRACE can be used to trace real devices. It can be used to diagnose hardware and timing problems. VM/XA SP has DATATRACE, which is similar to CCWTRACE. Data from CCWTRACE is written to the trace area, stopping other trace data from being written. These records can be formatted and printed using the CCWTRPRT module.

MAXIMISING NETWORK PERFORMANCE

In order to maximise the performance of any network it is necessary to understand how the network is set up and what it is being used for. This can be done using various measurement techniques that are discussed in other books on communications. In terms of VM and network performance the following suggestions are given:

- With HPO release 5 and above the TERM BREAKIN GUESTCL command can be used with VTAM terminals. This allows a unit of work to be completed rather than being interrupted when the user is in XEDIT mode when a message is sent to the terminal. This saves the work from having to be be re-keyed. If a message is sent to the terminal it remains in full screen mode and signals that there is a message by beeping.
- With HPO release 5 and above it is also possible to retrieve the previous command from the buffer by using the backward and forward options of the retrieve PF key, ie SET PF RET BACK/FORW. This saves time re-keying a previous command.
- If users working at 3270 terminals use Entry Assist, this can improve their productivity.
- The response times on remote 3270 devices can be improved if the SET REMOTE ON command is specified in the XEDIT profile.

OTHER TERMS

The following is a list of the software and terminology associated with communications that may be found in some VM environments but have not been covered already.

ADE

The Application Development Environment (ADE) runs across a network of PS/2s and AS/400s or S/370. ADE is loosely based on ADPS and will incorporate the Repository.

ADPS

The Application Development Project Support (ADPS) was written to provide an application development environment for VM. It is made up of a set of dialogues which support the planning, development and quality control of a development project.

DSU

The Distribution Services Unit (DSU) is a node in a SNADS network. A DSU may be an originator, recipient or an intermediate store-and-forward node.

ECF

The Enhanced Connectivity Facilities (ECF) are a suite of programs that transform VM/SP systems into information servers for PC users (virtual disks, virtual files, virtual print, file transfer with application/character format translation).

ISDN

Integrated Services Digital Network (ISDN) describes the CCITT digital services for both voice and data.

LEN

Low Entry Networking (LEN) refers to an SNA development that provides networks which are easier to manage and support than 'conventional' SNA networks (although with less comprehensive network management function).

NCO

The Network Conversion Offering (NCO) is provided for users converting non-IBM or non-SNA network to an SNA 372x or 3745 network. It can also be used at sites being upgraded from early versions of NCP to the latest version.

NETDA

The Network Design and Analysis (NETDA) package is a tool for SNA network development. It is written in APL and runs in a VM environment with GDDM.

NFS

The Network File System (NFS) is a set of Unix/AIX protocols for data sharing across a LAN.

NIA

The Network Interface Adaptor (NIA) is a protocol converter that allows SDLC products to attach through an X.25 network to an SNA host system.

NPA

The Network Performance Analyser (NPA) is a performance monitor. It is now superseded by NPM.

NPSI

NCP Packet Switching Interface provides FEP support for X.25 networks.

NVAS

NetView Access Services allows users to have several mainframe sessions running concurrently from a single terminal.

OSI

Open Systems Interconnection is a set of international standard protocols and services for communications systems. There are some overlaps in function between OSI and SNA, but they are in many ways incompatible. OSI has now been included as part of SAA.

OSI Layer

The OSI layer is a layer within the OSI Reference Model for Open Systems Interconnection. The seven layers, their names and functions are:

1 physical — the physical medium (wire, fibre optic, etc);
2 link — moving data reliably along the medium;
3 network — creating connections;
4 transport — ensuring end-to-end data integrity;
5 session — session set-up and termination, co-ordination of interaction between applications;
6 presentation — character sets/codes, screen displays;
7 application — high-level application or systems functions;

OSI/CS

The OSI Communications Subsystem is a VM product providing access to OSI, including: high-level language APIs (Application Program Interfaces), data conversion, session layer interface, network management. It is part of SAA.

OSME

The Open Systems Message Exchange (OSME) is an OSI electronic mail application for VM that uses X.400 between OSI environments and PROFS. It works directly with VTAM.

OSNS

The Open Systems Network Support (OSNS) is a VTAM application that supports use of the OSI network layer protocol. It is a prerequisite for use of OTSS.

OTSS

Open System Transport and Session Support (OTSS) implements layers 4 and 5 of the OSI model and provides an access method interface to the session layer. It requires OSNS.

RRAS

The Remote Resource Access Services (RRAS) is built on TSAF for distributed data management. It allows SQL databases to be marked as shared-system resources within 9370 clusters so that SQL/DS data can be accessed by a remote SQL/DS machine.

X.25

X.25 is the CCITT international standard for attachment to packet-switched networks. SNA host node access to X.25 networks is available using the NPSI facility in the FEP. X.25 is part of SAA.

XI

XI is software that allows X.25 packet-switched devices to be connected in an FEP network.

SECTION VI

Security and Performance Considerations

This final section of the book looks at the important aspects of security at a VM site and lastly examines various aspects of performance. These include how performance can be measured on the different versions of XA and the reports that can be produced from the data supplied by measuring.

13 Security

When the early VM systems were being developed some security considerations were built into them. However, because of the high degree of flexibility that is inherent in the system, ways of getting round the native security system were easily devised and successfully used. Indeed, many systems programmers successfully carry out user requests which 'theoretically' are 'impossible' using such tricks, and in the process earn themselves an image of awe-inspiring power. To overcome the flaws in the native security system External Security Management (ESM) packages were devised to extend the level of security. Because these security packages are add-ons to VM and not part of it, they may not address the areas required by a user or may not have the required degree of success.

SECURITY REQUIREMENTS

Many people adopt the principle of 'it will never happen to me' in relation to security at their sites. However, the degree of importance that the trade press has given to hacking, viruses, theft and other computer-related crimes has raised the level of public awareness of these issues.

The implementation of a security package at a site involves a great many trade-offs. This is because total security cannot be attained, and attempts to approximate to total security generally entail unacceptable costs and disruption. When applying protection the security administrator must take into account the following three considerations:

- the probability of a violation occurring;
- the cost of such a violation;

- the cost of protecting against such a violation.

When security systems are being installed, it must be borne in mind that the function of the DP department is to help the company to perform useful work that will enable it to make money and ensure that it is able to carry on its business. If a security system is installed that renders a particular system virtually unusable, it serves no useful purpose for the company.

Software packages cannot overcome problems associated with fire, flood, earthquake, explosions or loss of essential services (typically electricity). Nor can they cope with theft of equipment, physical damage or logic bombs. The areas that they do address are:

- preventing unauthorised access to data;
- preventing unauthorised use of programs;
- preventing unauthorised use of CPU cycles, I/O or storage media.

Some firms may feel that they do not hold any sensitive programs or data or that the only people who could access them are trusted employees and therefore do not require a security package.

NATIVE SECURITY

Native VM offers four types of security:

- Access security;
- Disk access security;
- Restrictions on commands available;
- Address space security.

Access Security

In order to log on to a VM system a user must know not only a user-id but also a password. If incorrect combinations of user-id and password are given, the user will be unable to access the system. The user-ids and their corresponding passwords are usually stored in a file called USER DIRECT. The user-id and password are allocated to the user by the system administrator. It is important that the password is kept secret. When a user logs on, the user-id will be displayed on the screen but the password will not be displayed. This will prevent anyone from being able to read the password. Users should change their passwords regularly so that, should another person discover their password, he will not be able to use it for long. The DIRMAINT utility program places the date the password was last changed as a comment next to the directory entry. It is possible for the system administrator to produce a list of those users who have not changed their passwords recently and remind them to do so. Users should never be allowed to stick a label on their terminal with their user-id and password written on it. One other weak point of this system is that the system administrator has access to all the passwords and therefore needs to be completely trustworthy.

Disk Access Security

Each virtual machine has mini-disks associated with it. These mini-disks are used to store files containing data, programs, EXECs, etc. The user has read/write access to the mini-disks owned by his virtual machine. There is usually a requirement to share data. One user may explicitly link to another user's mini-disk if the directory contains a link password for that user's mini-disk. It is possible to restrict the level of access that a user can have to another user's mini-disk by the use of passwords. There are three passwords available for use. These are:

- read password (R);
- write password (W);
- multiwrite password (M).

The read password allows a user to read the files on a mini-disk but not to update them. Many users can have read access to a mini-disk at the same time. The write password allows a user to read and write to the files on a mini-disk. The restriction is that only one user at a time can be writing to a disk. The multiwrite password allows more than one user to access a mini-disk at a time and also allows more than one user to be updating the data at a time. The fact that there is no mechanism by which CMS users can synchronise updates can lead to problems. The usual solution to the problem lies in using a security package. As with passwords associated with user-ids, it is necessary to ensure that the passwords associated with mini-disks are kept secret. A password of ALL allows data sharing by all other users. This is a reserved password.

In order for one user to access a mini-disk associated with another user it is necessary to use the CP LINK command. LINK commands can also be set up in the user's directory, for example a CMS user's LINK to MAINT's mini-disks. If no passwords are specified against a mini-disk in the directory, it is not possible to link to it dynamically using the CP LINK command.

One problem that the system administrator has when allocating mini-disks is to ensure that new ones are not allocated in the same location as existing ones. This would lead to a security breach because the owner of the second mini-disk would be able to read and write to the files belonging to the first user. This could be particularly serious if, for example, payroll files were involved.

Restrictions on Commands Available

Within the directory entry for each user the command classes that can be used by that person are specified. With VM releases before 4 there were only eight command classes available. Since release 4 there have been 32 command classes available. Each command class has a particular subset of the CP and CMS commands available to it (more details are given in Chapter 9). A user cannot issue a particular command if the user does not have that command class.

Address Space Security

Each user is allocated an area of virtual storage in which to process. This area is called an address space. By the use of tables it is possible for each address space to remain completely separate from every other address space and thus one user cannot see the contents of the memory of another user. With earlier releases of VSE, where only one address space exists, it is possible for a user in one partition to look at the contents of another partition. A systems programmer can get round this restriction.

DIRECTORY

The directory contains the user's log-on password, the command classes that can be used, and the passwords for any mini-disks associated with that user. The directory entries for all the users are combined in one source file called USER DIRECT. The stand-alone utility DIR, or the command DIRECT, can be used to create an object file which is placed on-line on part of the system disk (DRCT area). The USER DIRECT file can be updated using XEDIT but most sites use IBM's DIRMAINT. If an error should occur in the USER DIRECT file it could cause the system to crash and would prevent a re-IPL.

SECURITY PROBLEMS

With the native security that is available with VM there are a number of problems that can be identified in addition to the ones mentioned above.

User Location

It is very difficult to identify where users are located when they log on to the machine. This can be important in preventing unauthorised access to the system. When someone logs on there is no check about where they are logging on: only the password is checked. The problem is made more difficult if Passthrough is used. Passthrough uses the Logical Device Support Facility (LDSF) which means that the user's terminal address appears as Lxxx, where xxx is an arbitrary address, not a real address.

If a user DIALs into CICS or some other teleprocessing monitor system running under a guest-operating system, again the terminal is attached at an arbitrary address. This compromises any security checking that might have taken place on the location of the terminal.

Passwords

At many sites it is common practice for operators to share the passwords for production or service virtual machines so that they can log on to them as required. Because of this it is difficult to discover which individual actually logged on at any particular time. Changing the password is also a nuisance because so many people have to be informed.

Similar problems occur when a user wants only a small group of people to have access to a particular mini-disk. The mini-disk must be given a password and everyone in the group must be told what password to use. Should a member of the group leave, the laborious process of changing the password and informing all remaining members of the group must take place.

If a user has class-C authority he can modify VM control blocks and assume the identity of another user. If he then accesses the other user's mini-disks there will be no password checking.

Another problem with passwords is that they are not subject to checking for obvious values or repeating previous values. It is possible to write an Assembler exit to DIRMAINT to do this.

Other Problems

Auditing user activities is not as well advanced as it might be. For example, use of TAG and SPOOL commands is not recorded; successful AUTOLOGs and LOGONs are only recorded if the operator's console is being spooled. In the latter case the operator could turn spooling off, perform the illegal activity and start spooling again without any likelihood of being found out. If the appropriate parameters are specified in the SYSJRL macro of DMKSYS, the accounting file will record successful LINKs and unsuccessful AUTOLOGs, LOGONs and LINKs. However, the users must write a program to process these records.

Mode 0 files, which are supposedly hidden from users when placed on read-only disks *can* be accessed in a number of ways. The simplest method is probably to define a temporary mini-disk that is the same size as the original mini-disk and then use DDR (DASD Dump Restore program) to copy all the files across to the temporary disk. The previously hidden files can be read on the temporary disk.

If a CMS user has access to an MVS or VSE guest-system disk, the CMS user has access to all files on that disk. This, therefore, bypasses any security package that might be installed on the guest system.

USER IMPROVEMENTS

Improvements to security can be made by the user's making additions to the code supplied by IBM. Within the supplied code are dummy routines that can be replaced by user-written code that performs certain specified activities. These dummy routines are called user exits. There is also a range of parameter codes that are reserved for users. Comments in the source code explain how the code is to be used. Diagnose codes X'100' and X'1FC' are, for example, reserved for users. Some control blocks are reserved for users and can be used for enhancing security.

The following are some examples of user security:

- A table can be used to check whether a CMS user who has opened a VSE or MVS guest system file is allowed to access that file.
- When a message is sent it occupies free memory. If a lot of undelivered messages are being stored, a lot of free storage can be used up, thus reducing the performance of the system. It is possible to send messages without even being logged on, which makes message-sending a potential threat to the system. Many sites therefore restrict the number of messages that can be sent by a user.
- The DIAL command can be replaced by a CONNECT command. This requires users to DIAL guest virtual systems at addresses equal to the real ones. This means that the guest system 'knows' the location of all its users.
- An exit to Passthrough can be used to check the identity of any user from a remote site who wishes to use the local VM system. Usually the code requires that only authorised users who are logged on at known locations are given access.

There are also many ways in which the users can write code that can run alongside the VM system and help with security.

VM SECURITY PRODUCTS

In-house developed security products can be written which modify the module DMKCFC (the module which lists the CP commands and the names of the modules that process them), or which use the exits supplied in routines DMKRPD, DMKRPI and DMKRPW.

If a site decides to purchase a security product the choices that are currently available are:

- ALERT/VM from Goal Systems;
- CA-ACF2/VM from Computer Associates;
- CA-TOP SECRET from Computer Associates;
- OMNIGUARD from On-line Software;
- RACF/VM from IBM;
- VM/SECURE from Systems Center.

In addition VM/CMS Unlimited produce AUTOLINK, which controls mini-disk access. It works by eliminating mini-disk passwords and substituting a set of rules which the system administrator or the mini-disk owner can change dynamically. The new version of AUTOLINK now supports rules for log-on as well as LINK.

ALERT/VM

ALERT/VM was developed by Goal Systems solely for the VM environment. There are no MVS or VSE equivalents. ALERT/VM controls the use of the commands AUTOLOG, LOGON, SPOOL, STCP, TAG and TRANSFER. It can also be used to monitor other CP commands. It makes use of the access control interface and modifies DMKCFC so that its CP command-checking code is installed prior to normal command processing. All ALERT/VM databases are held on mini-disks and it is impossible to share the database with other systems. Passwords cannot be discovered by the security administrator. It is also possible to specify an encryption algorithm that is unique to each user, and is applied to three numbers that are displayed. If the command SET NORULE RULE DEFER is specified all commands issued by a user are passed to CP for checking in the normal way. If SET NORULE RULE FAIL is specified it will reject commands for which no rules exist. In this mode it is similar to CA-ACF2/VM in operation.

CA-ACF2/VM

ACF2 was originally developed by SKK, who were taken over by UCCEL, who were taken over by Computer Associates. In addition to the VM version there are MVS and VSE versions. The database for the VM version can be kept on a mini-disk but if it is to link to the VSE or MVS version the database must be kept in a VSAM dataspace.

CA-ACF2/VM can be used to control the use of any CP or CMS command or diagnose instruction. Access to resources can depend on the command parameters, eg VSE might be restricted to ATTACHing only the VSE disks to itself. CA-ACF2/VM uses the IBM-specified access control interface wherever possible. When this is not possible it uses a system of 'intercepts', in which the address of a CA-ACF2/VM routine is substituted for an IBM routine. It will then front-end, or replace the equivalent IBM code. With CA-ACF2/VM, passwords are encrypted using a one-way DES (US Bureau of Standards Data Encryption Standard) algorithm. All data is protected by default, which prevents a phased implementation of the package. Access is only possible to the system or data if rules are written.

CA-TOP SECRET

TOP SECRET was developed for the MVS environment and was later extended to protect the VM environment. The product is currently supplied by Computer Associates, who also supply CA-ACF2/VM. CA-TOP SECRET forms part of CA-UNICENTER and can interface to CA-DIRECTOR, which performs directory maintenance.

CA-TOP SECRET can control CP commands including AUTOLOG, LOGON, SPOOL, STCP, TAG and TRANSFER. In addition it can control other CP commands and diagnose codes. It does this by restricting the use of facilities to certain user-ids rather than checking parameter formats in any way. Other facilities include special treatment for the diagnose codes that load DCSSs that are also saved systems; and modifications to control the access of CMS users to OS datasets. CA-TOP SECRET does not control CMS files or datasets.

The VM and MVS versions of CA-TOP SECRET can share the same database and VM parameters can be updated from MVS, and MVS parameters from VM.

When CA-TOP SECRET is running it can be in one of four modes. These are:

- DORMANT — installed, but not being used to control accesses;
- WARN — when an invalid request is made a warning is issued;
- IMPL — all defined resources are protected; undefined resources use standard CP authority;
- FAIL — only authorised accesses are permitted.

OMNIGUARD

OMNIGUARD is supplied by On-line Software and is a development of their GUARDIAN product. It is designed to protect VM, VSE and CICS environments. OMNIGUARD protects the whole VM environment including terminals, mini-disks, spool files, CP and CMS commands, SVCs in the CMS environment, VSE and OS datasets. Passwords are stored in an irreversibly encrypted form. OMNIGUARD can be set to protect specified resources rather than all, at an installation.

RACF/VM

RACF/VM is supplied by IBM and was made available after the MVS version of the product. The RACF/VM code replaces dummy routines in modules DMKRPD, DMKRPI and DMKRPW with code that controls the CP environment. The database for the product is a single extent, non-VSAM OS format file. This allows the database to be shared with one or more RACF/MVS systems running either native or as guest systems under VM. RACF/VM manages the commands AUTOLOG, LOGON, SPOOL, STCP, TAG and TRANSFER. Log-ons for controlled user-ids can be restricted by terminal-id, date and time of day. With RACF/VM, passwords may be encrypted using a one-way DES standard. In order for a resource to be protected it must be explicitly defined as a RACF-defined resource.

VM/SECURE

VM/SECURE was developed specifically for the VM environment by Systems Center (VM Software as was). There is no MVS or VSE equivalent. VM/SECURE uses a number of CMS files on several mini-disks as its database. This database cannot be shared between different VM systems. VM/SECURE controls the AUTOLOG, LOGON, SPOOL, STCP, TAG and TRANSFER CP commands. It can also be used to control the DIAL command. VM/SECURE can be used instead of DIRMAINT for directory maintenance. VM/CYPHER can be used to encrypt CMS files. This uses a reversible implementation of the DES standard. VM/SECURE can be set up to protect everything or only specified objects. This can be done using the NORULE REJECT and NORULE ACCEPT parameters respectively.

OTHER CONSIDERATIONS

The password that a user gives in order to log on is stored in the directory. The passwords associated with any mini-disk are stored in the directory. A VM system is therefore only as secure as its USER DIRECT file. Anyone who can gain access to it could gain access to any file on any mini-disk anywhere on the system.

The system administrator must also be above suspicion. A corrupt system administrator could be giving away passwords to all and sundry.

To ensure that data integrity is maintained it is usual to perform back-ups to tape of files that are on mini-disks. Corruption of files on disk can be caused by:

- the DASD becoming unusable;
- the part of the DASD where the file is located becoming unusable;
- the part of the mini-disk containing the directory becoming unusable;
- the data in the file becoming accidentally corrupted or deleted;
- the data becoming deliberately corrupted or deleted during an unauthorised access;
- the computer site becoming unusable.

If taking a back-up can be considered to be like taking out an insurance policy, recovery (using the same analogy) would be like making a claim.

The back-up and recovery packages that are available for the VM environment include:

- Backup CMS from Boole & Babage/The European Software Company;
- CA-DYNAM/B from Computer Associates;
- DDR from IBM;
- DMS/VM from Sterling Software;
- Syback from Syncsort Inc.;
- VMBackup from Systems Center — also an IBM licensed product.

SELECTING A SECURITY PACKAGE

When a security package is being chosen it should be remembered that it is no substitute for good procedures. Furthermore, it will not necessarily solve all the security problems encountered. Before a package is selected, a list of features that are required should be drawn up. The criteria contained in this 'shopping list' should be compared to the facilities that are offered by the various products. The next thing to be done is to ask the suppliers what happens when the security package crashes and what will happen if the package does not start working. When a short-list of products has been drawn up they should be installed and tested. It is never a good idea to install more than one product at a time. One thing that must be ascertained is whether the product interfaces with any other security products that might be installed at a site. For example, a CICS security product may already be installed and in use on a CICS system running in a guest VSE system.

14 Performance Considerations

This chapter looks at monitoring and measuring techniques that are available with VM, in particular VM/XA, and considers performance information and what should be done with it.

BENCHMARKS

At one stage the way that the performance of two or more processors could be compared was to look at the number of MIPS (Million Instructions Per Second) that the processor delivered. MIPS is basically a way of expressing the number of machine cycles that a processor can get through in a second. Unfortunately, with a commercial workload a lot of time can be spent making use of the I/O subsystem and MIPS does not take this into account in any way.

If the workload consists almost purely of number-crunching, scientific/mathematical-type work, MIPS or the alternative FLOPS (Floating Point Operations Per Second — usually expressed as megaflops) might be considered an acceptable measurement of machine performance because the performance depends so much on the raw processing power of the CPU.

IBM occasionally quote RPV figures, where RPV stands for Relative Processing Value. It is generally accepted that 1 RPV is the same as 1 MIPS. Currently, however, IBM use the ITR (Internal Throughput Rate) as their basis for computer comparision. The value expressed is usually in terms of an older IBM box of the same architecture. The result is that the IBM 3090-600S is described as offering up to 56 per cent greater internal throughput rate than some earlier model. This would be fine if the value quoted always referred to the same older IBM box. However, IBM use a sliding scale which makes direct comparison difficult and makes comparison with non-IBM processors almost impossible.

In order to compare the way that two different processors perform work, benchmark tests were created. A benchmark typically consists of a standard workload that is representative of the type of work that is to be run on the machine. Using the results from a standard workload should make it easy to compare the performance of processors from different manufacturers. The problem with these standard workloads is that some were made public and some were not. IBM uses a benchmark known as RAMP-C (Rochester Approximation of Machine Performance) to compare the performance of its mid-range machines, ie 9370s and 4300s. Unfortunately there is no independent verification of the figures produced because IBM has not released the source code for this benchmark. For on-line transaction processing systems the 'standard' test used by most other companies is called Debit-Credit or sometimes ET-1.

PROBLEMS IN BENCHMARKING VM

With a new or upgraded system running VM, the usual criteria that are applied at a site when comparing the new system to the old system would include the following:

- total CPU utilisation;
- number of active users on the system (Q1 and Q2);
- paging-related data;
- I/O related data.

Unfortunately, these are neither accurate nor valid as a means of comparing processor performance. The problem is that most statistics are dependent on the multiprogramming level. The multiprogramming level can be affected by the length of timeslice used. The calculation of the timeslice is dependent on a variety of factors that make it inaccurate as a basis for comparison.

The scheduler maintains three queues made up of virtual machines (eg CMS users) that would like to process. Q1 contains those virtual machines that have completed their last task in a short time; Q2 contains virtual machines that took longer to complete their last task; and Q3 contains very long-running tasks and is typically associated with guest-operating systems. Q1 virtual machines are selected for processing by the scheduler eight times more frequently than Q2 virtual machines and 64 times more frequently than Q3 machines. Q3 users get eight times longer to process than Q2 users and 64 times longer than Q1 users. The problems with processor comparison are a direct result of this timeslicing. The length of time that a Q1 user can spend processing can be different for every processor.

The timeslice is calculated, at IPL time, by timing how long the processors take to execute a complex subset of instructions. The time taken for an 'average' instruction to process is calculated and compared to the time taken to process the instruction on a 370/145. From this result the 'speed' of the processor is calculated and the value for the timeslice (quantum) determined.

Although between 5000 and 6000 machine instructions are carried out, the size and complexity of the instructions do not accurately measure processor speed. Factors that can affect the time taken for an instruction to be executed include variation in:

- processor cycle times;
- storage access cycle times;
- high-speed buffer-cycle time.

The level and type of microcode assists installed can also vary with different processors and therefore the instructions that are assisted (speeded up) can vary.

If the length of a timeslice is longer on one processor than the other it can cause an alteration in the elapsed execution time for some virtual machines. The reason for this is that a user in Q1 will be placed in Q2 if a particular transaction does not complete by the end of a timeslice. If the timeslice is longer, the user will not be placed in Q2 and will continue to process in Q1. Q1 users are selected for execution eight times more frequently than Q2 users. Staying in Q1 can dramatically reduce the elapsed time for execution of a sequence of instructions. The length of a timeslice can, therefore, affect the multiprogramming level, ie a short timeslice will result in fewer users in Q1 and more in Q2.

If the timeslices were identical for two processors being compared, this might still not give valid results because different numbers of instructions might be executed in a given timeslice on the different processors.

Any statistic that can be affected by the multiprogramming level cannot be used to compare processor performance. This makes any comparison of VM systems extremely difficult.

TYPES OF MONITOR

Monitors are used to measure what is going on inside the VM system. Their use carries with it an overhead because when they are active they are using machine resources.

Monitors may be classified as either event-driven or time-driven, although there are a few that are a combination of both. Event-driven systems produce records containing status information after any critical events have occurred to a task. Time-driven monitors collect status information at regular time intervals.

Software monitors can be broadly categorised into two groups. These are:

- On-line monitors, which measure specified resources and report immediately;
- Historical monitors, which collcct data for later analysis.

On-line Monitors

On-line monitors are most frequently used by the operations group, because they continuously measure system resources and can be used by the operators for problem determination and system tuning. The monitors usually report when a site-determined threshold is exceeded. Each site must first determine what criteria should be the basis for acceptable performance so that the monitor has some values to compare the sampled data against. The reports are usually displayed on a screen, and corrective action can be taken immediately to return the system to the preferred state.

A drawback with many on-line monitors is that they have no data storage facilities which means that they cannot be used for trend reporting, historical analysis or capacity planning.

Historical Monitors

Historical monitors sample the state of the system at regular intervals and record the data which can be analysed later. A choice must be made regarding which resources are to be measured and how often.

CP MONITOR

There is an internal monitor in VM that can be used to obtain on-line information about system performance. This can be used to give data to on-line and historical monitors; it can also give information dynamically when it is interrogated using the INDicate and Query commands.

INDicate

The most useful, in terms of performance information, of the INDicate commands are:

- IND FAVOR;
- IND I/O;
- IND LOAD;
- IND PAGing;
- IND Queues;
- IND USER.

IND FAVOR

IND FAVOR will display information about those users who have had the SET FAVOR command issued for their virtual machines. Against the user-id it says whether the user was favoured by the SET FAVOR user-id command, or the SET FAVOR user-id percent command. In the latter case it will give the percentage value and an approximate percentage value for CPU utilisation over the previous eight minutes.

IND I/O

IND I/O will display information about those users that are in an I/O wait, and also the device they are waiting for.

IND LOAD

IND LOAD will display information about:

- CPU utilisation;
- average number of Q1 and Q2 users;
- the ratio of number of pages in store for in-queue virtual machines against the number of available page frames;
- a measure of the delay caused by processor and storage contention;
- paging rate;
- percentage of page reads that were associated with a page steal from an in-queue user;
- a measurement of system load — a measurement of system time used for page services.

IND PAGing

IND PAGing gives information about those users who are in pagewait and whether they are on high or low speed paging devices. Information is also provided about spooling.

IND Queues

IND Queues provides information about a user's position within the various system queues. Some of the possible states are given below:

EX — the user is in an instruction simulation wait.

IO — the user is in an I/O wait.

PG — the user is in page wait.

PS — the user is in a PSW wait.

PA — the user is currently executing on the non-IPL processor in an MP environment.

RA — the user is currently executing on an attached processor.

RU — the user is currently executing on the main processor.

All responses to this command are given in priority order within queues, starting with eligible Q1 then Q2, followed by despatchable Q1 then Q2.

IND USER

IND USER gives information to individual users about their execution profile. This information includes:

- resident page count;
- working-set size;
- page reads/writes;
- page locations.

Query

The most useful of the Query commands are given below. Many of them give information that can be changed using the SET commands.

- Q SRM SWAPQTIME
- Q SRM PGMACT
- Q SRM MAXPP
- Q SRM DSPSLICE
- Q SRM APAGES
- Q SRM MAXWSS
- Q USERS
- Q FRAMES
- Q PAGing
- Q PRIORITY user-id
- Q QDROP

Q SRM SWAPQTIME

With HPO releases up to 5, Q SRM SWAPQTIME will show the actual times spent by users on the interactive and non-interactive swap queues. It is useful as an indicator of the way that paging and swapping are being carried out and whether the values specified by the SET SRM SWPQTIME command are being met.

Q SRM PGMACT

Q SRM PGMACT can be used with HPO to display the amount of page migration activity.

Q SRM MAXPP

Q SRM MAXPP can be used with HPO to display the percentage of the preferred paging area that may become full before automatic page migration occurs.

Q SRM DSPSLICE

Q SRM DSPSLICE displays the timeslice value used by the despatcher for each of the three queues.

Q SRM APAGES

Q SRM APAGES displays the number of DPA page frames that are available for user pages.

Q SRM MAXWSS

Q SRM MAXWSS displays the maximum working-set size value that is allowed, if any value has been specified.

Q USERS

Q USERS displays which virtual machines are logged on at a given time. This can be used as a rough indication of how busy the system is.

Q FRAMES

With XA, the Q FRAMES command displays the number of free storage page frames that have been obtained from the Dynamic Paging Area.

Q PAGing

Q PAG displays the control variables used by CP for paging calculations.

Q PRIORITY User-id

Q PRIORITY user-id displays the priority of a particular virtual machine.

The lower the value specified the better the priority of the user.

Q QDROP

Q QDROP displays queue drop information.

ANALYSING THE MONITOR DATA

With SP and HPO the analysis of the data that has been collected using the VM monitor is usually done using VMMAP (VM Monitor Analysis Program). VMMAP provides detailed analysis of the system and maintains historical data over periods of time which can be used for capacity planning. It also has a GDDM interface. VMMAP produces graphs of:

- channel loadings;
- device loadings;
- location on DASD of I/O;
- peak values;
- seek maps.

SMART, the VM Real Time Monitor (VM/RTM), is used to give short-term analysis while the system is running. It uses DIAGNOSE 4 to sample data within CP. It then processes the data and gives frequent running values of most key values. It gives useful information about peaks and will report when threshold limits are exceeded. It will also display values on demand. SMART can act as an early warning system for some conditions, and can be used to remove from the system users who are idle for a specified time period. SMART features include:

- CP trace table displays;
- exception reporting;
- history data;
- message logs;
- performance information.

The SP and HPO sampled data is grouped into classes and these classes are summarised in Figure 14.1.

Class	Resource measured
PERFORM	general performance counters
RESPONSE	data from terminal I/O
SCHEDULE	scheduler queue manipulation data and resource allocation strategies
USER	user resource consumption data
INSTSIM	instruction simulation events
DASTAP	samples I/O device activity; provides data on tape and DASD usage
SEEKS	provides DASD I/O data; indicates contention by channel, control unit and device; also gives arm movement statistics
SYSPROF	system profile

Figure 14.1 Non-XA Monitor Classes

Monitor data may be collected by state sampling or event recording. State sampling refers to the process of taking a snapshot of the system at predefined intervals. It takes place when PERFORM, USER or DASTAP are activated. They have a small impact on the system. Event recording refers to the process of monitoring all activity after a particular event has occurred. It is used only when trying to resolve a specific situation. This is due to the high overhead when INSTSIM, RESPONSE, SCHEDULE or particularly SEEKS are used. They do, however, provide a lot of information.

A choice must be as to which of the numerous variables that are possible from the monitor classes DASTAP, PERFORM and USER are to be kept.

Many third-party monitors access the trace tables to gain data which they utilise in the production of statistics and reports.

VM/XA MONITOR

With XA a facility similar to VMMAP is available called VMPRF (Performance Reporting Facility) that can be used to produce reports on resource and channel usage, response times, throughput, and disk and tape activity. The XA monitor is controlled by the MONITOR command. It can be used for both sample and event data collection. The monitor uses DOMAINs rather than CLASSes as with SP. Figure 14.2 shows the differences between the classes and domains that are available and also shows the sampling frequency. MONITOR EVENT and MONITOR SAMPLE commands allow the user to monitor selectively at the device or user-id level for the domains I/O, USER, SCHEDULER and SEEK. The command only affects the option specified (whereas SP requires the user to respecify all the classes that are to be enabled).

The monitor command can be used to change:

- the domains for which data will be collected;
- the high-frequency recording interval;
- the sample interval;
- the I/O and virtual devices for which data will be recorded.

The command will also control the amount of data collected (data volume and granularity) by altering the length of the data-collection interval.

	SP		XA	
	Classes	Frequency	Domains	Frequency
0	PERFORM	SAMPLE	SYSTEM	SAMPLE
1	RESPONSE	EVENT	MONITOR	EVENT/SAMPLE
2	SCHEDULE	EVENT	SCHEDULER	EVENT
3	SWAP	EVENT	STORAGE	EVENT/SAMPLE
4	USER	SAMPLE	USER	EVENT/SAMPLE
5	INSTSIM	EVENT	PROCESSOR	EVENT/SAMPLE
6	DASTAP	SAMPLE	I/O	EVENT/SAMPLE
7	SEEKS	EVENT	SEEK	EVENT
8	SYSPROF	SAMPLE		

Figure 14.2 Monitor Classifications

Data Collection

Monitor data is not written to disk or tape but is written into page frames within a user-defined saved segment. The monitor records must be smaller than pages. When the page frame is full of records an end-of-frame record is added and data is then written to the next page. There are no spanned records.

The size of the monitor CPDCSS (Control Program DisContiguous Saved Segment) suggested by IBM is considered by many to be too large. An alternative suggestion is to take the amount of disk space used to hold data for a non-XA system and use this value as the maximum size of the CPDCSS. Smaller starting values around half this size can be used. The monitor CPDCSS can be defined by

DEFSEG name 300-AFF SC RTSD

When specifying the CPDCSS it is possible to determine how much is to be reserved for sample data and how much for event data.

To specify that four event 4K blocks are to be filled before writing out to the virtual collection machine the following command is given:

MONITOR START 4 PARTITION 1024

The command also specifies that 1024 4K blocks are to be reserved for event data and any remaining blocks in the CPDCSS are to be allocated to sample data.

Pages in the monitor CPDCSS are locked/unlocked in real storage as CP records event and sample data. When either a user-defined number of event 4K blocks or a sample interval has occurred, CP notifies a virtual collection machine (using the *MONITOR system service, which issues an IUCV interrupt) that data is ready for downloading. CP passes the location of the segments to the application using IUCV. The virtual collection machine then downloads the data and writes it to disk. Another IUCV interrupt tells CP that the CPDCSS page is available. An application can only receive monitor data if it allocates the shared segment that is defined for monitor data recording.

If problems occur with the virtual collection machine due to lack of resources so that it cannot process the data from the CPDCSS then recording will stop once the sample and event portions of the CPDCSS are full. To prevent such an occurrence IBM recommend that

SET SHARE user-id ABSOLUTE 3%

is specified for the virtual collection machine.

MONWRITE is the name of the application program that downloads data from the CPDCSS to disk (or tape). An example of the directory entry for MONWRITE is given in Figure 14.3.

When the monitor is started the SYSTEM and MONITOR domains are automatically started and cannot be terminated.

Domains

The following section overviews the domains that are available with the XA monitor and how they can be used.

SYSTEM

The SYSTEM domain provides an overview of system performance, resource consumption and resource utilisation. Fourteen different records

```
USER MONWRITE password 1M 1M EG
AUTOLOG AUTOLOG1 MAINT MONITOR VCOLLECT
SHARE ABS 3%
ACCOUNT
IPL CMS PARM AUTOCR
IUCV *MONITOR MSGLIMIT 255
NAMESAVE MONDCSS
CONSOLE 009 3215 T PROP71
SPOOL 00C 2540 READER A
SPOOL 00D 2540 PUNCH A
SPOOL 00E 1403 A
LINK DASDPOOL 002 002 MW
LINK MAINT 190 190 MR
MDISK 191 3380 785 100 XASPOL MR rpass wpass upass
LINK MAINT 19D 19D RR
```

Figure 14.3 MONWRITE Directory Entry

are provided and these can be used for general peformance monitoring. It also provides information on how well CP is managing work based on scheduler and despatcher parameters.

The following records are provided:

- *System data* provides counts for each processor on activities such as DIAGNOSE instructions, external interrupts, machine checks, real I/O instructions and interrupts, SIGPs (signal processor), simulated instructions, soft abends, system page and spool operations.
- *Processor data* provides CPU information for each processor. The information includes fast path instruction simulations, page faults, problem and supervisor state time, SIE intercepts passed to CP and SIE instructions executed, vector facility time, VMDBKs that were despatched with hard affinity, and wait state time.
- *Measurements of real and expanded storage* provide information for each processor. The information includes the numbers of vir-

tual machines in wait for page read, the number of DPA pages that have been taken by free storage extends, the number of pages moved to and reclaimed from expanded storage, pages used by CP for page areas, and the sizes of the various areas that CP has allocated.

- *Communication activity for IUCV and VMCF* provides information for each processor. The data contains counts of how often data was successfully or unsuccessfully transferred between IUCV or VMCF partners.
- *Records of scheduler data* contain information about the number of virtual machines added to the despatch list for each queue type.
- *Records about auxiliary storage* contain information about CP-owned volumes including the sizes of the various system areas that are used for paging and spooling and the proportion of each that is used, the number of spool files that have been created or purged, and the number of times an area was more than 90 per cent full.
- *Records about shared segment use* include the number of active DCSSs and named saved segments, and the number of active shared page frames.
- *User data records* include logged-on and dormant user counts, counts of trivial transactions completed for UP, MP and QUICKDSP virtual machines, and CPU consumption for virtual machines.
- *Records on channel path contention* include information about the number of times any channel path was busy and the number of channel paths that were concurrently busy.
- *Records on the global scheduler* include information about counts of virtual machines in scheduler lists, despatch queue stay times and factors, and the total of all absolute and relative shares for virtual machines in the despatch list.
- *Records on user wait states* provide information on the number of virtual machines in a wait state (ie console function, CPU, I/O, page, SVM and simulation).

MONITOR

The MONITOR domain details the configuration of the monitor itself.

I/O

The I/O domain provides data about changes in the I/O configuration. It includes I/O subsystem changes, eg terminal enable/disable or volume attached to system; details about cache controllers; I/O counts, and busies.

PROCESSOR

The PROCESSOR domain provides data about changes in the CPU configuration and despatcher information such as VMDBK steal and despatcher long path taken.

SCHEDULER

The SCHEDULER domain allows a virtual machine to be traced through the scheduler using system interactions and scheduler list transactions. These include eligible list to despatchable list transitions, modification of scheduling algorithm parameters for the virtual machine, terminal I/O and overall system parameter data.

SEEK

The SEEK domain provides additional data on DASD devices. It can be used to find out the activity of a volume at the cylinder and head level.

STORAGE

The STORAGE domain provides data on memory use and its allocation, expanded storage use, and paging. This includes available list replenishment thresholds and replenishment scans, block paging statistics, CP free storage subpool utilisation, CP-owned volume I/O counts and configuration changes, shared segment detail and shared segment use.

USER

The USER domain provides data about virtual machines and the VMDBKs associated with the virtual machine. The data includes details of log-on/log-offs, interval ends and transaction ends.

Data Volume

The amount of data produced depends on which domains are enabled for both sample and event data collection. The following formula can be used to estimate the size of the CPDCSS required to store the data:

Sample Data

SYSTEM

450 × number of on-line processors

I/O

140 × number of on-line processors
240 × number of cache devices

PROCESSOR

120 × number of on-line processors

STORAGE

80 × number of NSSs and DCSSs
80 × number of CP paging and spooling areas
250 × number of on-line processors
50 × number of expanded storage users

USER

400 × number of logged-on virtual machines running in UP mode
400 × number of virtual CPUs defined to all logged-on MP mode virtual machines

Event data

The total for each domain should be summed and multiplied by a factor of 20. To this value 400 should be added and the total rounded up to the nearest megabyte.

PROCESSOR

200

SCHEDULER

132,000 × number of virtual machines

SEEK

200 × number of devices

STORAGE

150

USER

600 × number of virtual machines

Data Reduction

Data can be merged to provide a system view. If it is, it is necessary that the time stamp on the first record is applied to all the records that are merged. The amount of data collected initially can be reduced by using the MONITOR command not to monitor so many domains or so many devices. Once the data has been used it can be archived to tape to reduce the amount of storage space used.

PERFORMANCE INFORMATION

At most sites using a monitor the same core of data is collected for input into a performance report. This data usually covers such areas as:

- attached processors;
- resource utilisation;
- wait times;
- I/O interrupts;
- multi-processors;
- I/O subsystems;
- storage utilisation;
- paging;
- swapping;

- spooling information;
- number of I/Os;
- I/O wait time;
- I/Os per device;
- I/Os per channel;
- I/Os per control unit;
- storage utilisation;
- amount of storage used;
- steal rates;
- maximum number of users logged on;
- maximum number of in-queue users;
- page rate;
- wait time per page;
- user's working-set sizes.

From this data selected records can be kept for the various subsystems, eg:

- CPU usage;
- I/O;
- network;
- paging and swapping;
- spooling;
- user information;
- performance in general.

The following list contains a brief summary of the type of data that would be collected in each area; each site will need to determine what information is particularly relevant.

CPU Usage

The type of data about CPU usage could include such topics as:

- TVRATIO for guest systems — total time/virtual time;
- percentage CPU utilisation;
- time spent in supervisor or problem program state;
- wait states;
- storage utilisation;
- multi-processors.

I/O

The type of data about I/O could include such topics as

- I/O interrupts;
- number of I/Os;
- I/O wait time;
- I/Os per channel;
- I/Os per device;
- I/Os per control unit.

Network

Typical information about the network that would be collected would include:

- number of transactions;
- response times or host delay

  minimum/maximum/average

  standard deviation

  number above threshold one/two;
- poll delay;
- network delay.

Paging and Swapping

The type of data about paging and swapping could include such topics as:

- page rates;
- steal rates;
- working-set sizes;
- wait times per page;
- system queue utilisation (ie Q1, Q2 and Q3).

Spooling

The type of data about spooling could include such topics as:

- number of print, punch and reader files;
- how full the spool area becomes over time;
- average size of spool files;
- oldest spool file.

User Information

The type of user information produced could include:

- maximum number of users logged on;
- maximum number of in-queue users;
- user working-set sizes.

Performance in General

An overall view of the way the hardware and software has been performing can be produced using the above information. This composite can be used to give a summary of performance to interested parties, eg senior management, end-user department managers, etc, and it can be used as the basis for comparison when new systems are implemented or new hardware is installed. For example, if 200 new terminals are brought on-line, this could be a reason for a decrease in general performance being observed.

Additional Measurements

In addition to accurately measured system data produced by a monitor, it can be useful to include manual input from logs, records and verbal communication with operators when measuring performance.

DATA EVALUATION

Once all the measurements have been made the second stage is the analysis of the results. It should be remembered that each system will be different and any assessment of system load, contention and system utilisation depends on the capacity of the system, its configuration and the performance objectives that have been specified.

Additional information may be derived from the data if it can be analysed by:

- time;
- virtual machine;
- log-on session;
- application.

The load on the system indicates how much work that the system is doing and can be thought of in terms of the rate at which work arrives at a system resource. As load increases so service levels tend to decrease. Indicators of system load include: total number of logged-on users; total number of active users; and the virtual machine I/O rate. In a balanced system the rate at which work arrives is equal to or less than the speed of the device.

Work can defined as a request for a particular function to be performed.

Contention can be defined as work requests having to wait for a resource to become available because other work requests are currently using the resource. Contention can be identified when a task takes longer to process that some 'ideal' length of time. A bottleneck occurs when a large number of tasks are waiting for the same resource to become available.

Utilisation can be defined as the amount of time that a resource is busy relative to the overall elapsed time. The figure is usually expressed as a percentage and can be used to specify threshold values for some monitors. Processor busy times are slightly different because the processor could be in supervisor state or problem state (ie processing work). CPU utilisation may not therefore be a true reflection of the amount of work that is being done.

Analysing the measurement data should identify any bottlenecks or potential bottlenecks. The four most common areas for bottlenecks are:

- CPU;
- central storage;
- paging;
- I/O.

On many occasions it is not easy to identify which resource is the cause of a bottleneck because of the complex interrelationship of the four resources mentioned above, eg, a page-in operation will necessarily involve an I/O operation.

The next stage is to consider actions that would solve any bottlenecks that have been identified or simply improve overall performance. The impact on the system of any change that could be made (or of making no change at all) should be evaluated in depth before that change is implemented. Often an improvement in one system leads to a deterioration in another system. Any solutions will also have an associated cost that should be evaluated at this point to establish whether the gains will be worth the expenditure.

It is a general rule that the removal of one bottleneck leads eventually to the identification of another one and that 80 per cent of any success in tuning occurs in the first 20 per cent of the time spent.

Appendix 1

Glossary

Access mode letter — Each CMS mini-disk is allocated a letter either at IPL time or when the ACCESS command is used. This letter is used as part of the filemode for a file on that mini-disk.

ACONS — A specific memory reference in a program that is not relocatable is referred to as an ACONS (Address CONStant).

Active Disk Table — *see* ADT

Active File Table — *see* AFT

Address — Every page in virtual storage and every device is allocated an address so that a record can be kept of what it is and where it is.

Addressing — This is a technique used by the system to locate every instruction and every device. An instruction to be executed must be located somewhere in a page. Part of the address identifies this displacement. Another part is used to indicate which page and a third part indicates which segment. 370 systems use 24-bit addressing; XA systems use 31-bit addressing.

Device addressing makes use of a three-digit number which indicates the channel, control unit and device being referred to. Virtual machines have virtual addresses for virtual devices.

Address space — An address space is an area of virtual storage allocated to a particular virtual machine.

Address translation — This is the process used to find the exact location of a page in virtual storage. It involves looking up the address in the appropriate segment and page tables.

ADT — The Active Disk Table is a control block that is created when a mini-disk is accessed. It contains information about the disk, eg blocksize and number of files.

Advanced Program to Program Communication — *see* APPC

AFT — The Active File Table is a control block that is created when a disk file is opened.

AIX/370 — This is the current IBM version of Unix which runs only as a guest under VM.

ALOCBLOK — ALOCBLOKs are control blocks stored in cylinder 0 of DASD and contain information about areas allocated on the disk.

Alternate path — If there is a second route from the processor to a device this is called an alternate path. The use of an alternate path when the primary path is busy can result in performance improvements.

APAR — An Authorised Program Analysis Report is a report to IBM of a bug. The term is typically used to refer to the fix to the problem which is sent out on a PUT. A zap is used to install the fix.

APPC/VM — Advanced Program to Program Communication/VM is an SNA facility that allows program-to-program communication. The VM version does not support LU6.2 and is used in TSAF.

APPC/VM VTAM Support — *see* AVS

Application System — *see* AS

AS — Application System is an interactive applications development, decision support and personal computing facility. It provides graphics, statistical functions, business modelling and forecasting. Version 2 was announced as part of Office Vision/VM.

Authorised Program Analysis Report — *see* APAR

AUTOLOG1 — When VM is IPLed a service virtual machine called AUTOLOG1 is started. This can be used to start other disconnected virtual machines, using the AUTOLOG command, and issue commands automatically.

AUX file — When the system is updated using a PTF the AUX file contains the updates to be applied.

Auxiliary storage — Auxiliary storage is storage outside real storage and is usually located on DASD. It is formatted into 4K page slots and is used to store the pages of virtual machines that are running under CP.

AVS APPC/VM VTAM Support is the VTAM version of TSAF. It allows the connection of APPC programs running in non-VM systems.

Binary Synchronous Communication *see* BSC

Bottleneck If more requests for a service occur than can be satisfied by a device, a bottleneck is said to have been created. Bottlenecks usually cause a decrease in system performance.

BSC Binary Synchronous Communication is a synchronous communication protocol that is older and slower than SDLC.

CCS The Console Communication Services is an IUCV system service.

CCW Channel Command Word is 8 bytes long and issued by the processor to give instructions to channels on how to perform a particular I/O operation.

CF Search/370 Contextual Search/370 is a CMS product that enables text searching through CMS files based on full text indexing.

Channel Command Word *see* CCW

Channel To Channel Adaptor *see* CTCA

CICS/VM A version of the Customer Information Control System for CMS users. It offers many of the facilities of CICS at a price.

CMS Conversational Monitor System is an operating system that runs under VM and offers users interactive facilities. It can be used for program development; PROFS, SQL/DS and CICS/VM run under it.

CNTRL file — During source code maintenance the CNTRL file specifies which AUX files are to be used to update a module, which MACLIBS to use during Assembly, and which filetype to use for the TEXT file that is produced.

Common Programming Interface for Communications — *see* CPI-C

Console Communication Services — *see* CCS

Control block — An area in memory used to store specific pieces of information is a control block.

Control Program — *see* CP

Control Program Assist — *see* CPA

Control Unit — A control unit is placed between I/O devices, eg between tape drives and a channel. It ensures that data from the channel passes to the correct device and groups data from devices into blocks for transmission to a channel.

Conversational Monitor System — *see* CMS

Core table — The core table records the contents of all the page frames within real storage (ie it acts as a page-frame table).

CP — Control Program is the name given to the collection of software that controls the real devices and allows virtual machines to exist.

CP/67 — An early operating system for the 360/370 which eventually evolved into VM.

CPA Control Program Assist is a microcode assist available on some processors.

CPI-C The Common Programming Interface for Communications is a superset of IBM communications verbs containing bits of APPC/VM, TSAF and SRPI (Server Requestor Protocol Interface). It provides a high-level interface to APPC, and consists of 30 standard calls available in SAA high-level languages and other SAA subsystems.

CTCA A Channel To Channel Adaptor is hardware used to link processors to allow them to communicate. With VM it is possible to have virtual channel-to-channel adaptors.

Customer Information Control System/VM *see* CICS/VM

DASD Direct Access Storage Devices are typically disk devices used to store data on-line.

DASD Dump Restore *see* DDR

DAT Dynamic Address Translation is the method used to translate virtual addresses into real addresses. This is necessary for virtual storage to exist.

Database Management System *see* DBMS

Data Facility Storage Management Subsystem/Virtual Machine *see* DFSMS/VM

DBEXTENT A DBEXTENT is the SQL equivalent of a CMS mini-disk.

DBMS DataBase Management System is software that controls the placement of data

	and retrieval of data in a relational database. An example is SQL/DS.
DBSPACE	With SQL/DS, DBSPACEs are located in DBEXTENTs and contain SQL tables.
DCSS	Discontiguous Saved Segments are areas of virtual storage used to hold a single copy of shared code. With shared segments space savings can be achieved by keeping a single copy of shared code in virtual storage. DCSSs must not overlap.
DDR	DASD Dump Restore program is used to back-up and restore data from disks. At many sites back-up and restores are performed using VMBACKUP-MS or other third-party software.
Dedicated channel	A dedicated channel is one that is directly attached to a guest-operating system rather than under the control of VM. This can lead to performance improvements because VM does not have to translate the addresses of virtual devices on that channel.
Demand paging	After a page fault occurs the system demands that the next pages containing instructions for a virtual machine are moved into real storage.
Despatcher	DMKDSP is the part of CP responsible for selecting the next virtual machine to be processed.
Despatch list	The despatch list contains the names of the virtual machines that are competing for a timeslice.
DFSMS/VM	The Data Facility Storage Management

	Subsystem/Virtual Machine makes migration of mini-disks to new real disks faster.
DIAGnose	The DIAGnose instruction set allows virtual machines to request CP services. The command format is DIAG X 'code'.
DIOF	The Display Input/Output Facility is a full-screen I/O facility for 3270 devices with VM/SP or VM/XA.
Direct Access Storage Device	*see* DASD
Directory	The directory contains a list of all virtual machines that can log on to the VM system, and their characteristics.
DIRMAINT	The DIRectory MAINTenance program is used to maintain the system directory.
Discontiguous Saved Segment	*see* DCSS
Display Input/Output Facility	*see* DIOF
Display Management System	*see* DMS
Display Write/370	*see* DW/370
DMKRIO	A CP module that specifies the real I/O device configuration.
DMKSEL	With HPO the DMKSEL macro is used to select real storage page frames that can be put on the freelist.
DMKSNT	A CP module (System Name Table) that contains references to, amongst other things, saved systems, eg CMS.
DMKSYS	A CP module that contains many macros which directly affect VM performance.
DMS	The Display Management System is an

	older product used to create panels or menus.
DPA	The Dynamic Paging Area is part of real storage that contains pages from processing virtual machines. The larger the size of the DPA the better the performance of the VM system.
DRCT	DRCT is an area on a CP-owned DASD that contains the system directory.
Dump Viewing Facility	*see* DVF
DVF	Dump Viewing Facility is a problem analysis system available with XA. It is the equivalent of IPCS.
DW/370	DisplayWrite/370 is a word-processing package sometimes used with PROFS.
Dynamic Address Translation	*see* DAT
Dynamic Paging Area	*see* DPA
ECPS	The Extended Control Program Support is microcode available on medium-sized machines that improves performance.
ED/VM	Executive Decisions/Virtual Machine allows users to access, analyse and communicate critical business information. It is based on OS/2 extended edition. It is IBM's version of EIS.
EIS	The Executive Information System is an end-user system for decision-making people.
Eligible list	The eligible list contains information about virtual machines that would like to execute but are not placed on the

despatchable list because of the current load on the system.

Environmental Reporting, Editing and Printing — *see* EREP

EREP — The Environmental Reporting, Editing and Printing program is a problem-analysis tool that reads the error messages sent to the error-recording area.

EVMA — Extended Virtual Machine Assist is a microcode extension to VMA.

EXEC/EXEC2 — Before the introduction of REXX, these two procedural languages existed within CMS.

Executive Decisions/VM — *see* ED/VM

Executive Information System — *see* EIS

Expanded Storage — An area within the processor complex that can be used for paging with HPO and XA. It can be cache mini-disks with XA.

Extended Control Program Support — *see* ECPS

Extended Virtual Machine Assist — *see* EVMA

Filemode — The filemode is the third part of a CMS filename and is made up of a letter and number. The letter identifies on which mini-disk the file is located; the number indicates the type of access that is permitted. The default filemode is A.

Filename — The filename is the name of the file given to it by a user. It can be up to a maximum of eight characters in length.

File Status Table	*see* FST
Filetype	The filetype is the second part of a filename and can be used to indicate the type of file, eg EXEC indicates that the file contains procedural language.
Flushlist	The flushlist is part of the core table and contains pointers to page frames that could be put on the freelist.
Freelist	The freelist is part of the core table and contains a list of those page frames that are free for use.
Free Storage Area	*see* FSA
Free storage extends	When the FSA fills up it takes space from the DPA. This reallocation of real storage page frames is called a free storage extend.
FSA	The Free Storage Area is part of real storage. It contains most of the control blocks and tables used to control virtual machines.
FST	The File Status Table is a control block located on disk which is used to describe a CMS file. The control block is loaded into storage when the file is ACCESSed.
GCS	The Group Control System is software running under VM that allows VTAM to execute under VM. Other communication software runs under GCS, eg NetView.
GDDM	The Graphical Data Display Manager is a package that allows graphics to be created and displayed on a terminal.
Graphical Data Display Manager	*see* GDDM

Group Control System — *see* GCS

Handshaking — Handshaking is a method of improving the performance of a guest-operating system by reducing the VM overhead.

HCPSYS — The XA equivalent of DMKSYS.

High Performance Option — *see* HPO

HPO — The High Performance Option is required to run MVS/SP guest-operating systems successfully with VM/SP. It contains many performance benefits over VM/SP.

Hypervisor — VM is sometimes referred to as a hypervisor because it is a superior form of supervisor software that controls virtual machine address spaces.

IFS — Interactive File Sharing was software that allowed a few VSAM files to be shared under VM.

Input Output Configuration Dataset — *see* IOCDS

Input Output Configuration Program — *see* IOCP

Interactive Executive/370 — *see* IX/370

Interactive File Sharing — *see* IFS

Interactive Problem Control System — *see* IPCS

Interactive Productivity Facility — *see* IPF

Interactive System Productivity Facility — *see* ISPF

Inter-User Communication Vehicle — *see* IUCV

Inter System Facilities *see* ISF

IOCDS The Input Output Configuration Dataset contains the I/O configuration and is used by XA systems. A new I/O device cannot be used unless defined in the IOCDS.

IOCP The Input Output Configuration Program is used to write to the IOCDS the I/O configuration.

IPCS Interactive Problem Control System is problem-determination software that runs under CMS. With XA, it has been replaced by DVF.

IPF The Interactive Productivity Facility provides screen panels and utility programs.

ISF Inter System Facilities is a package that allows up to 4 HPO systems to share mini-disks and spool files. It allows a 'cluster' of processors to be created.

ISPF Interactive System Productivity Facility is a menu and screen management system for CMS environments. It provides facilities for developing and running menu-driven dialogue systems from terminals.

IUCV Inter-User Communication Vehicle is used to transfer messages between virtual machines, or between CP and a virtual machine.

IX/370 Interactive eXecutive for the 370 is an older Unix implementation that runs as a guest under VM. Its replacement AIX/370 has been announced.

LDSF The Logical Device Support Facility was used to allow programs to emulate terminals. This made the use of Passthrough possible. Many of its functions are now provided by CCS.

LOADLIST When the system is being generated the LOADLIST specifies all the modules that are to be used to make up the nucleus.

Load Map A file on disk called CPNUC MAP contains a map of modules in storage, and pointers to them.

Logical Device Support Facility *see* LDSF

Logical Unit of Work *see* LUW

Look-aside entries As a method of enhancing performance, CMS re-orders its list of nucleus-resident functions so that the more recently used ones are at the top and can be found more quickly.

LUW A Logical Unit of Work is the amount of work that must be completed before any modification to data in a database takes place, eg with CICS or SQL.

MAINT The MAINT virtual machine is used by systems programmers for system maintenance.

MHPG Multiple High Performance Guests are available with VM/XA SP. Up to six guest-operating systems can achieve near-native levels of performance. MHPG uses SIE assists.

Mini-disk Real disk packs can be logically divided into a number of small areas called mini-disks. These mini-disks function like real disks and are assigned to virtual machines. Users store files on the mini-disks.

Module — A module is a non-relocatable executable program stored on disk. When it is called it is loaded into virtual storage and executed.

Multiple High Performance Guests — *see* MHPG

Named Saved Segment — *see* NSS

NCCF — Network Communications Control Facility is now part of NetView.

NCP — The Network Control Program is a part of SNA that is loaded into the communications controller (eg 3745). It communicates with the mainframe through ACF/VTAM using a channel interface, and communicates with terminals or another communications controller using TP lines. NCP offloads certain line protocol and routeing functions from the host CPU.

NETPARS — NETwork Performance And Reporting System is a batch program which is used to analyse performance data collected by NPM.

NetView — NetView is an SNA network management product which also offers a degree of automated operations. It runs under GCS.

NetView Access Services — *see* NVAS

NetView Performance Monitor — *see* NPM

Network Communications Control Facility — *see* NCCF

Network Control Program — *see* NCP

Network Logical Data Manager — *see* NLDM

Network Management Productivity Facility *see* NMPF

Network Performance and Reporting System *see* NETPARS

Network Problem Determination Application *see* NPDA

NLDM Network Logical Data Manager is an NCCF application which is used to detect network faults not explicitly picked up by other network management tools. It is now part of NetView.

NMPF The Network Management Productivity Facility is now part of NetView.

NPDA The Network Problem Determination Application runs under NCCF and provides network error analysis. It is now part of NetView.

NPM NetView (was Network) Performance Monitor monitors the performance of SNA networks.

NSS A Named Saved Segment is a copy of the memory occupied by a system after it has been loaded, and then saved to disk. It can be IPLed by name, eg IPL CMS.

Nucleus The system programs that are loaded in at IPL time are the core of VM. They make up the nucleus. Nucleus programs may be stored in the non-pageable nucleus or the pageable nucleus.

Nucleus extensions The use of nucleus extensions can improve the performance of CMS by building logical extensions to the CMS nucleus. Modules can be loaded in to real storage (using the NUCXLOAD command) and used when a program needs to call another user area program. Nucleus extensions can be identified using the NUCXMAP command. They can be removed using the NUCXDROP command.

NUCON The NUcleus CONstant area is a control block located in a CMS address space from address 0 to X'A000'. It is used to store information about the active CMS session.

NVAS The NetView Access Service enables users to have several sessions running concurrently from a single terminal. Its only connection with NetView is the name.

OCO Much of XA is distributed as Object Code Only. This means that users cannot modify the source code.

OfficeVision IBM's family of office products is a series of server-requester products; server on OS/2, VM, MVS (XA or ESA) or OS/400, and requester on OS/2 EE or DOS. OfficeVision is being introduced in a phased fashion. The final phase is to wean users off the old office products (DISOSS, Personal Services, STAIRS, DisplayWrite, etc) and to turn OfficeVision into a true cooperative application based solely on OS/2 workstations.

OfficeVision/VM *see* OV/VM

OV/VM OfficeVision/VM is a version of OfficeVision using a VM system as a server. It provides document preparation, calendar, E-mail, decision support and library services. At the VM end it is little more than a combination of PROFS, PASF, AS (Application System) and DW/370. There is a new SAA front end on the workstation.

PAGE
Part of CP-owned DASD is allocated as a PAGE area which is used for auxiliary storage.

Page
A page is 4K in size. When a virtual machine logs on it is allocated virtual storage space, which is formatted into 4K pages. A page is the unit of data that is moved between real and auxiliary storage during a page-in or page-out operation.

Page fault
If the next instruction to be processed for a program is in a page that is not in real storage, a page fault occurs. Demand paging takes place as the contents of the required page on auxiliary storage is copied into a free page frame. Because the program cannot continue processing until thc page-in takes place, it is interrupted and another program is processed.

Page frame
Real storage is subdivided into 4K units called page frames. A reference to each page frame is maintained by the core table.

Page-in/page-out
Copying a page from auxiliary storage to real storage is called a page-in operation. Copying a page from real storage to auxiliary storage is called a page-out operation.

Page slot
Auxiliary storage is divided up into 4K areas called page slots. These contain the pages of virtual machines that are logged on.

Page stealing Page stealing occurs when page frames that have been allocated to one virtual machine are reallocated by CP to another virtual machine.

Page tables The page tables are used to identify each of the 4K pages in a segment. They are pointed to by segment tables. After a page fault occurs, the page tables are updated to reflect the new location of the page.

Paging The process of copying pages between real storage and auxiliary storage is called paging.

PASF The PROFS Application Support Feature is a set of optional extras for PROFS.

Passthrough Passthrough allows remote terminal users to log on to VM as easily as local terminal users. Passthrough runs in its own server virtual machine PVM.

PC/VM Bond These two programs (PC Bond and VM Bond) together enable a VM host to act as a PC file server.

PERM Part of the CP-owned DASD is allocated as the PERM area. It contains CP nucleus, warm start, saved system and error recording areas.

PL/AS PL/AS is an IBM system programming language that is sometimes used instead of Assembler for development work on VM.

PMA The Preferred Machine Assist is microcode that is available with HPO as a way of improving the performance of guest systems (particularly MVS/SP).

PMAV PMAV is an enhancement to PMA microcode that enhances the performance of guest-operating systems.

Preferred Machine Assist *see* PMA

Prefixed Storage Area *see* PSA

Privop If a guest-operating system tries to perform a privileged operation (privop) an exception is taken and VM or microcode assists will simulate the effect of the privop.

Problem state VM is said to be in problem state when it is processing work from a virtual machine rather than when processing its own work, ie supervisor state.

Processor Resource/System Manager *see* PR/SM

Professional Office System *see* PROFS

Profile When a CMS user logs on a profile EXEC is executed. This profile can be used to specify the environment the person wants to work in, eg set up PF keys. A profile XEDIT can be used to tailor a user's XEDIT environment.

PROFS PRofessional OFfice System provides services such as diary, text management and messaging.

PROFS Application Support Feature *see* PASF

Programmable Operator *see* PROP

Program Status Word *see* PSW

Program Temporary Fix *see* PTF

Program Update Tape *see* PUT

PROP PRogrammable OPerator allows some automation of routine operator activities to take place by automating responses to arriving transactions.

PR/SM Processor Resource/System Manager allows the logical partitioning of a single mainframe (3090E and above) into seven logical partitions (LPARs). It makes use of the SIE assists.

PSA The Prefixed Storage Area is a control block that maps page zero of real storage and contains pointers and flags used by CP.

Pseudo page fault When a page fault occurs for an address space or partition running in a guest-operating system under VM the guest system would stop processing. However, if the guest receives a pseudo page fault from VM it will continue processing and despatch another address space.

PSW The Program Status Word is a double word (ie 8 bytes) that indicates the state of the processor and gives the address of the next instruction to be processed.

PTF A Program Temporary Fix is fix-to-source code sent out on a PUT.

PUT A Program Update Tape is a tape sent out periodically by IBM. It contains PTFs and APARs.

PVM The Passthrough Virtual Machine is the Passthrough server machine used to allow remote terminal users access to VM.

Queue drop At the end of the allotted time for the current runuser a process called queue drop takes place. The virtual machine is put on an appropriate queue and some of its pages may become free for use. The size of its working set when next despatched is calculated.

Queues CP maintains three despatchable queues (referred to as Q1, Q2 and Q3). Q1 contains interactive users, Q2 contains interactive users who are no longer entering data but require more time to complete the current work, and Q3 contains guest-operating systems, as a rule.

RACF Resource Access Control Facility is a security and access control system used to control access to resources such as mini-disks and CMS log-on, etc.

RCHBLOKs When DMKRIO is assembled the status of real channels is stored in the RCHBLOKs control blocks.

RCTBLOKs When DMKRIO is assembled the status of real control units is stored in the RCTBLOKs control blocks.

RDEVBLOKs When DMKRIO is assembled the status of real devices is stored in the RDEVBLOKs control blocks.

Real storage Real storage is the name given to the space available for processing programs within the CPU. It is made up of 4K page frames. It is divided up into a number of specialised areas including FSA, trace tables, DPA and nucleus. SP can address main memory up to 16MB, HPO can address up to 64MB, and XA can address up to 2GB.

Remote Spooling Communication Subsystem *see* RSCS

Resource Access Control Facility — *see* RACF

Response Time Monitor — *see* RTM

Restructured extended executor — *see* REXX

REXX — The Restructured EXtended eXecutor is a combined programming and job-control language. It is now part of SAA.

RMSIZE — With HPO systems the RMSIZE is specified in the DMKSYS SYSCOR macro. It specifies the size of the DPA to be available above the 16MB line.

RSCS — Version 1 of the Remote Spooling Communication Subsystem runs in its own address space; version 2 runs under GCS. It allows VM to transfer spool files to remote unit record devices (ie printers and card readers) and other CPUs.

RSSIZE — The RSSIZE option on the DMKSYS SYSCOR macro is used with HPO systems to specify the size of the extended V=R area.

RTM — The Response Time Monitor is a hardware facility that is optional on some terminal control units. It collects ranges of response times for each device. The information can be sent to NLDM or NetView.

Runuser — The virtual machine that is currently being executed is referred to as the runuser.

SAA — Systems Application Architecture is a set of standard interfaces developed by

IBM to allow programs written for one operating system to run on another.

Scheduler DMKSCH arranges virtual machines that are logged on, into queues for despatching. It is a component of the SRM.

SDF The System Data File in XA contains information about DCSSs and NSSs.

SDLC Synchronous Data Link Control is the communication protocol used with SNA. It is faster than BSC.

SE The Software Engineering facility controls and manages source code, object code, documentation, etc during software development.

Segments A virtual storage segment is 64K in size for SP and HPO systems and 1024K for XA. Segments are made up of 4K pages. Segment tables contain pointers to segments.

Segment tables Segment tables contain pointers to page tables and are used to locate pages in real storage.

Server (service) machine A service machine is a virtual machine that is available for use by other virtual machines. Examples include DIRMAINT, SFS, SMART, SQL/DS.

Serviceability Enhancement Support stage II (SES-II) Automates the maintenance procedure with XA systems.

SFBLOK A spool file control block contains information about files in the spool.

SFS The Shared File System allows file-sharing at the file level rather than at the mini-disk level. SFS files are held in pools and managed by a file-server machine.

Shadow page tables Shadow page tables are used by CP as a mechanism for mapping from guest-operating system virtual addresses to real addresses.

Shadow Table Bypass Assist *see* STBA

Shared File System *see* SFS

SIE The Start Interpretive Execution command is used by VM/XA SP to start the execution of a guest system.

SIO The Start I/O command was issued by virtual machines to initiate an I/O operation.

SIOF The Start I/O Fast is used by guest-operating systems as a way of allowing them to continue despatching another partition or address space while the I/O request from the first one is queued.

SIPO/E The System Installation Productivity Option/Extended was introduced to make the installation of new VM systems straightforward.

Small Programming Enhancement *see* SPE

SMART The run-time name for VM/RTM is SMART. It runs in a server virtual machine and gives on-line information about the state of the system.

SNA Systems Network Architecture is a set of definitions from IBM about the protocols for communication between terminals, applications and programs.

Software Engineering *see* SE

SolutionPac A SolutionPac is an attempt to integrate a range of products (eg menus have been made more consistent) to make installation and initial use easier.

SPE A Small Programming Enhancement is an enhancement to CP sent out on a PUT.

SPOOL Part of the TEMP area on CP-owned DASD is used to store spool files. It is called the SPOOL.

Spool files Spool files are made up of reader, printer and punch files. They are stored in the SPOOL.

SQL The Structured Query Language is a standard language used to access relational databases, particularly SQL/DS.

SQL/DS Structured Query Language/Data System is a relational database that runs under VM and VSE.

SRM The System Resource Manager is responsible for the optimisation of work throughput and resource usage. Its subcomponents are the scheduler and the despatcher.

SSCH Activity in a subchannel is started by the processor in XA systems using the Start SubCHannel command.

Start Input/Output *see* SIO

Start Input/Output Facility *see* SIOF

Start Interpretive Execution *see* SIE

Start Subchannel *see* SSCH

STBA The Shadow Table Bypass Assist is microcode that improves the performance of guest systems that despatch more than one address space (eg MVS).

Structured Query Language *see* SQL

Structured Query Language/Data System *see* SQL/DS

Supervisor state When the processor is despatching instructions from CP rather than from a virtual machine it is said to be in supervisor state.

SWAP With HPO, groups of pages called swap sets can be moved from real storage to an area of auxiliary storage defined as the SWAP area. SWAP areas exist on CP-owned DASD.

Swapping The movement of blocks of pages from real storage to auxiliary storage (swap-out) or from auxiliary storage to real storage (swap-in) is called swapping. This process is available on HPO systems as a way of improving performance.

Swap queue Swap queues exist for interactive and non-interactive users with HPO. Users on the swap queue may have their pages swapped out.

Swap tables Swap tables contain pointers to the location of swapped pages on disk.

Synchronous Data Link Control *see* SDLC

SYSCOR The maximum real storage size that VM can utilise is specified by the SYSCOR macro.

SYSGEN SYStem GENeration refers to the process of creating a new operating system. The SYSGEN is also carried out after modifications have been made to an existing system.

SYSJRL The SYSJRL macro specifies the options to be used when recording (journalling) resource usage.

SYSMON The SYSMON macro specifies what performance monitoring data is to be collected.

SYSOPR The SYSOPR macro specifies the userids of the system operator, and the user to receive a system dump in the event of a restart.

SYSOWN The SYSOWN macro informs CP which are the CP-owned volumes.

SYSPAG The SYSPAG macro in DMKSYS specifies parameters to be used in paging and swapping.

SYSRES The SYSRES macro sets up the IPL (SYSRES) volume. It specifies the unit address and device type, and also areas for the nucleus programs, error recording and warm-start areas.

System Data File *see* SDF

System Installation Productivity Option/Extended *see* SIPO/E

System Resource Manager *see* SRM

Systems Applications Architecture *see* SAA

Systems Network Architecture *see* SNA

TDSK Part of the CP-owned DASD is allocated as TDSK. This space can be used by virtual machines for the creation of temporary mini-disks.

TEMP Part of the CP-owned DASD is allocated as TEMP. It is used for spooling and paging.

Thrashing If the load on the system forces CP to page heavily it may be forced to steal pages. If this occurs too often the system is described as thrashing, it spends more time in supervisor state than problem state and performance deteriorates.

Timeslice A timeslice is a unit of time that is allocated to virtual machines. If they do not complete all the required instructions within that timeslice the virtual machine may be moved into a different queue (eg from Q2 to Q3). The length of the timeslice depends on the processor.

Trace table The trace table is located in real storage and stores information about recent events. The information can be used when debugging. Information is stored in a wraparound manner so that new data overwrites existing data.

Transient area The transient area exists in a CMS virtual machine. It is 8K in size (addresses X'E000' to X'FFFF') and can be used to store nucleus extension programs that can be invoked from the user area.

Transparent Services Access Facility *see* TSAF

Trimming Trimming refers to pages from the working set of a user being placed on the flushlist. The pages are the ones that have not been referenced and have not been placed in a swap set.

Trim set The trim set refers to pages from a virtual machine that could be trimmed.

TSAF Transparent Services Access Facility is the peer-to-peer network software that runs under VM. It provides transparent user access to multiple (up to eight) 370 devices.

TTIME TTIME refers to the total time taken for a guest system to complete a piece of work. It includes the time spent in supervisor state.

User area The user area is part of a CMS address space in which most applications run.

V=F Virtual=Fixed refers to the up to five guest systems that can be run in fixed real storage with XA.

V=R Virtual=Real refers to running a guest-operating system within VM's real storage.

VCNA VTAM Communication Network Application ran under VTAM in a guest system (VSE or VS1) and provided access to VM applications from SNA terminals. It was replaced by VSCS.

VCTBLOK The Virtual ConTrol unit BLOK contains information about the status of each control unit in a virtual machine's configuration.

VDEVBLOK The Virtual DEVice BLOK contains information about the status of each I/O device in a virtual machine's configuration.

Virtual address A virtual address refers to either a virtual storage location or to a virtual I/O device.

Virtual Communication Network Application *see* VCNA

Virtual device Each virtual machine is defined in the directory with a number of devices.

	These devices do not actually exist but to the user of the virtual machine they appear to exist.
Virtual Interval Timer Assist	*see* VITA
Virtual Machine Assist	*see* VMA
Virtual Machine Communication Facility	*see* VMCF
Virtual RSCS Network Application	*see* VRNA
Virtual storage	The storage space available to logged-on virtual machines that appears to be in the CPU is called virtual storage. Virtual storage spans real storage and auxiliary storage.
Virtual Storage Access Method	*see* VSAM
Virtual Telecommunications Access Method	*see* VTAM
VITA	The Virtual Interval Timer Assist is a microcode that improved the performance of some older operating systems running under VM.
VM	The Virtual Machine hypervisor controls real devices and allows operating systems (CMS, MVS, etc) to run under it using the real devices.
VMA	The Virtual Machine Assist is microcode that improves the performance of guest systems.
VMBLOK	The VMBLOK is a control block that contains detailed information about each virtual machine that is logged on to VM, including its user-id. The XA equivalent is VMDBK.

VMCF The Virtual Machine Communication Facility allows the transfer of data between virtual machines.

VMDBK VMDBK is an XA control block that is equivalent in function to the VMBLOK.

VM/ESA The Enterprise Systems Architecture version of VM is predicted as the successor to current VM products on large mainframes.

VMFASM The VMFASM program is used to combine source code and PTFs.

VMFLOAD The VMFLOAD program is used to create a new CP nucleus.

VM/IS Virtual Machine/Integrated System is an easy-to-install version of SP for small machines (9370s).

VMMAP VMMAP is used with SP and HPO systems as an historical monitor. It produces reports of what has happened to the system.

VM/PPF The VM Performance Planning Facility is a performance modelling tool that can be used with SP and HPO.

VM/PRF The VM Performance Reporting Facility is the XA equivalent to VMMAP.

VM/RSP VM Remote System Programming Support is a support service available at VM/IS installation.

VM/RTM The VM Real Time Monitor is an online monitor that is better known as SMART.

VM SNA Console Support *see* VSCS

VM/SP The VM (System Product) is the basic version of VM that is used on small and medium systems. It is sometimes called 'vanilla'.

VM/SP HPO VM/SP with High Performance Option is used on larger systems that are running MVS/SP as a guest system.

VM/XA SF The System Facility version of VM/XA (eXtended Architecture) was used to support MVS/XA as a guest but it also required a VM guest to provide CMS and other functions.

VM/XA SP A full function version of VM utilising 31-bit addressing and giving up to 2 GB of storage. It allows MVS/XA or MVS/ESA systems to run as guests and provides an enhanced version of CMS and other facilities.

VRNA The VTAM RSCS Network Application is a supplement to RSCS allowing data to be routed to applications under non-VM operating systems.

VSAM The Virtual Storage Access Method is available as VSE/VSAM for CMS users. It is a complex system for data storage and retrieval on disk.

VSCS VM SNA Console Support runs under GCS and allows applications from SNA terminals to access VM.

VTAM The Virtual Telecommunications Access Method is a component of SNA that runs under GCS. It manages data flow between terminals and applications.

VTAM Communication Network Application *see* VCNA

VTAM RSCS Network Application — *see* VRNA

VTIME — VTIME is the time that a guest system takes to complete an operation. It does not include any time spent by VM in supervisor state.

Working set — The working set for a virtual machine is the number of page frames in real storage that it currently has allocated to it or that it will require in order to process. The working-set size required for a virtual machine is recalculated at queue drop time.

XEDIT — The eXtended EDITor is a comprehensive editor available to CMS users.

Appendix 2

Bibliography

Christopher D, *Tools and Methods Available for In-depth VM Performance Analysis,* CMG, 1988

Dunshire R, *Processor Performance Comparison Problems in VM/SP and VM/SP HPO,* CMG, 1988

Eckols S, *VM/CMS Commands and Concepts,* Mike Murach, 1988

Eckols S, *VM/CMS XEDIT Commands and Features,* Mike Murach, 1988

Eddolls T, *VM Performance Management,* McGraw-Hill, 1989

Fosdick H, *VM/CMS Handbook for Programmers, Users and Managers,* Hayden Books, 1987

The Handbook of IBM Terminology, Xephon, 1989

McClain G R, *VM and Departmental Computing,* McGraw-Hill, 1988

McClain G R, ed, *VM Applications Handbook,* McGraw-Hill, 1989

New Directions in VM, Xephon, 1987

Owen R, *Analysing the New VM/XA Monitor Records,* UKCMG, 1989

Page J G, *VM/XA Monitor Data: An Architected Data Source,* CMG, 1988

Planning for Capacity, UKCMG, 1988

Ryall P R, *CMS Performs,* UKCMG, 1988

Shum A, *Modelling PR/SM, MDF, and VM,* UKCMG, 1989

Software Performance Monitors, Xephon, 1987

VM Performance, Xephon, 1988

VM Performance in Practice, Xephon, 1986

VM Software in Practice, Xephon, 1989

VM Update, Xephon, 1986

Walmsley A, *Interpreting RMF Reports under VM,* UKCMG, 1989

Index

24-bit addressing 28, 105
26-bit addressing 105
31-bit addressing 27, 28, 105
360/67 24
370/145 94, 255
370E—SET command 62
3080 27, 31, 62, 90, 200, 205
3082 7
3087 19
3089 19
3090 5, 7, 27, 29, 31, 62, 90, 99, 100, 200, 205, 253
3092 7
3094 28
3270 211
3274 17
3275 17
3380 11, 201
3420 8
3480 8
3725 17
3800 31
3880 11
4300 24, 62
4341 31

4381 31, 60, 90
7171 211, 225
8232 225
9370 25, 31, 60, 70

abend 77, 105, 266
ACCESS 16, 159
ACONS 146
active wait 90
address translation 103
ADE 234
ADPS 234
ADSTOP command 81
ADT 51
affinity—SET command 62
AFT 51
AIX 21
ALOCBLOK 41, 51
ALU 5, 100
AMSERV 150
APAGES—SET SRM command 66
APAR 71-72, 73, 114
API 218
APL 30
APPC/VM 188, 218
archive 8
ASCII 211, 224
assists 57-62
autodump 77
AUTOLOG1 50, 54-55
autopoll—SET command 64
AUX file 71-73, 75
auxiliary storage 99-103, 121, 122, 131
AUXLCL 75
AUXSP 75
AUXTMT 75
AVS 27, 28, 219

back-up 8, 39
benchmarks 253-256
block paging 122, 129
BMX—SET command 64
BSC 212-214, 219, 221, 224

BSEPP	24
BTAM	62, 214
bucket	73
cache	11, 27, 28
CCS	218
CCW	62, 131, 201, 212
CEC	5
central storage	5
channel	25, 27, 61, 64, 199, 201
channel path	7
CICS	186, 212
CKD	13, 189, 195
CKPT start	39, 54
CMS	3, 4, 16, 19, 20, 24, 29, 31, 38, 42, 43, 55, 70, 72, 73, 83, 112, 114, 117, 139-189, 194, 195, 199, 212, 225-227, 244, 247
CMS commands	158-165
CMSSTOR	146
CNMI	223
CNTRL file	70, 73, 75, 76
COLD start	45, 54
command classes	141-142
connect time	203
console	5, 23, 139, 143
console block	50-51, 81, 112, 144, 245
control register	7
COPY command	159, 166, 189
core storage	5, 99
core table	103, 123, 125
CP (Control Program)	3, 36, 43, 44, 48, 50, 53, 55, 58, 61, 69, 73, 87, 89, 94-96, 102, 103, 105, 112, 124, 134, 194, 205, 212, 244, 266, 267, 269
CP FMT module	83
CP FORMAT command	70

CP-owned DASD 35-43, 47, 116, 122, 143, 154, 193, 195, 268
CP-system DASD 193, 194
CP/40 23, 24
CP/67 24
CPA assist 58, 60
CPDCSS 117, 118, 264-265, 269
CPDUMP 80
CPE 7
CPEREP 38
CPI 218
CPNSS 117
CPTRAP 81, 233
CPU 5, 64, 214, 254
CRT 16
CTCA 214, 218, 219

DASD 5, 11, 13, 19, 27, 36, 99, 126, 184, 193-210, 251, 268
DAT 91
data evaluation 274-275
DCF 181, 182
DCSS 40, 45, 110, 116-118, 165, 166, 181, 184, 224, 226, 267
DCSS-M 117
DCSS-S 117
DDR 83, 195, 246
deadline priority 93, 96
DEBUG 77
debugging 81
DEFINE 161, 195
DEFSEG 116
DEFSYS 116
demand paging 100
despatchable list 93
despatcher (DMKDSP) 19, 95
despatching priority 96-97
DETACH 16, 159
DFSMS 188
DIAGNOSE 43, 61, 80, 117, 195, 205, 246, 266

DIAL 146, 212, 245, 247
DIRECT command 42, 83
directory 13, 41, 83, 118, 140-144, 187, 188, 194, 242-243, 244-245, 250, 251
DIRMAINT 42, 243, 246
disabled wait state 44, 77-79
disaster recovery 81-83
DISKMAP 42
DISPLAY H 81
DMK prefix 69, 71
DMKBOX 73, 146
DMKCFC 247
DMKCKP 70
DMKCPE 70, 105
DMKDEF 41
DMKFCB 46
DMKFMT 35, 36, 41, 42, 47, 48, 193
DMKFREE 115
DMKFRET 115
DMKIOQ 205
DMKIOS 80
DMKIOT 80
DMKPGT 41
DMKRIO 43, 44, 51, 69, 73, 105, 118, 194, 205
DMKRPD 247
DMKRPI 247
DMKRPW 247
DMKSEL 124
DMKSNT 43, 44-46, 69, 73, 115, 116, 194
DMKSYS 36, 40, 41, 43, 46-48, 69, 73, 110, 111, 115, 118, 126, 193, 246
DMKUCB 46
DMKUCC 46
DMKUSS 46
DMS 178
DMS prefix 69
DOS—SET command 84, 150

DPA 69, 100, 105, 109, 110-111, 112, 114, 115, 116, 118-119, 121, 123, 126
DPR 200, 201, 267
DRAIN 54
DRCT 35, 36, 41-43, 48, 193
DSE 7
DSF module 83
DSNX 223
DSPBUF—SET SRM command 66
DSU 234
DSX 223
DUMP 35, 43, 81
dumps 80-81
DVF 19
DW/370 181-182

EBCDIC 211
ECF 234
ECPS assist 58, 60
eligible list 93
eligible queue 67
eligible user 91
ENA 218
enabled wait state 77-80
EP 17
ERASE 163
EREP 48
EVMA assist 58, 60
EXDC 7, 200
EXEC 42, 70, 73, 114, 144, 162, 165, 167, 172, 194, 225, 243
EXECDROP 162
EXECLOAD 162, 165
execution element 5-7
execution wait (EX) 89
expanded Storage (XSTOR) 5, 28, 99, 103
external interrupt 90

FAVOR—SET command 64
FBA 13, 189, 195

FCB 40, 46
FEP 17, 62, 193, 214-218, 224
FILEDEF command 77, 83, 162
filemode 150
filename 150
filetype 42, 150
FLOPS 253
flushlist 122, 123
FORCE 114
FORCE start 39, 54
FORMAT 161, 193-195
formatting 83
free storage extend 112
freelist 123-125
FRETRAP 114
FSA 16, 112-115, 118, 182, 194
FST 51
full duplex 8

GCS 20, 21, 214, 218, 221, 225-232
GENMOD command 83, 146
GLOBAL command 77, 83
GLOBALV 162, 166
guest-operating system 129-135

handshaking 129-131
HCPDEV 51
HCPFRE 115
HCPRIO 43, 44
HCPSYS 43, 48-50, 110, 111, 118, 129
HDA 13
hypervisor 3, 21

I/O 193-210
I/O interrupt 90, 91
I/O path 199-200
I/O performance 207-210
I/O wait 89
IABIAS—SET SRM command 66

IAE 7
IBUF—SET SRM command 66
IDLE wait 88
idle user (dormant) 91
IML 53
IND command 257-259
information centre 31
instruction element 7
interrupts 90-91, 102
IOWAIT 204
IOASSIST 64
IOCDS 44
IOCP 83, 207
IPCS 19, 24
IPF 55
IPL 35, 36, 39, 44, 53-55, 58, 70, 94, 115, 116, 123, 131, 142, 143, 148, 216
ISDN 234
ISMF 189
ISPF 177-178, 181
ITR 253
IUCV 109, 184, 220-221, 265, 267
IUCV assist 58, 60

LAN 224-225
LDSF 211, 212, 245
LDUBUF—SET SRM command 66
LEN 234
LINK 16, 140, 144, 159, 198, 244
LISTFILE 163
load map 51
LOADER 70
LOADLIST 69, 70, 105, 118
LOCK 119
loops 80
LOPER 57
LPAR 29, 62
LU 217-218, 224
LUW 184, 185

matching check interrupt	90
MACLIB	74, 77, 83
macro file	73, 74
main storage	5, 100
MAINT	42, 55, 71, 72, 140, 144, 194, 219, 244
MAXPP—SET SRM command	66
MAXUSER—SET command	64
MAXWSS—SET SRM command	66
MDISK	42, 143-144
MHPG	30, 135
MIGRATE	114, 118
mini-disk	4, 11, 13, 16, 140, 150, 159, 166, 183, 185, 194-199, 243, 250, 251
MINNUMSS—SET SRM command	66, 122, 123
MINWS—SET command	64, 122
MIPS	253
modem	17
module	19, 43, 70, 75, 83, 165
monitor	111, 256-270, 265
MSG	162
MSNF	214
multiple address space	27, 29, 61
multiplexing	8
multiprocessing	100
multiprogramming	100, 255
MVS	3, 21, 24, 27, 28, 29, 30, 31, 61, 67-68, 94, 109, 131, 134, 143, 172, 177, 183, 187, 188, 205, 212, 214, 215, 246, 247
NAME3800	44-45, 194
NAMELANG	44-45, 194
NAMENCP	44-45, 194
NAMES command	57
NAMESYS	44-45, 194
NAU	217-218
NCCF	221
NCO	234-235
NCP	17, 215, 216, 217, 224

NETDA 235
NETPARS 223
NetView 21, 221
NetView DM 223
NFS 235
NIA 235
NLDM 221
No-op 58
non-paging mode 131
NOTE 162
NOTRANS—SET command 131
NPA 235
NPDA 221
NPM 223
NPSI 235
NRF 224
NSI 224
NSS 40, 45, 114, 115-118, 225, 269
NT 217
NTO 224
NUCEXT 146
nucleus 19, 36, 69, 70, 73, 105-106
NUCON 144
NUCXLOAD 165
NVAS 235

OCCF 221
OSI 235, 236
OSI/CS 236
OSME 236
OSNS 236
OTSS 236
OV/VM 182
OVRD 35, 43

PAGE 38, 41, 47-48, 126
page addresses 129
page fault 122, 123
page frame 66, 100, 102, 121-124
page slot 100, 129
page stealing 102

page table 102-103, 113, 122, 135
page wait 89
page-in 66, 100, 102, 121, 123
page-out 100, 123, 126, 128
PAGEX—SET command 64, 131
PAGING—SET command 64-65
paging 38, 66, 184
parity 10
PASF 20, 181
passthrough 21, 57, 212-213, 245, 247
PE 72
PEEK 162
PER command 81
performance information 270-273
PERM 35, 36-38, 47, 116, 193
PF key 161, 167, 233
PGMBK 112
PGULL—SET SRM command 67, 128
PLSPIOPR 38
PLSPIOPW 38
PLSPIOSR 38
PLSPIOSW 38
PMA assist 30, 58, 61
PMAV assist 58, 61
PR/SM 30, 62, 135
PREPAGE—SET SRM command 67
PRIORITY—SET command 65
priority calculation 96-97
privileged operations (PRIVOPS) 58
problem diagnosis 77
problem state 87, 102
profile 55, 167, 168, 225
PROFS 19, 20, 113, 114, 181-183, 209
program interrupt 90
program testing 83
PROP (programmable operator) 55-57
protocol 204
PSA 50
pseudo page fault 131
PSW 44, 79, 81, 91, 95, 96, 103, 116

PSW wait 90
PTF 71, 72
PU 217
PURGE 45, 114, 162
PUT 71-73, 83, 114
PVM 21, 212

Q0 97
Q1 93-94, 97, 122, 123, 125, 254, 255
Q2 93, 94, 95, 97, 122, 123, 125, 254, 255
Q3 93, 94, 95, 97, 255
QDROP—SET command 65, 185
quanta 255
QUERY 45, 158, 259-261
queue drop 93, 96
queue time 201
queuing sequence 94-95
QUICKDSP—SET command 65

RBT 19
RCHANNEL 44
RCHBLOK 51
RCTBLOK 51
RCTLUNIT 44
RDEVBLOK 51, 210
RDEVICE 44
real storage 5, 25, 27, 28, 99-115, 121, 122, 126-127, 131
RECEIVE 162
recovery 8
register 103, 116
RELEASE 16, 159
REMOTE—SET command 65, 233
RENAME command 161
RESERVE—SET command 65, 119, 185
restart interrupt 91
restore 8, 39
REXX 42, 172-177, 225
RIOGEN 44
RJE 19
RMSIZE parameter 111

RPS 203
RRAS 236
RSCS 19, 21, 24, 55, 162, 213-214
RSSIZE parameter 110
RU 217

SAA 29, 172, 218
SAD 16
saved system 38
SAVEFD 166, 209
scheduler (DMKSCH) 19, 91-93, 254
SDF 117
SDLC 213
security 241-252
seeking 202
segment table 102-103, 113, 122, 135
segments 102, 117
SEPP 24
SET commands 55, 62, 167
SFBLOK 39, 40, 51
SFS 27, 28, 60, 187-188, 199
shadow page table 67-68, 131-134
SHARE—SET command 65-66
shutdown 54
SIE assist 30, 58, 61-62, 64, 135, 266
SIO 205, 207, 232
SIOF 204, 205, 232
SLU 71, 72
SMART 20, 60, 261
SNA 20, 212, 214, 215, 221
SNA/FS 223
SNCP 217
SNI 217
SolutionPac 25, 70
SORT 166
SPE 71
SPOOL 39, 154
spool 17
spool file 39
spooling 38, 39-40, 154-158

SPTAPE 39, 40, 45
SQL/DS 19, 20, 183-186
SRM 19, 21, 87, 91
SSCH 207
SSCP 217-218
stand-alone dump 77
start I/O 204-205
start type 54
STBA assist 58, 61
STBYPASS—SET command 61, 67-68, 131, 134
STMULTI—SET command 68, 134
STORBUF-SET SRM command 67
subchannel system 28, 44, 199, 201
supervisor state 87, 102
SVC interrupt 91, 96
SWAP 47-48, 122, 123, 126, 129
swap queue 67, 122, 123, 125
swap set 122, 124
swap table 113, 122
swap-in 66, 123
swapping 102, 121, 122, 128
SWPQTIME—SET SRM command 67, 124-125
SYSCKP 48, 194
SYSCLR 48
SYSCOR 46, 110, 111, 118, 119
SYSCPVOL 129
SYSERR 38, 48, 194
SYSFCN 46, 47
SYSGEN 44, 45, 61, 194
SYSJRL 46, 47, 246
SYSMON 46, 47
SYSNAME 45
SYSNUC 36, 48, 193
SYSOPR 46, 47
SYSOWN 36, 38, 41, 46, 47, 126
SYSPAG 36, 46, 47-48, 122, 126, 194
SYSPCLAS 46, 48
SYSPGCT 45
SYSRES 36, 40, 46, 48, 70, 83
SYSSPOOL 40
SYSSTART 45

SYSSTORE 110, 111, 118
SYSTYPE 48
SYSVOL 45, 48
SYSWRM 36, 48, 194

TCP/IP 224
TDSK 16, 35, 36, 40-41, 47, 83, 193, 195
TELL command 57
TEMP 35, 38-40, 41, 47, 81, 126, 143, 193
terminal 4, 5, 17, 23
terminal cluster controller 5, 16-17
terminal status 148-149
TEXT file 70, 74-77
thrashing 102, 126
timeslice 93-95, 97, 255-256
TPNS 223
TRACE command 111, 118
trace table 80, 111, 261
transient area 144, 146
trim set 122
trimming 122
TRN 224
TSAF 218-219
TTIME 88
TVRATIO 88
TXTLCL filetype 70
TXTLIB 76
TXTTMP filetype 70
TYPE command 161

UCS 40, 46
Unix 21
UPDATE 74
User area 144-146

V=F 110, 135
V=R 61, 109-110, 131, 135
V=R free area 110
VAE 31
VCHBLOK 51
VCNA 57, 218

VCTLBLOK 51
VDEVBLOK 51
VDU 16
virtual devices 4, 139
virtual machines 3
virtual storage 99-103, 139
VITA assist 58, 60
VM Batch 178-181
VM/370 24
VM/ESA 29
VM/IS 25, 27, 29, 31
VM/RTM 20
VM/SP 24, 25, 27, 29, 31, 38, 43, 66, 100, 102, 105, 109-111, 119, 121, 125, 126, 134, 200, 203
VM/SP HPO 24, 25, 27, 29, 31, 38-40, 43, 47, 55, 61, 62, 64-67, 100, 102, 105, 109-112, 119, 121, 125, 126, 134, 200, 203
VM/XA SP 19, 24, 25, 27-31, 38, 40, 43, 44, 61, 64-67, 100, 102, 105, 109-112, 116, 119, 121, 129, 134, 188, 199, 200, 203, 207, 263
VMA assist 58-60, 134
VMBLOK 50, 81, 110
VMCF 221, 267
VMDBK 50, 81, 112, 266, 268
VMDUMP 77, 80
VMFASM 73, 74, 75, 76
VMFLOAD 69, 70, 73
VMFMAC 74
VMFPLC2 72
VMMAP 20, 60, 261, 263
VMPRF 263
VMSERV 73
VMUTIL 55
VNCA 223
VRFREE 110
VRNA 214

VSAM 83, 150-153, 187, 199
VSCS 218
VSE 3, 21, 27, 29, 30, 31, 61, 64, 94, 131, 177, 187, 199, 205, 212, 215, 246, 247
VTAM 20, 21, 60, 212-220, 226
VTIME 88

wait state 88-90
WAKEUP 55, 57
warm start 36, 54
working set 66, 93, 100, 102

X.25 218, 237
XEDIT 19, 65, 159, 166, 167-172, 181, 212
XI 237

ZAP 71, 74